ESSAYS

PATTERNS AND
PERSPECTIVES

Judith Barker-Sandbrook

Toronto

OXFORD UNIVERSITY PRESS

Oxford University Press
70 Wynford Drive, Don Mills, Ontario M3C 1J9

*Oxford New York Athens Auckland Bangkok Bombay Calcutta
Cape Town Dar es Salaam Delhi Florence Hong Kong Istanbul
Karachi Kuala Lumpur Madras Madrid Melbourne Mexico City
Nairobi Paris Singapore Taipei Tokyo Toronto*

and associated companies in
Berlin Ibadan

Canadian Cataloguing in Publication Data

Barker-Sandbrook, Judith
  Essays : patterns and perspectives

ISBN 0-19-540839-X

1. English language—Rhetoric.   2. English
language—Composition and exercises.   3. Essays.
I. Title.

PE1471.B37 1992   808.4   C91–095221–3

Oxford is a trademark of Oxford University Press

Editor: Loralee Case
Design: Marie Bartholomew
Typesetter: Colborne, Cox & Burns
Printed in Canada by Gagné Printing

  6 7   99

Acknowledgements

....

Thanks to the following educators for their constructive comments in reviewing the manuscript:

John J. Picone, St. Thomas Aquinas High School,
Oakville, Ontario

Peter Prest, John Diefenbaker High School, Calgary, Alberta

Don Stone, Windsor Board of Education, Windsor, Ontario

Jon Terpening, Burnaby School District, Burnaby, British Columbia

Thanks also to the following students for their contributions:

Reviewers: Sir Oliver Mowat Collegiate Institute, Scarborough, Ontario—
Sam Blythe, Andrea Chisholm, Kris Janssen, Mike McGregor, Leigh Murtha, Kalle Radage, Andy Sinclair

Essays: Sir Oliver Mowat Collegiate Institute, Scarborough, Ontario—
Talin Arzumanian, Andrea Chisholm, Brenda Chow, Andrew Coletto, Erik Savas, Stumpie Stavropoulis

Student Tips: Alpha Secondary School, Burnaby, British Columbia—
Tom Borugian, Clara Cristofaro, Alice Ho, Christopher Li, Nicole Ruddy

Sir Winston Churchill High School, Calgary, Alberta—
Julie Anne Abbott, Alyssa Becker, Ender Cheung, Phuong Ngo

Additional thanks to the following students who submitted Student Tips:

School District No. 41, Burnaby North, British Columbia—
Carmen Choy, Monica Gunn, Elaine Wong

Cariboo Hill Secondary School, Burnaby, British Columbia—
Nicole Batistic, Myken Jensen, Kavita Srivastava

Alpha Secondary School, Burnaby, British Columbia—
Dana Birkenthal, Teresa Fadden, Harmel Singh Guram, Jason Henwood, Mike James, Tina S. Lee, Wendy Leung, Juliana Ng, Karaleen Reid, Cristina Toso, Marnie Wolfe, Melissa Wong

Sir Winston Churchill High School, Calgary, Alberta—
Darren Milne

Thanks to the following teachers for encouraging their students to participate in this book:

Steven Bailey, Burnaby School District No. 41, British Columbia

Penny Martel, Cariboo Hill Secondary School, Burnaby, British Columbia

Sarah McManus, Alpha Secondary School, Burnaby, British Columbia

Kathleen Weir, Sir Winston Churchill High School, Calgary, Alberta

Special thanks to Kris Janssen of Sir Oliver Mowat Collegiate Institute who acted as both reviewer and research assistant.

J.S.

Judith Barker-Sandbrook, M.A., B.Ed., is an Ontario Academic Course teacher of English. She has been an instructor of writing workshops for the Scarborough Board of Education and piloted the Ontario Ministry of Education's "Contact North" teleworkshop writing program. She was awarded the Distinguished Achievement Award for Excellence in Educational Journalism (1989) by the Educational Press Association of America. She is the author of *Thinking Through Your Writing Process* (McGraw-Hill Ryerson, 1989). She co-authored *Thinking Through the Essay* (McGraw-Hill Ryerson, 1986), and *101 Independent Study Projects for the OACs in English* (OSSTF Resource Books, 1986).

Contents

SO WHAT'S THIS BOOK ABOUT?

This book is about essays—essays of many shapes and types, textures and flavours. This genre was conceived by the French essayist Montaigne in the sixteenth century. But what *is* an essay?

The essay is non-fiction.

. . . a short written composition in prose that discusses a subject or proposes an argument without claiming to be a complete or thorough exposition. The essay is more relaxed than the formal academic dissertation.

The Concise Oxford Dictionary of Literary Terms

Okay, that's a dictionary definition. But what do essays have to do with you?

You've probably written essays in history and English, and perhaps even in your politics, economics, or geography classes. Indeed, you may associate essays with evaluation.

But this anthology offers you a different perspective on the essay. It presents the essay as a multi-faceted form of non-fiction and shows how it may offer you an opportunity for *extended personal expression*.

Why Will You Enjoy This Book?

This anthology invites you to explore essay patterns and perspectives. You will enjoy a student-centred approach to building communications and thinking skills. Students in grades 11 and 12 chose the selections and reviewed the activities. You'll notice many student voices, including student essays and tips. You'll also read a variety of distinctive voices from across Canada. And you'll be given the opportunity to respond creatively to essays in your own voice. You and your teacher may develop activities, or you may select from the suggestions designed to encourage your extended personal responses to other writers' perspectives on issues, ideas, people, and literary works. In either case, you'll initiate, create, and discover what essays can mean to you.

How Do You Use This Book?

This anthology invites you and your teacher to choose *how* to use it. "Patterns" offers four core essays by professional writers, accompanied by four student response essays and four supplementary essays for your reading enjoyment. The essays represent narration, exposition, argumentation, and persuasion—four basic essay patterns which interlock or overlap, as illustrated on page ix.

For each group of essays, you'll find an introduction to the essay type along with activities at the end of each section to assist you in your explorations and to help you apply these techniques to your oral and written work.

- An introduction explains each essay pattern.
- *Talking Points* suggests pre-reading activities.
- *First Reactions* invites individuals and groups to engage in informal personal response in oral or written form.
- *The Writing Folder* suggests options for expressing your voice in written assignments which you may revise, edit, and polish, or leave in first-draft form.
- *Media Extensions* encourages you to extend your reactions in media format.
- *Independent Learning* suggests related projects for individuals and/or groups.
- *Connections* links your learning to others—your peers and community and cultural resources.

"Perspectives" invites you to explore and respond to a diverse selection of voices from Canada and abroad. Whether or not you've studied the four basic patterns, you'll enjoy the perspectives of both student and professional writers on such themes as adolescence, media and society, relationships, and science and technology. The "Guide to Themes" (page 209) and the "Responding to the Essay" questions (page 174) are intended to help you explore these perspectives.

"Resources" rounds off the collection with a practical potpourri of guides, checklists, student tips, and "how-to" essays to help you work through the learning process.

NOTE: For information about suggested approaches to using this anthology, see the "Guide to Themes" (page 209) and the "Guide to Patterns" (page 211).

Essay Patterns: A Continuum of Options

Both essay purposes and patterns can overlap. Few writers write with just one purpose in mind; similarly, essay patterns today rarely exist in their pure form. You might view these essay patterns as a continuum of interlocking options. As you work through the groupings in "Patterns" and refer to the "Guide to Patterns" (page 211), remember that the labels are not mutually exclusive and that they represent a tendency more than a template carved in stone.

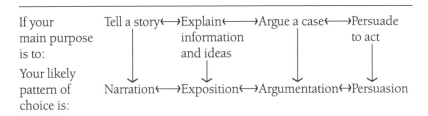

If your main purpose is to:	Tell a story⟷Explain information and ideas	Argue a case⟷Persuade to act
Your likely pattern of choice is:	Narration⟷Exposition⟷Argumentation⟷Persuasion	

PATTERNS

CONTENTS

TELLING A TALE

Let's suppose you want to share a humorous true story about your dog's shabby behaviour on a recent trip to the vet. Your aim is to entertain readers who've never met Chimo—to make her come alive for your audience. If you tell the tale as an engaging narrative essay, chances are your readers will empathize with the experience.

That's partly because narrative essays tell a story. And just about everyone loves a well-told tale. In fact, you may have difficulty determining whether a narrative is an essay or a short story. Only the author knows for sure whether characters such as Chimo are real or imaginary and whether the events are literally true or slightly embroidered.

Before reading the sample narratives and student response essay, you may want to consider the writing variables (see page 183) and discuss this pattern's characteristics.

The Narrative Essay

Purpose	To entertain and perhaps illuminate
Audience	Anyone old enough to enjoy a story
Tone	Various, but generally personal and often subjective
Mood	Various
Language	Generally informal, even colloquial, often with generous use of figurative language and rhetorical devices which invite the reader's empathy
Voice	Expressive and individualistic

E. B. White

....

Afternoon Of An American Boy

Talking Points

1. Relate an amusing or embarrassing anecdote to a partner or share it with the class.

2. What universal anxieties do you think both boys and girls share about first dates? You might view and discuss a film such as Thanks for the Ride *(NFB) based on Alice Munro's short story.*

3. List characteristics of a good story. Rank them in order of your personal priorities.

When I was in my teens, I lived in Mount Vernon, in the same block with J. Parnell Thomas, who grew up to become chairman of the House Committee on Un-American Activities. I lived on the corner of Summit and East Sidney, at No. 101 Summit Avenue, and Parnell lived four or five doors north of us on the same side of the avenue, in the house the Diefendorfs used to live in.

Parnell was not a playmate of mine, as he was a few years older, but I used to greet him as he walked by our house on his way to and from the depot. He was a good-looking young man, rather quiet and shy. Seeing him, I would call "Hello, Parnell!" and he would smile and say "Hello, Elwyn!" and walk on. Once I remember dashing out of our yard on roller skates and executing a rink turn in front of Parnell, to show off, and he said, "Well! Quite an artist, aren't you?" I remember the words. I was delighted at praise from an older man and sped away along the flagstone sidewalk, dodging the cracks I knew so well.

The thing that made Parnell a special man in my eyes in those days was not his handsome appearance and friendly manner but his sister. Her name was Eileen. She was my age and she was a quiet, nice-looking girl. She never came over to my yard to play, and I never went over there, and, considering that we lived so near each other, we were remarkably uncommunicative; nevertheless, she was the girl I singled out, at one point, to be of special interest to me. Being of special interest to me involved practically nothing on a girl's part—it simply meant that she was under constant surveillance. On my own part, it meant that I suffered an astonishing disintegration when I walked by her house, from embarrassment, fright, and the knowledge that I was in enchanted territory.

In the matter of girls, I was different from most boys of my age. I admired girls a lot, but they terrified me. I did not feel that I possessed the peculiar gifts or accomplishments that girls liked in their male companions—the ability to dance, to play football, to cut up a bit in public, to smoke, and to make small talk. I couldn't do any of these things successfully, and seldom tried. Instead, I stuck with the accomplishments I was sure of: I rode my bicycle sitting backward on the handle bars, I made up poems, I played selections from "Aïda" on the piano. In winter, I tended goal in the hockey games on the frozen pond in the Dell. None of these tricks counted much with girls. In the four years I was in the Mount Vernon High School, I never went to a school dance and I never took a girl to a drugstore for a soda or to the Westchester Playhouse or to Proctor's. I wanted to do these things but did not have the nerve. What I finally did manage to do, however, and what is the subject of this memoir, was far brassier, far gaudier. As an exhibit of teen-age courage and ineptitude, it never fails to amaze me in retrospect. I am not even sure it wasn't un-American.

My bashfulness and backwardness annoyed my older sister very much, and at about the period of which I am writing she began making strong efforts to stir me up. She was convinced that I was in a rut, socially, and she found me a drag in her own social life, which was brisk. She kept trying to throw me with girls, but I always bounced. And whenever she saw a chance she would start the phonograph and grab me, and we would go charging around the parlor in the toils of the one-step, she gripping me as in a death struggle, and I hurling her finally away from me through greater strength. I was a skinny kid but my muscles were hard, and it would have taken an unusually powerful woman to have held me long in the attitude of the dance.

One day, through a set of circumstances I have forgotten, my sister managed to work me into an afternoon engagement she had with some others in New York. To me, at that time, New York was a wonderland largely unexplored. I had been to the Hippodrome a couple of times with my father, and to the Hudson-Fulton Celebration, and to a few matinées; but New York, except as a setting for extravaganzas, was unknown. My sister had heard tales of tea-dancing at the Plaza Hotel. She and a girl friend of hers and another fellow and myself went there to give it a try. The expedition struck me as a slick piece of arrangement on her part. I was the junior member of the group and had been roped in, I imagine to give symmetry to the occasion. Or perhaps Mother had forbidden my sister to go at all unless another member of the family was along. Whether I was there for symmetry or for decency I can't really remember, but I was there.

The spectacle was a revelation to me. However repulsive the idea of dancing was, I was filled with amazement at the setup. Here were tables where a fellow could sit so close to the dance floor that he was practically on it. And you could order cinnamon toast and from the safety of your chair observe girls and men in close embrace, swinging along, the music playing while you ate the toast, and the dancers so near to you that they almost brushed the things off your table as they jogged by. I was impressed. Dancing or no dancing, this was certainly high life, and I knew I was witnessing a scene miles and miles ahead of anything that took place in Mount Vernon. I had never seen anything like it, and a ferment must have begun working in me that afternoon.

Incredible as it seems to me now, I formed the idea of asking Parnell's sister Eileen to accompany me to a tea dance at the Plaza. The plan shaped up in my mind as an expedition of unparalleled worldliness, calculated to stun even the most blasé girl. The fact that I didn't know how to dance must have been a powerful deterrent, but not powerful enough to stop me. As I look back on the affair, it's hard to credit my own memory, and I sometimes wonder if, in fact, the whole business isn't some dream that has gradually gained the status of actuality. A boy with any sense, wishing to become better acquainted with a girl who was "of special interest," would have cut out for himself a more modest assignment to start with—a soda date or a movie date—something within reasonable limits. Not me. I apparently became obsessed with the notion of taking Eileen to the Plaza and not to any darned old drugstore. I had learned the location of the Plaza, and just knowing how to get to it gave me a feeling of confidence. I had learned about cinnamon toast, so I felt able to cope with the waiter when he came along. And I banked heavily on the general splendor of the surroundings and the extreme sophistication of the function to carry the day, I guess.

I was three days getting up nerve to make the phone call. Meantime, I worked out everything in the greatest detail. I heeled myself with a safe amount of money. I looked up trains. I overhauled my clothes and assembled an outfit I believed would meet the test. Then, one night at six o'clock, when Mother and Father went downstairs to dinner, I lingered upstairs and entered the big closet off my bedroom where the wall phone was. There I stood for several minutes, trembling, my hand on the receiver, which hung upside down on the hook. (In our family, the receiver always hung upside down, with the big end up.)

I had rehearsed my first line and my second line. I planned to say, "Hello, can I please speak to Eileen?" Then, when she came to the phone, I planned to say, "Hello, Eileen, this is Elwyn White." From there on, I figured I could ad-lib it.

At last, I picked up the receiver and gave the number. As I had suspected, Eileen's mother answered.

"Can I please speak to Eileen?" I asked, in a low troubled voice.

"Just a minute," said her mother. Then, on second thought, she asked, "Who is it, please?"

"It's Elwyn," I said.

She left the phone, and after quite a while Eileen's voice said "Hello, Elwyn." This threw my second line out of whack, but I stuck to it doggedly. "Hello, Eileen, this is Elwyn White," I said.

In no time at all I laid the proposition before her. She seemed dazed and asked me to wait a minute. I assume she went into a huddle with her mother. Finally, she said yes, she would like to go tea-dancing with me at the Plaza, and I said fine, I would call for her at quarter past three on Thursday afternoon, or whatever afternoon it was—I've forgotten.

I do not know now, and of course did not know then, just how great was the mental and physical torture Eileen went through that day, but the incident stacks up as a sort of unintentional un-American activity, for which I was solely responsible. It all went off as scheduled: the stately walk to the depot; the solemn train ride, during which we sat staring shyly into the seat in front of us; the difficult walk from Grand Central across Forty-second to Fifth, with pedestrians clipping us and cutting in between us; the bus ride to Fifty-ninth Street; then the Plaza itself, and the cinnamon toast, and the music, and the excitement. The thundering quality of the occasion must have delivered a mental shock to me, deadening my recollection, for I have only the dimmest memory of leading Eileen onto the dance floor to execute two or three unspeakable rounds, in which I vainly tried to adapt my violent sister-and-brother wrestling act into something graceful and appropriate. It must have been awful. And at six o'clock, emerging, I gave no thought to any further entertainment, such as dinner in town. I simply herded Eileen back all the long, dreary way to Mount Vernon and deposited her, a few minutes after seven, on an empty stomach, at her home. Even if I had attempted to dine her, I don't believe it would have been possible; the emotional strain of the afternoon had caused me to perspire uninterruptedly, and any restaurant would have been justified in rejecting me solely on the ground that I was too moist.

Over the intervening years (all thirty-five of them), I've often felt guilty about my afternoon at the Plaza, and a few years ago, during Parnell's investigation of writers, my feeling sometimes took the form of a guilt sequence in which I imagined myself on the stand, in the committee room, being questioned. It went something like this:

PARNELL: Have you ever written for the screen, Mr. White?

ME: No, sir.

PARNELL: Have you ever been, or are you now, a member of the Screen Writers' Guild?

ME: No, sir.

PARNELL: Have you ever been, or are you now, a member of the Communist Party?

ME: No, sir.

Then, in this imaginary guilt sequence of mine, Parnell digs deep and comes up with the big question, calculated to throw me.

PARNELL: Do you recall an afternoon, along about the middle of the second decade of this century, when you took my sister to the Plaza Hotel for tea under the grossly misleading and false pretext that you knew how to dance?

And as my reply comes weakly, "Yes, sir," I hear the murmur run through the committee room and see reporters bending over their notebooks, scribbling hard. In my dread, I am again seated with Eileen at the edge of the dance floor, frightened, stunned, and happy—in my ears the intoxicating drumbeat of the dance, in my throat the dry, bittersweet taste of cinnamon.

I don't know about the guilt, really. I guess a good many girls might say that an excursion such as the one I conducted Eileen on belongs in the un-American category. But there must be millions of aging males, now slipping into their anecdotage, who recall their Willie Baxter period with affection, and who remember some similar journey into ineptitude, in that precious, brief moment in life before love's pages, through constant reference, had become dog-eared, and before its narrative, through sheer competence, had lost the first, wild sense of derring-do.

**Erik
Savas**
·······

WHEN BOY MEETS GIRL

**Student response essay to
E.B. White's "Afternoon of an American Boy"**

Talking Points

*1. In small groups, devise a chart listing similarities and differences
between a first date in 1920 and today. Share your list.*

2. Why does snappy dialogue enhance a narrative essay?

*3. Read aloud a poem such as P.K. Page's "Adolescence" or discuss a film
portrayal of the teenage years such as* Dead Poets Society *or* Heathers.

"So, what're you waiting for, Erik?"

"Just shut up, man."

"If you haven't got the guts—"

"I'm working on my approach, creep. First impressions, you know?"

"Whatever, Dr. Ruth. I'm tired of this jerking around."

Unimpressed with my stalling, my bronzed brother, Mike, abandons the
steamy white sand for the crashing North Carolina surf.

This retrospective of my first boy-meets-girl story floods my mind as I
read E.B. White's tale of his awkward first date. It's true, you know—some
things just never change.

It's August, and as the sun's rays weaken, I recall the penultimate memory
of my mental album, "The Summer of '88." The object of my fantasy—and
my dispute with Mike—is a wonderful girl. She dozes comfortably on the
beach, her long cream hair caressing her right arm, not quite reaching the
pink bikini top.

But the three feet between me and this princess seem longer than the
Mount Vernon block which the youthful E.B.—Elwyn—White shared with
his heart-throb, Eileen. I, too, grasp for "the right words" to attract the object
of my affection. As anxiety swells, two tiny beads of perspiration fall from
my brow. A shiver descends down my spine as I ponder the stocky male
hoisting metal nearby. Her boyfriend, perhaps? Shrieking ambulances and
full-length body casts cloud my mind. As White would be the first to admit,
approaching a girl takes nerve, and lots of it.

At that same moment she rolls over onto her side and slowly, gently, runs her long fingers through her hair. Suddenly, I take the plunge. Grabbing the orange frisbee half-buried by our cooler, I toss it in her direction.

"Ouch!"

"So sorry," I proclaim, the soul of innocence. "My friend . . . he apologizes."

"So who's your friend?" Her eyes scan the length of the shore behind me.

"Huh?" Silently cursing my mindlessness, I recall Mike's still ocean-paddling. Only a few forlorn umbrellas dot the sand.

"Well, here ya' go." She hands me the orange dish which, only moments ago, bounced off her behind.

"Thanks. I'm Erik."

"Cheryl. You from outta' town?"

Wow! Interest. And no degrading opening line.

"No," I lied. "Want a soda?" I venture.

"Sure."

Together in the sand, I savour every word spilling from her mouth. Much to my surprise, my ferocious anxiety gives way to bliss. Our laughter outlives our sodas as the sun dips into the ocean, the sky smoldering yellows and reds, the surf licking our toes. White would have been proud of me. Soothed by her reassuring persona, I pop The Question.

"Cheryl, how'd you like to go for ice cream tonight?"

"Sure, I'd love to."

To this very day I cringe as I recall lunging at her hand and shaking it gleefully like a salesperson shakes the hand of a satisfied customer. She merely smiles as I blurt, "Thank you so much! You won't regret it!"

I watch my date stroll home, imagining Mike's envy when he learns that his fuzzy-faced younger brother has a date with a stunning college sophomore that night.

As I giddily ready myself for this night of nights, I marvel at the stark change in my mood. Throughout the afternoon, I could have sworn that ice water was pulsing through my veins. But now, as I button my shirt in our hotel room mirror, my hands quiver so feverishly that Mike shouts:

"What's wrong, lover boy, nervous?"

"Ah, stuff it, Mike."

Shuffling along the wooden walk to Cheryl's room, vicious questions taunt me with doubt about the evening. Is this a typical first date? Was Cheryl merely putting me on? And worst of all, what do we do *after* the ice cream? Having answered none of my questions, I reach her door. I stand motionless, silent, staring at the door for so long that a spider begins constructing his home around my frozen elbow.

I must have rapped on the door because she appears before me.

"Hi, Erik!"

"Uh . . . Hi . . . These are for you."

She grins at the three daisies I thrust at her, having swiped them from the hotel's flower box on my journey.

"You're very sweet," she breathes, kissing me lightly on the cheek.

The most delicious rush of my life engulfs my chest and my knees buckle beneath me. But manly to the death, I take her arm, leading our way to nourishment. As we stroll through the hotel parking lot and past the front office, I hear a women yell, "What happened to my daisies, Bruno?"

Unlike Elwyn and Eileen, we've no need to hop a train to our destination. But my memories are many and vivid. I recall the softness of her hand in mine and her hair spilling across my shirt as she rests her head on my skinny shoulder. I recall the tiny drop of strawberry ice cream I wipe from the tip of her nose and my fear that I'd forgotten to shave as she rests her cheek against mine.

I'm more fortunate than E.B. White. My first date is a mixture of both warm and embarrassing memories. As I tuck a wilted daisy behind her ear, I impulsively nuzzle her neck. And Cheryl doesn't even seem to mind the sandy grit that rubs from my flushed cheek onto hers.

George
Orwell

·········

SHOOTING AN ELEPHANT

Talking Points

1. If you've experienced being a member of a visible minority, what were your initial feelings? Did they change? Why or why not?

2. Have you ever felt pressured into doing something you later regretted? Why did you succumb to pressure? How did you feel afterwards?

3. Under what circumstances, if any, is it morally acceptable for a foreign power to police another country's citizens? You might begin by discussing a film portrayal of colonialism such as The Jewel in the Crown *or* Out of Africa.

In Moulmein, in Lower Burma, I was hated by large numbers of people—the only time I have been important enough for this to happen to me. I was subdivisional police officer of the town, and in an aimless, petty kind of way anti-European feeling was very bitter. No one had the guts to raise a riot, but if a European woman went through the bazaars alone somebody would probably spit betel juice over her dress. As a police officer I was an obvious target and was baited whenever it seemed safe to do so. When a nimble Burman tripped me up on the football field and the referee (another Burman) looked the other way, the crowd yelled with hideous laughter. This happened more than once. In the end the sneering yellow faces of young men that met me everywhere, the insults hooted after me when I was at a safe distance, got badly on my nerves. The young Buddhist priests were the worst of all. There were several thousands of them in the town and none of them seemed to have anything to do except stand on street corners and jeer at Europeans.

All this was perplexing and upsetting. For at that time I had already made up my mind that imperialism was an evil thing and the sooner I chucked up my job and got out of it the better. Theoretically—and secretly, of course—I was all for the Burmese and all against their oppressors, the British. As for the job I was doing, I hated it more bitterly than I can perhaps make clear. In a job like that you see the dirty work of Empire at close quarters. The wretched prisoners huddling in the stinking cages of the lock-ups, the grey, cowed faces of the long-term convicts, the scarred buttocks of the men who had been flogged with bamboos—all these oppressed me with an intolerable sense of guilt. But I could get nothing into perspective. I was young and ill-educated and I had had to think out my problems in the utter silence that is imposed on every Englishman in the East. I did not even know that the British Empire is dying, still less did I know that it is a great deal better than the younger empires that are going to supplant it. All I knew was that I was stuck between my hatred of the empire I served and my rage against the evil-spirited little beasts who tried to make my job impossible. With one part of my mind I thought of the British Raj as an unbreakable tyranny, as something clamped down, in *saecula saeculorum*, upon the will of prostrate peoples; with another part I thought that the greatest joy in the world would be to drive a bayonet into a Buddhist priest's guts. Feelings like these are the normal by-products of imperialism; ask any Anglo-Indian official, if you can catch him off duty.

One day something happened which in a roundabout way was enlightening. It was a tiny incident in itself, but it gave me a better glimpse than I had had before of the real nature of imperialism—the real motives for which despotic governments act. Early one morning the sub-inspector at a police station the other end of the town rang me up on the 'phone and said that an elephant was ravaging the bazaar. Would I please come and do something about it? I did not know what I could do, but I wanted to see what was happening and I got on to a pony and started out. I took my rifle, an old .44 Winchester and much too small to kill an elephant, but I thought the noise might be useful *in terrorem*. Various Burmans stopped me on the way and told me about the elephant's doings. It was not, of course, a wild elephant, but a tame one which had gone "must." It had been chained up, as tame elephants always are when their attack of "must" is due, but on the previous night it had broken its chain and escaped. Its mahout, the only person who could manage it when it was in that state, had set out in pursuit, but had taken the wrong direction and was now twelve hours' journey away, and in the morning the elephant had suddenly reappeared in the town. The Burmese population had no weapons and were quite helpless against it. It had already destroyed somebody's bamboo hut, killed a cow, and raided some fruit-stall and devoured the stock; also it had met the municipal rubbish van, and, when the driver jumped out and took to his heels, had turned the van over and inflicted violences upon it.

The Burmese sub-inspector and some Indian constables were waiting for me in the quarter where the elephant had been seen. It was a very poor quarter, a labyrinth of squalid bamboo huts, thatched with palm-leaf, winding all over a steep hillside. I remember that it was a cloudy, stuffy morning at the beginning of the rains. We began questioning the people as to where the elephant had gone, and, as usual, failed to get any definite information. That is invariably the case in the East; a story always sounds clear enough at a distance, but the nearer you get to the scene of events the vaguer it becomes. Some of the people said that the elephant had gone in one direction, some said that he had gone in another, some professed not even to have heard of any elephant. I had almost made up my mind that the whole story was a pack of lies, when we heard yells a little distance away. There was a loud, scandalized cry of "Go away, child! Go away this instant!" and an old woman with a switch in her hand came round the corner of a hut, violently shooing away a crowd of naked children. Some more women followed, clicking their tongues and exclaiming; evidently there was something that the children ought not to have seen. I rounded the hut and saw a man's dead body sprawling in the mud. He was an Indian, a black Dravidian coolie, almost naked, and he could not have been dead many minutes. The people said that the elephant had come suddenly upon him round the corner of the hut, caught him with its trunk, put its foot on his back, and ground him into the earth. This was the rainy season and the ground was soft, and his face had scored a trench a foot deep and a couple of yards long. He was lying on his belly with arms crucified and head sharply twisted to one side. His face was coated with mud, the eyes wide open, the teeth bared and grinning with an expression of unendurable agony. (Never tell me, by the way, that the dead look peaceful. Most of the corpses I have seen looked devilish.) The friction of the great beast's foot had stripped the skin from his back as neatly as one skins a rabbit. As soon as I saw the dead man I sent an orderly to a friend's house nearby to borrow an elephant rifle. I had already sent back the pony, not wanting it to go mad with fright and throw me if it smelt the elephant.

The orderly came back in a few minutes with a rifle and five cartridges, and meanwhile some Burmans had arrived and told us that the elephant was in the paddy fields below, only a few hundred yards away. As I started forward practically the whole population of the quarter flocked out of the houses and followed me. They had seen the rifle and were all shouting excitedly that I was going to shoot the elephant. They had not shown much interest in the elephant when he was merely ravaging their homes, but it was different now that he was going to be shot. It was a bit of fun to them, as it would be to an English crowd; besides they wanted the meat. It made me vaguely uneasy. I had no intention of shooting the elephant—I had merely sent for the rifle to defend myself if necessary—and it is always unnerving to have a crowd following you. I marched down the hill, looking and feeling a fool, with the rifle over my shoulder and an ever-growing army of people jostling at my heels. At the bottom, when you got away from the huts, there was a metalled road and beyond that a miry waste of paddy fields a thousand yards across, not yet ploughed but soggy from the first rains and dotted with coarse grass. The elephant was standing eight yards from the road, his left side towards us. He took not the slightest notice of the crowd's approach. He was tearing up bunches of grass, beating them against his knees to clean them, and stuffing them into his mouth.

I had halted on the road. As soon as I saw the elephant I knew with perfect certainty that I ought not to shoot him. It is a serious matter to shoot a working elephant—it is comparable to destroying a huge and costly piece of machinery—and obviously one ought not to do it if it can possibly be avoided. And at that distance, peacefully eating, the elephant looked no more dangerous than a cow. I thought then and I think now that his attack of "must" was already passing off; in which case he would merely wander harmlessly about until the mahout came back and caught him. Moreover, I did not in the least want to shoot him. I decided that I would watch him for a little while to make sure that he did not turn savage again, and then go home.

But at that moment I glanced round at the crowd that had followed me. It was an immense crowd, two thousand at the least and growing every minute. It blocked the road for a long distance on either side. I looked at the sea of yellow faces above the garish clothes—faces all happy and excited over this bit of fun, all certain that the elephant was going to be shot. They were watching me as they would watch a conjurer about to perform a trick. They did not like me, but with the magical rifle in my hands I was momentarily worth watching. And suddenly I realized that I should have to shoot the elephant after all. The people expected it of me and I had got to do it; I could feel their two thousand wills pressing me forward, irresistibly. And it was at this moment, as I stood there with the rifle in my hands, that I first grasped the hollowness, the futility of the white man's dominion in the East. Here was I, the white man with his gun, standing in front of the unarmed native crowd—seemingly the leading actor of the piece; but in reality I was only an absurd puppet pushed to and fro by the will of those yellow faces behind. I perceived in this moment that when the white man turns tyrant it is his own freedom that he destroys. He becomes a sort of hollow, posing dummy, the conventionalized figure of a sahib. For it is the condition of his rule that he shall spend his life in trying to impress the "natives," and so in every crises he has got to do what the natives expect of him. He wears a mask, and his face grows to fit it. I had got to shoot the elephant. I had committed myself to doing it when I sent for the rifle. A sahib has got to act like a sahib; he has got to appear resolute, to know his own mind and do definite things. To come all that way, rifle in hand, with two thousand people marching at my heels, and then to trail feebly away, having done nothing—no, that was impossible. The crowd would laugh at me. And my whole life, every white man's life in the East, was one long struggle not to be laughed at.

But I did not want to shoot the elephant. I watched him beating his bunch of grass against his knees, with that preoccupied grandmotherly air that elephants have. It seemed to me that it would be murder to shoot him. At that age I was not squeamish about killing animals, but I had never shot an elephant and never wanted to. (Somehow it always seems worse to kill a large animal.) Besides, there was the beast's owner to be considered. Alive, the elephant was worth at least a hundred pounds; dead, he would only be worth the value of his tusks, five pounds, possibly. But I had got to act quickly. I turned to some experienced-looking Burmans who had been there when we arrived, and asked them how the elephant had been behaving. They all said the same thing: he took no notice of you if you left him alone, but he might charge if you went too close to him.

It was perfectly clear to me what I ought to do. I ought to walk up to within, say, twenty-five yards of the elephant and test his behaviour. If he charged I could shoot, if he took no notice of me it would be safe to leave him until the mahout came back. But also I knew that I was going to do no such thing. I was a poor shot with a rifle and the ground was soft mud into which one would sink at every step. If the elephant charged and I missed him, I should have about as much chance as a toad under a steam-roller. But even then I was not thinking particularly of my own skin, only of the watchful yellow faces behind. For at that moment, with the crowd watching me, I was not afraid in the ordinary sense, as I would have been if I had been alone. A white man mustn't be frightened in front of "natives"; and so, in general, he isn't frightened. The sole thought in my mind was that if anything went wrong those two thousand Burmans would see me pursued, caught, trampled on, and reduced to a grinning corpse like that Indian up the hill. And if that happened it was quite probable that some of them would laugh. That would never do. There was only one alternative. I shoved the cartridges into the magazine and lay down on the road to get a better aim.

The crowd grew very still, and a deep, low, happy sigh, as of people who see the theatre curtain go up at last, breathed from innumerable throats. They were going to have their bit of fun after all. The rifle was a beautiful German thing with cross-hair sights. I did not then know that in shooting an elephant one would shoot to cut an imaginary bar running from ear-hole to ear-hole; actually I aimed several inches in front of this, thinking the brain would be further forward.

When I pulled the trigger I did not hear the bang or feel the kick—one never does when a shot goes home—but I heard the devilish roar of glee that went up from the crowd. In that instant, in too short a time, one would have thought, even for the bullet to get there, a mysterious, terrible change had come over the elephant. He neither stirred nor fell, but every line of his body had altered. He looked suddenly stricken, shrunken, immensely old, as though the frightful impact of the bullet had paralysed him without knocking him down. At last, after what seemed a long time—it might have been five seconds, I dare say—he sagged flabbily to his knees. His mouth slobbered.

An enormous senility seemed to have settled upon him. One could have imagined him thousands of years old. I fired again into the same spot. At the second shot he did not collapse but climbed with desperate slowness to his feet and stood weakly upright, with legs sagging and head drooping. I fired a third time. That was the shot that did for him. You could see the agony of it jolt his whole body and knock the last remnant of strength from his legs. But in falling he seemed for a moment to rise, for as his hind legs collapsed beneath him he seemed to tower upwards like a huge rock toppling, his trunk reaching skywards like a tree. He trumpeted, for the first and only time. And then down he came, his belly towards me, with a crash that seemed to shake the ground even where I lay.

I got up. The Burmans were already racing past me across the mud. It was obvious that the elephant would never rise again, but he was not dead. He was breathing very rhythmically with long rattling gasps, his great mound of a side painfully rising and falling. His mouth was wide open—I could see far down into caverns of pale pink throat. I waited a long time for him to die, but his breathing did not weaken. Finally I fired my two remaining shots into the spot where I thought his heart must be. The thick blood welled out of him like red velvet, but still he did not die. His body did not even jerk when the shots hit him, the tortured breathing continued without a pause. He was dying, very slowly and in great agony, but in some world remote from where not even a bullet could damage him further. I felt that I had got to put an end to that dreadful noise. It seemed dreadful to see the great beast lying there, powerless to move and yet powerless to die, and not even to be able to finish him. I sent back for my small rifle and poured shot after shot into his heart and down his throat. They seemed to make no impression. The tortured gasps continued as steadily as the ticking of a clock.

In the end I could not stand it any longer and went away. I heard later that it took him half an hour to die. Burmans were bringing dahs and baskets even before I left, and I was told they had stripped his body almost to the bones by the afternoon.

Afterwards, of course, there were endless discussions about the shooting of the elephant. The owner was furious, but he was only an Indian and could do nothing. Besides, legally I had done the right thing, for a mad elephant has to be killed, like a mad dog, if its owner fails to control it. Among the Europeans opinion was divided. The older men said I was right, the younger men said it was a damn shame to shoot an elephant for killing a coolie, because an elephant was worth more than any damn Coringhee coolie. And afterwards I was very glad that the coolie had been killed; it put me legally in the right and it gave me sufficient pretext for shooting the elephant. I often wondered whether any of the others grasped that I had done it solely to avoid looking a fool.

Suggested Activities

First Reactions

Tip • For suggestions about using your Response Notebook, see page 183 of Resource One.

1. In your Response Notebook, react to an idea, person, or event in one of these essays. You might express your ideas in a poem, expository paragraph, monologue, skit, or speech. Accompany your written work with a line drawing or cartoon.

2. If you've read White's and/or Savas's work, assume the role of the girl in either essay. In your Response Notebook, depict her reaction to the date.

3. If you've read more than one essay, compare the techniques each writer uses to create vivid characters and evaluate the success of each.

4. With a partner, discuss the form of one (or more) essays. Include its style and/or structure and the "little touches" that help you "hear" the writer's voice. What tips for writing effective narrative essays can you assemble for future use?

Tip • The checklist on page 3 may help you begin.

The Writing Folder

Tip • You may wish to discuss your progress with a partner as you revise, edit, and polish your writing, or you may prefer to leave your work in first-draft form. Resource Two, which begins on page 181, will help you with the revision process.

5. In small groups, brainstorm imaginative written activities stimulated by the White and/or Savas essays. Experiment with one suggestion from a composite class list, or adapt one of the following ideas to meet your needs:

   a) Compose an interview with White, Savas, or Orwell. Answer as you think the author would.
   b) Draft a narrative essay about your first date, your visit to a different culture, or another memorable personal experience.
   c) In a formal essay, assess the effectiveness of one narrative essay. Be sure to state specific criteria and include textual references and brief quotations.

Tip* • *For assistance, see page 182.

d) Read a second narrative essay by Orwell or White. In a comparative essay, argue which work is the most effective.

Media Extensions

Tip* • *Resource Five, which begins on page 190, may be of help with your media assignment.

6. Adapt a topic from your Writing Folder or Response Notebook, using a media format, or alter one of these assignments to suit your circumstances:

   a) Compose a storyboard for the videotaping of one essay or shoot stills and assemble a photostory with text.
   b) Compose a photostory (text and stills) about teenage relationships in your school.

7. How successful are television commercials or "yellow-journalism" television and "rag" newspapers at enticing and/or entertaining viewers by employing narrative techniques?

Independent Learning

Tip* • *Resource One, which begins on page 178, may help you devise and complete your project.

8. With the assistance of your peers and teacher, develop a project of personal interest. Read a collection of narrative essays or another form of non-fiction prose and express your learning in a format negotiated with your teacher—perhaps a literary analysis, a photostory, or an anthology of favourites introduced by a preface.

Connections

9. Share a true story with a small group or the class. Sitting in a circle helps establish a suitable atmosphere. Or you may wish to invite a grandparent or a professional storyteller to share a narrative tale with your class.

Tip* • *Bob Barton's* Tell Me Another One: Storytelling and Reading Aloud at Home, at School, and in the Community *(Markham, Ont.: Pembroke Publishers, 1986) is a useful "how-to" resource.

NOTE: *For additional activities, see "Responding to the Essay" (page 174).*

Explaining The World

Let's suppose that your dog, Chimo, is a puppy and you need information about training and diet. You'd consult "how-to" resources about coping with young spaniels. Because these publications explore, explain, define, and classify readers' concerns, they're labelled exposition.

An expository essay is centred around a main idea expressed in the first paragraph. The essay's body elaborates upon the main idea with a blend of fact and opinion; the writer's purpose, audience, and tone determine this balance. For example, a formal scholarly exposition relies on facts. But a satirical approach to a subject is more often tinged with opinion.

But how do you distinguish between fact and opinion? A fact is verifiable information about which most reasonable people would agree. An opinion is a personal interpretation about which people may disagree. For example, Chimo is a spaniel. This is a fact. However, if we were to say that spaniels are the most cuddly dogs in the world, this is an opinion.

Before reading the sample expository essays and student response essay, you may want to consider the writing variables (see page 183) and discuss this pattern's characteristics.

The Expository Essay

Purpose	To explain, explore, classify, or define
Audience	May be specialized according to interest
Tone	Varies from serious through humorous
Mood	Various
Language	Formal through informal, unadorned and objective through figurative and subjective
Voice	Neutral through expressive

Judy
Syfers
·······

WHY I WANT A WIFE

Talking Points

1. Working with a partner, explain a "how-to" process with which you are familiar. Your partner should listen carefully for omissions. Reverse roles.

2. Make class lists of those subjects which are and are not appropriate for satirical treatment; or view a satirical film such as The Awful Fate of Melpomenus Jones *(NFB).*

3. How should household chores be divided among family members? Argue your case or role-play your conflicts and resolutions.

I belong to that classification of people known as wives. I am A Wife. And, not altogether incidentally, I am a mother.

Not too long ago a male friend of mine appeared on the scene fresh from a recent divorce. He had one child, who is, of course, with his ex-wife. He is looking for another wife. As I thought about him while I was ironing one evening, it suddenly occurred to me that I, too, would like to have a wife. Why do I want a wife?

I would like to go back to school so that I can become economically independent, support myself, and, if need be, support those dependent upon me. I want a wife to take care of my children. I want a wife to keep track of the children's doctor and dentist appointments. And to keep track of mine, too. I want a wife to make sure my children eat properly and are kept clean. I want a wife who will wash the children's clothes and keep them mended. I want a wife who is a good nurturant attendant to my children, who arranges for their schooling, makes sure that they have an adequate social life with their peers, takes them to the park, the zoo, etc. I want a wife who takes care of the children when they are sick, a wife who arranges to be around when the children need special care, because, of course, I cannot miss classes at school. My wife must arrange to lose time at work and not lose the job. It may mean a small cut in my wife's income from time to time, but I guess I can tolerate that. Needless to say, my wife will arrange and pay for the care of the children while my wife is working.

I want a wife who will take care of *my* physical needs. I want a wife who will keep my house clean. A wife who will pick up after my children, a wife who will pick up after me. I want a wife who will keep my clothes clean, ironed, mended, replaced when need be, and who will see to it that my personal things are kept in their proper place so that I can find what I need the minute I need it. I want a wife who cooks the meals, a wife who is a *good* cook. I want a wife who will plan the menus, do the necessary grocery shopping, prepare the meals, serve them pleasantly, and then do the cleaning up while I do my studying. I want a wife who will care for me when I am sick and sympathize with my pain and loss of time from school. I want a wife to go along when our family takes a vacation so that someone can continue to care for me and my children when I need a rest and change of scene.

I want a wife who will not bother me with rambling complaints about a wife's duties. But I want a wife who will listen to me when I feel the need to explain a rather difficult point I have come across in my course of studies. And I want a wife who will type my papers for me when I have written them.

I want a wife who will take care of the details of my social life. When my wife and I are invited out by my friends, I want a wife who will take care of the babysitting arrangements. When I meet people at school that I like and want to entertain, I want a wife who will have the house clean, will prepare a special meal, serve it to me and my friends, and not interrupt when I talk about things that interest me and my friends. I want a wife who will have arranged that the children are fed and ready for bed before my guests arrive so that the children do not bother us. I want a wife who takes care of the needs of my guests so that they feel comfortable, who makes sure that they have an ashtray, that they are passed the hors d'oeuvres, that they are offered a second helping of the food, that their wine glasses are replenished when necessary, that their coffee is served to them as they like it. And I want a wife who knows that sometimes I need a night out by myself.

I want a wife who is sensitive to my sexual needs, a wife who makes love passionately and eagerly when I feel like it, a wife who makes sure that I am satisfied. And, of course, I want a wife who will not demand sexual attention when I am not in the mood for it. I want a wife who assumes the complete responsibility for birth control, because I do not want more children. I want a wife who will remain sexually faithful to me so that I do not have to clutter up my intellectual life with jealousies. And I want a wife who understands that *my* sexual needs may entail more than strict adherence to monogamy. I must, after all, be able to relate to people as fully as possible.

If, by chance, I find another person more suitable as a wife than the wife I already have, I want the liberty to replace my present wife with another one. Naturally, I will expect a fresh, new life; my wife will take the children and be solely responsible for them so that I am left free.

When I am through with school and have a job, I want my wife to quit working and remain at home so that my wife can more fully and completely take care of a wife's duties.

My God, who *wouldn't* want a wife?

Talin
Arzumanian
·············

PORTRAIT OF A MODERN MARRIAGE

Student response essay to
Judy Syfers's "Why I Want a Wife"

Talking Points

1. *In your experience, which of Syfers's observations about the male's expectations of females apply to girlfriend-boyfriend relationships?*

2. *Discuss your current perception of marriage and whether evidence suggests the institution benefits one sex more than the other. You might view a film such as* Careers and Cradles *(NFB, Media and Society, II)*

3. *Research the origins of the words "husband" and "wife."*

I belong to that classification of people known as students. I've never been married, nor, not "altogether incidentally," do I intend to marry in the near future. But I belong to a happy and loving family.

Yet, my immediate reaction to Judy Syfers's essay, "Why I Want a Wife," was impassioned agreement with all her sentiments. I adamantly felt—indeed, hotly declared—that I'd remain single my entire life. After all, who wants to become a slave? But when I cooled down, I more calmly scrutinized my initial response. Why has Syfers written such a biting satire of marriage and family life? Even given the satirist's hyperbole, or poetic licence, I gather she and many of her peers aren't living the fairy tale version of wedded bliss.

Of course, many people believe (and most of them seem to be male) that once you're married, you can kiss your freedom goodbye. And others—again usually males—speculate that marriage is a surefire path to living hell. Let's face it. There are various philosophies about "holy matrimony," many of which are derived from jaded couples. You hardly ever hear from the happiest of partners; after all, what would they whine or grumble about? Literature, movies, and talk shows thrive on conflict, not harmony.

So who's to speak up for marriage and the family? These institutions must have something going for them. After all, most divorced people remarry within three years, we're told, and many bravely forge ahead with a second—or third—set of offspring. Also, matrimony is an ancient institution dating back to early human history. Finally, recent studies show that married men report greater personal happiness than bachelors and that married men between 45 and 60 suffer fewer deaths than their unwed counterparts.

As an unmarried senior student, my thoughts are fresh and, I suspect, relatively untainted. I feel equal to the task of offering my humble thoughts about wedlock, matrimony, betrothal, responding particularly to some of Syfers's satirical swipes at the institution. I feel that since modern marriage is a partnership of equals, each and every family member must contribute to running a balanced, happy household.

First of all Ms. Syfers gripes about children, although I've no doubt about her love for her brood. Apparently, she and many of her female counterparts assume almost total responsibility for their offsprings' lives; what with keeping track of medical appointments, nourishing, clothing, entertaining, and nursing them when they fall ill, there's little time for less altruistic pursuits. Whew! What a lot of work, and all of it *has* to be done—by someone.

But children are a *couple's* future. They embody the wife's *and* husband's loving union. Children may be viewed as the couple's gift to the world—an opportunity to rear well-mannered, morally literate social individuals. Now, if wives are burdened with the total responsibility of child-rearing—the slaves of the "second shift" after paid employment—they might remind their husbands that children need equal time and role-modeling from both parents. If a reasonable approach doesn't do the trick, the mother might casually mention that the children seem to be developing into little anarchists and need another firm hand.

Next on the agenda is that nasty business of housework, a sure-fire war starter. So who *likes* scrubbing the toilet bowl? I'm sure everyone's shaking their heads, right? Yes, there *are* a few clean freaks out there who are actually refreshed by housework, but the great bulk of humanity is reluctant to pick up the duster.

Now, according to Ms. Syfers, today's wives are stuck cleaning the house, picking up after husband and children, and washing, ironing, and mending clothes. They must also play the nourishing Earth Mother; in today's world, that means deciphering labels for nasty preservatives, standing in long supermarket lines, preparing gourmet meals between 6:10 and 6:17, and stacking the dishwasher so it doesn't clog. If so, mums are completing 100 percent of the work while dads read the paper and kids watch TV and talk to a dozen friends via call waiting.

If husbands and children don't understand this situation, wives should establish that any toilet-trained family member is expected to contribute constructively to household chores. No, that standard mealtime refrain, "I'm starved! What's for dinner, Ma? Not meatloaf again," doesn't count as a contribution, folks. As a last resort, wives can always cook meals the family loves to hate. One final healthy approach a teacher-friend reports is claiming they're all getting too plump; she serves large helpings of fat-free banana-cum-tofu yogurt layered in alfalfa sprouts—three nights in a row. Dessert? A raised eyebrow and a comment such as, "Have you forgotten about the world's starving children?", usually crushes the mob's sugar cravings.

Now, when it comes to socializing, why not enjoy your mate's companion-ship in the company of friends? "Adult time" is very important for marital happiness. But if it means, as Ms. Syfers suggests, yet another unshared burden, that's another matter. No. The objective here is to enjoy your marriage without either of you going the slave route. If it should happen that a wife is constantly required to undertake all the social arrangements—despite her mate's promises to the contrary—she does have plenty of opportunities to botch things up. Burnt roasts, curdled sauces, lumpy potatoes, and salty puddings may ruin an event, but they make a more important point to one's "significant other" in the long run. Husbands and wives, wives and husbands. Families. Who needs them? We all do. But not if the relationships involve the slavery Ms. Syfers implies in "Why I Want a Wife." That's not wedlock, it's deadlock.

In my view, a wife offers love, honour, and respect to her mate and a husband reciprocates. And that means sharing everything—the bliss and the blues.

Stephen
King
....

WHY WE CRAVE HORROR MOVIES

Talking Points

1. What evidence, if any, supports the belief that human beings are naturally aggressive or territorial? You might view an NFB film such as Neighbours *or* The Wanderer.

2. Adopt a position about a subject of interest and explain your reasoning to a partner. Reverse roles.

3. If you're familiar with other work by Stephen King, speculate on whether this topic seems a likely one for him to write about.

I think that we're all mentally ill; those of us outside the asylums only hide it a little better—and maybe not all that much better, after all. We've all known people who talk to themselves, people who sometimes squinch their faces into horrible grimaces when they believe no one is watching, people who have some hysterical fear—of snakes, the dark, the tight place, the long drop . . . and, of course, those final worms and grubs that are waiting so patiently underground.

When we pay our four or five bucks and seat ourselves at tenth-row center in a theater showing a horror movie, we are daring the nightmare.

Why? Some of the reasons are simple and obvious. To show that we can, that we are not afraid, that we can ride this roller coaster. Which is not to say that a really good horror movie may not surprise a scream out of us at some point, the way we may scream when the roller coaster twists through a complete 360 or plows through a lake at the bottom of the drop. And horror movies, like roller coasters, have always been the special province of the young; by the time one turns 40 or 50, one's appetite for double twists or 360-degree loops may be considerably depleted.

We also go to re-establish our feelings of essential normality; the horror movie is innately conservative, even reactionary. Freda Jackson as the horrible melting woman in *Die, Monster, Die!* confirms for us that no matter how far we may be removed from the beauty of a Robert Redford or a Diana Ross, we are still light-years from true ugliness.

And we go to have fun.

Ah, but this is where the ground starts to slope away, isn't it? Because this is a very peculiar sort of fun, indeed. The fun comes from seeing others menaced—sometimes killed. One critic has suggested that if pro football has become the voyeur's version of combat, then the horror film has become the modern version of the public lynching.

It is true that the mythic, "fairy-tale" horror film intends to take away the shades of gray . . . It urges us to put away our more civilized and adult penchant for analysis and to become children again, seeing things in pure blacks and whites. It may be that horror movies provide psychic relief on this level because this invitation to lapse into simplicity, irrationality and even outright madness is extended so rarely. We are told we may allow our emotions a free rein . . . or no rein at all.

If we are all insane, then sanity becomes a matter of degree. If your insanity leads you to carve up women like Jack the Ripper or the Cleveland Torso Murderer, we clap you away in the funny farm (but neither of those two amateur-night surgeons was ever caught, heh-heh-heh); if, on the other hand, your insanity leads you only to talk to yourself when you're under stress or to pick your nose on the morning bus, then you are left alone to go about your business . . . though it is doubtful that you will ever be invited to the best parties.

The potential lyncher is in almost all of us (excluding saints, past and present; but then, most saints have been crazy in their own ways), and every now and then, he has to be let loose to scream and roll around in the grass. Our emotions and our fears form their own body, and we recognize that it demands its own exercise to maintain proper muscle tone. Certain of these emotional muscles are accepted—even exalted—in civilized society; they are, of course, the emotions that tend to maintain the status quo of civilization itself. Love, friendship, loyalty, kindness—these are all the emotions that we applaud, emotions that have been immortalized in the couplets of Hallmark cards and in the verses (I don't dare call it poetry) of Leonard Nimoy.

When we exhibit these emotions, society showers us with positive reinforcement; we learn this even before we get out of diapers. When, as children, we hug our rotten little puke of a sister and give her a kiss, all the aunts and uncles smile and twit and cry, "Isn't he the sweetest little thing?" Such coveted treats as chocolate-covered graham crackers often follow. But if we deliberately slam the rotten little puke of a sister's fingers in the door, sanctions follow—angry remonstrance from parents, aunts and uncles; instead of a chocolate-covered graham cracker, a spanking.

But anticivilization emotions don't go away, and they demand periodic exercise. We have such "sick" jokes as, "What's the difference between a truckload of bowling balls and a truckload of dead babies?" ("You can't unload a truckload of bowling balls with a pitchfork . . . " a joke, by the way, that I heard originally from a ten-year-old). Such a joke may surprise a laugh or a grin out of us even as we recoil, a possibility that confirms the thesis: If we share a brotherhood of man, then we also share an insanity of man. None of which is intended as a defense of either the sick joke or insanity but merely as an explanation of why the best horror films, like the best fairy tales, manage to be reactionary, anarchistic, and revolutionary all at the same time.

The mythic horror movie, like the sick joke, has a dirty job to do. It deliberately appeals to all that is worst in us. It is morbidity unchained, our most base instincts let free, our nastiest fantasies realized . . . and it all happens, fittingly enough, in the dark. For those reasons, good liberals often shy away from horror films. For myself, I like to see the most aggressive of them—*Dawn of the Dead*, for instance—as lifting a trap door in the civilized forebrain and throwing a basket of raw meat to the hungry alligators swimming around in that subterranean river beneath.

Why bother? Because it keeps them from getting out, man. It keeps them down there and me up here. It was Lennon and McCartney who said that all you need is love, and I would agree with that.

As long as you keep the gators fed.

SUGGESTED ACTIVITIES

First Reactions

Tip • For suggestions about using your Response Notebook, see page 183 of Resource One.

1. In your Response Notebook, react to Syfers's and/or Arzumanian's essay(s) in a form of your choice—perhaps in a satirical poem or dialogue or a comparison chart. You might focus on a thesis statement or another generalization, or begin with this quotation:

   Why does a woman work ten years to change a man's habits and then complain he's not the man she married?

   Barbra Streisand

2. In your Response Notebook, write King a letter supporting, refuting, or qualifying his thesis or another point of interest.

3. With a partner, consider which writer's voice you prefer and why. What distinguishes the "sound" of each? What tips about style and voice might you pick up to enliven your own writing?

The Writing Folder

Tip • You may wish to discuss your progress with a partner as you revise, edit, and polish your work, or you may prefer to leave your work in first-draft form. Resource Two, which begins on page 181, will help you with this process.

4. Working alone or in small groups, brainstorm topics for both serious and humorous expository essays. After creating a mind map or web of ideas for one topic, discuss your preliminary ideas with a partner. Determine whether you'll proceed with a rough draft or experiment with another topic.

Tip • Check your Response Notebook for ideas; for example, polish your letter to Stephen King and send it to his publisher or hone your satirical entry.

5. Rewrite a narrative essay in expository form. Which version do you prefer? Why?

Media Extensions

Tip* • *Resource Five, which begins on page 190, may be of help with your media assignment.

6. Bring to class titles of television and radio programs which use expository techniques, or clip several effective examples of expository writing from newspapers and magazines for group discussion. Be prepared to explain your choices and justify the label of exposition.

Tip* • Only the News That Fits (NFB) *explains the forces that shape news reporting.

7. View several documentary films or television programs. Take notes on how sound, text, and shots create the exposition. (You might compare two depictions of the same event, such as *Have I Ever Lied to You Before?* and *An Unremarkable Birth* [NFB, *Media and Society*, I].) Or you may prefer to create a visual response—perhaps a collage or cartoon strip—reacting to the content of one of the documentaries.

Independent Learning

Tip* • *Resource One, which begins on page 178, may help you devise and complete your project.

8. With the assistance of your teacher and a peer, adapt one of the above topics into an independent study project, or alter one of these ideas to suit your needs and interests.

a) After studying the genre, make a documentary film which uses expository techniques.
b) After reading many well-written expository essays, assemble an anthology of your preferences, along with an introduction, conclusion, and explanation of each essay.

Connections

9. Invite a visitor to explain the "how-to's" of a specific task. For example, a student services counsellor or parent might explain job-searching techniques or resumé writing.

NOTE: *For additional activities, see "Responding to the Essay" (page 174).*

ARGUING YOUR CASE

Suppose you want to convince a friend that your spaniel, Chimo, is better trained than her dog, Emilio. You'd present your case through argumentation, a form of exposition that adopts a position to be proved. If you've detected an element of argumentation in King's and Syfers's essays, remember that these patterns overlap.

There are two routes to convincing your audience—through the head and through the heart. Argumentation in its pure form appeals primarily to the intellect; the writer builds a logical case through verifiable evidence.

The second route, persuasion, which relies on the emotions, is the subject of the next section. Of course, argument is not totally without emotion. It's a question of emphasis and intensity.

There are two methods of building a sound argument. Inductive reasoning begins with a specific instance and moves through to a general conclusion. For example, if you board Chimo at a kennel and she returns once with fleas, you can't draw a valid conclusion about their source. However, if Chimo returns with fleas several times, you may validly decide to find a new kennel. With deduction, *you apply a general concept to a specific instance to arrive at a general conclusion. For example, you might reason that all dogs have fleas and Chimo is a dog; therefore, Chimo has fleas. Of course, if the basic assumption is false, so is your conclusion.*

Before reading the sample argumentation essays and student response essay, you may want to consider the writing variables (see page 183) and discuss this pattern's characteristics.

The Argumentative Essay

Purpose	*To convince an audience of the validity of a thesis*
Audience	*Anyone old enough to reason*
Tone	*Objective but determined*
Mood	*Varies according to subject*
Language	*Formal through informal; impersonal through colloquial; connotative and denotative*
Voice	*Neutral through expressive*

Harry
Bruce
••••••••

AND MAY THE BEST CHEATER WIN

Talking Points

1. Is honesty always the best policy? Do you agree with Thomas Jefferson that "honesty is the first chapter of the book of wisdom"?

2. What is the most appropriate way for an educational institution to deal with plagiarism?

3. Is cheating acceptable in your peer group? If so, what rules apply? View a film such as TV Sale *(NFB, Media and Society, I).*

Every youth knows he can get into deep trouble by stealing cameras, peddling dope, mugging winos, forging cheques, or copying someone else's answers during an exam. Those are examples of not playing by the rules. Cheating. But every youth also knows that in organized sports across North America, cheating is not only perfectly okay, it's *recommended*. "The structure of sport . . . actually promotes deviance," says U.S. sport sociologist D.S. Eitzen.

The downy-cheeked hockey player who refuses to play dirty may find himself fired off the team. The boy soccer player who refuses to rough up a superior striker to "throw him off his game" may find himself writhing under a coach's tongue-lashing. The basketball player who refuses to foul a goal-bound enemy star in the last seconds of a close game may find himself riding the bench next week. Thus, we have that cynical paradox, "the good foul," a phrase that makes about as much sense as "a beneficial outbreak of bubonic plague."

If organized sports offer benefits to youngsters, they also offer a massive program of moral corruption. The recruiting of college athletes in the United States, and the use of academic fraud to maintain their "eligibility," stunk so powerfully in 1980 that *Newsweek* decided "cheating has become the name of the game," and spoke of the fear on U.S. campuses of "an epidemic of corruption." But the epidemic had already arrived, and what really worried *Newsweek* was national acceptance of corruption as normal: "Many kids are admitting that they have tried to take the bribes and inducements on the sleazy terms with which they are offered. Their complaints are not so much that illegalities exist, but that they aren't getting their share of the goodies."

Fans, alumni, coaches, college administrators, players, and their parents all believed nothing could ever be more important than winning (or more disgraceful than losing), and that cheating in victory's cause was therefore commendable.

"Candidates for big-time sport's Hall of Shame have seemed suddenly to break out all over like an ugly rash," William Oscar Johnson wrote last year in *Sports Illustrated*. He constructed a dismal catalogue of assaults on cops, drunken brawls, adventures in the cocaine trade, credit-card frauds, and other sordid activities by rich professional athletes who, in more naïve times, might have earned the adulation of small boys. Jim Finks, then Chicago Bears general manager, speculated that the trouble with the younger lawbreakers was that they had "been looked after all the way from junior high school. Some of them have had doctored grades. This plus the affluence [astronomical salaries] means there has never been any pressing need for them to work things out for themselves. They have no idea how to face reality."

No one in all their lives had taught them about fair play. "In the early days of playground and high-school leagues, one of the key issues was moral regulation," says Alan Ingham, a teacher at the University of Washington. "You got sports, and you got Judeo-Christian principles thrown in, too." Now, however, "the majority of things taught in sports are performance things." John Pooley of the School of Recreation, Physical and Health Education at Dalhousie University, Nova Scotia, asked Calvin Hill, a former Dallas Cowboy, what percentage of all the football rookies he'd ever met had said that, as college players, they'd encountered no cheating. Hill's reply was short: "None."

So here we have the most powerful nation in the world, and it blithely corrupts children so they'll mature as athletic machines without an ounce of the moral sense that might prevent their sniffing cocaine or complicate their lust for victory. Pray for nuclear disarmament, fans.

Still, Canadians are little better. We all know who invented the game that inspired Paul Newman to star in *Slap Shot*, a black and bloody comedy about butchery on ice. We can't argue that it's only American coaches who teach peewees to draw tripping penalties rather than let an enemy player continue a breakaway on your goal. Moreover, I happen to live in Halifax, where only last winter St. Mary's University was disgraced for allowing a ringer from Florida to play varsity basketball. The coach of a rival but inferior team ferreted out the truth about the player's ineligibility. In doing so, he imported one of the fine old traditions of amateur sports in the States: if you can't beat them, hire a private dick. Oh well, that's what universities are supposed to be all about: the pursuit of truth.

Pursuing another truth, Pooley of Dalhousie surveyed recent graduates of three down-east universities. The grads were both men and women, and they had all played intercollegiate field hockey, ice hockey, soccer or basketball. "With one exception [a woman field hockey player], all felt there was immense pressure to win," Pooley said. Typical responses: "Winning is everything in university sport. . . . The measure of success was not how well you played but the win-loss record. . . . There is incredible pressure to perform because there are always two or three guys on the bench ready to take your place."

Half said their coaches had urged "winning at any cost." One grad revealed, "Some coaches send their players 'out to get' a good player on the other team." Another described "goon coaches who stressed intimidation and rough play." Coaches had not only condoned tactical fouls, but had actually taught the arts of fouling during practice. A player who had competed against British and Bermudian teams said they played "intensely but fairly" while the Maritimers "sometimes used dirty tactics" or "blatantly tried to stop a player."

Pooley wondered if the grads, after years in intercollegiate sport, felt it had promoted fair play. Only the field-hockey players said yes. Answers from the others were shockers: "Everyone cheats and the best cheater wins. . . . Fair play and sportsmanship are *not* promoted. This is a joke. . . . You did whatever you could to win. . . . You are taught to gain an advantage, whatever it takes." Such cynicism, from people so young they've barely doffed their mortarboards, confirms the sad opinion of one Kalevi Heinila, who told a world scientific congress in 1980 that fair play was "ripe to be dumped in the waste basket of sport history."

The irony in all this—and it's both ludicrous and nauseating—is that universities defend their expensive programs for intercollegiate sports with lip service to the notion that keen teamwork in clean competition nurtures good citizens. Fair play in sports, don't you know, spawns fair players for the world of politics, the professions, and business.

That's a crock. What intercollegiate sport really teaches is how to get away with murder, how to be crooked within the law. Just listen to one of the fresh-faced grads in Pooley's survey as he sets out to make his way in the world, his eyes shining with idealism: "University sport teaches you to play as close to the limits as possible; and this is the attitude that will get you ahead in the business world." Another acknowledged that his "concept of fair play decreased"; but, on the other hand, he had learned to "stretch the rules to my advantage." A young woman confided, "University sport has made me tough, less sensitive to other people's feelings." Still others stressed that college sport had prepared them for "the real world," for "real life," in which winning was all.

Cheating in amateur sport, Pooley says, "gives it a hollow feeling. Many coaches do not have integrity. I'm still sickened by that. It upsets me, at all levels." A tall, talkative, forceful man with a bony face and a thick brush of steely hair, Pooley has coached soccer in six countries, once played for professional teams in Britain, and now, at 53, cavorts on a team for men over 35. "I'm still playing league soccer," he wrote in a paper for the 1984 Olympic Scientific Congress in Eugene, Oregon, "because: a) I helped to organize and plan my own youth soccer experiences; b) coming second or being beaten was okay; c) I was always much more interested in playing well than playing to win; d) I never minded playing less well than I'd earlier played; and e) I always felt successful at the level played."

Those are highly un-American reasons for playing any sport, but Pooley is originally from northern England, the nation that invented "fair play" and knew that certain things just weren't cricket. That was in a time long before Americans institutionalized cheating even in soap box derbies, before athletes gobbled steroids, before universities invented courses in weight lifting and raquetball so quarterbacks could qualify as "students." Moreover, Pooley believes that the few adults who stick with team sports until middle age do so because, as youngsters, "They preferred the feel of the ball, the pass well made, the sweetness of the stroke or the power in the shot, rather than whether they won or lost the game." Such people don't need to cheat.

Some scholars believe that the sleaziness of organized sports simply reflects the sleaziness of our entire culture. Pooley points out, for instance, that one sociologist offers two reasons why cheating in sports shouldn't be "disproportionately reprimanded." The first is that it's "endemic in society," and the second is that even more cheating probably occurs in other fields. Pooley disagrees. He says this argument is like saying you should not disproportionately reprimand the clergy for being dishonest. Poor Pooley. He has such quaint ideas about sports. He actually believes they should not be immoral, and should be fun.

Andrea
Chisholm
••••••••••••

THE "HIGH" OF AN HONEST WIN

Student Response Essay to
Harry Bruce's "And May the Best Cheater Win"

Talking Points

1. Outline several constructive strategies for dealing with a rule or law you feel is unfair. You might view a film about a tactic called civil disobedience. See, for example, I Have a Dream *about Martin Luther King or* Walden *about Henry David Thoreau.*

2. If you observe someone cheating during a sports match in which you're a player, what do you do about it?

3. Discuss the meaning of the following terms: self-concept, self-esteem, and integrity. What people or forces help us form each of these attributes?

After our class discussed Bruce's essay about cheating in sports, I got to thinking about some of my peers' comments and values about scholastic cheating. There are two central concerns. First, what is happening to our school system and the individuals within it? And second, why is it happening? To answer these issues, I conducted independent research—minor in comparison to Pooley's—but it's indicative of what transpires among teens. The bald fact is this: most students reported cheating to "survive" at school. The moral and social consequences are far-reaching. In so doing, they're not only cheating the system, but worse, they also condone their own actions and deprive themselves of the satisfaction of a good mark, honestly earned.

Let's begin with some hard statistics from my survey conducted at a typical upper-middle class high school. *Fact:* 71 percent of high-school students interviewed have skipped a class and lied about it to school officials. *Fact:* 100 percent of these students have copied homework to pass a homework check. *Fact:* 100 percent have attempted to find out test questions and answers from students who have previously written it.

"Avoiding punishment by parents and teachers" is one of the reasons Karen, one typical "A" student, lied about skipping class. "I had a doctor's appointment," she said with a straight face to her history teacher. Did she follow the rules and bring a note or sign out? She "forgot." However, because her plight *sounded* sincere, and she'd developed a reputation of a "good and trustworthy student," the teacher relented and did not call home. So she, and many compatriots, get off the hook, so to speak—at least temporarily.

Annette, a graduating student, neatly summed up students' sentiments: "People—students *or* adults—cheat and lie because they can usually get away with it. If people were caught and punished more often, fewer would cheat on tests—or income taxes."

One major problem is attitudinal; few contemporary high-school students take homework—or school—very seriously. "I'll do that tomorrow" is a common sentiment. Procrastination is part of the problem, but today's teens tend to hold different values from earlier generations who often didn't take education as a right. And they fool themselves into thinking that the cheating will happen "just this once." Finally, priorities are just plain different: "My girlfriend and my job come first," George admitted. "But that's the way most of us guys feel. Hey, why not?"

This to-heck-with-the consequences attitude prevails before tests, too. Here's a typical high-school scenario. It's lunch hour and Susan has a biology test next class. In fact, it's the one her best friend, Jennifer, has just finished.

SUSAN: So, was the test hard? What was on it?

JENNIFER: Oh, some diagrams and essay-type things. You know.

SUSAN: Like what?

JENNIFER: Well . . .

Jennifer proceeds to disclose test details. They're cheating, but may not affix that label. The girls merely convince themselves of the need for this "discussion," rationalizing their actions as "survival tactics," as one graduating student put it.

Most students who themselves cheat certainly *appear* to condone cheating among others. Almost everyone, it seems, is guilty. And even if you don't cheat, you're reluctant to be stigmatized as a "squealer." Let's say you're in the middle of a major chemistry test. You observe the pair in front of you exchanging answers. But the teacher seems to be dozing at the front of the room. So you decide to ignore them and concentrate more intently on your paper. None of *my* business, you rationalize. And at the end of class, you leave, feeling only slightly guilty for not reporting the incident to the teacher. Are *you*, then, a cheater, too?

In a sense, yes. "Guilt by association," it's called. Allowing someone to cheat is as unethical as if *you'd* opted to cheat. *Fact:* 99 percent of the high-school students interviewed wouldn't inform the teacher they'd witnessed cheating. The social consequences are too high for most teens to bear. But if this isn't cheating the students who studied late into the night and kept their eyes on their own paper, what is?

But what of that 1 percent who don't condone and may report cheating? It seems that if one's self interest is *directly* involved, a report may be filed. For example, a teacher told me of a case several years ago in which two students reported a third who'd purchased an independent study project worth 20 percent of her final course mark. Indeed, they provided the evidence for the zero which was awarded. Why did they take this action? "We're competing for the same scholarships and prizes as Sally. She's getting an unfair advantage." When money's at stake among graduating students, a different "morality" takes charge.

Whether we like to admit it or not, most of us cheat in one way or another. We may involve ourselves with cheaters. Or we may participate directly in activities which permit others to cheat. Yet few people perceive themselves as cheaters. Most of us feel we're honest human beings. *Fact:* 100 percent of high-school students interviewed *claimed* they did not condone cheating. Bruce's argument seems to apply to the classroom, as well as to the locker room. It sometimes looks as if the best cheater does "win." Wrong.

Fact: they're only "the best cheater" of their self-respect.

Harry
Waters
. . . .

WHAT TV DOES TO KIDS

Talking Points

1. Compare TV viewing habits with your classmates.

2. What restrictions, if any, have your parents placed on your TV viewing over the years? When you're a parent, do you expect to follow the same policy?

3. Does viewing television violence and sex-role stereotyping increase our tolerance for such behaviour? Discuss. You may wish to view a film such as The Question of Television Violence (*NFB, Media and Society, III*).

His first polysyllabic utterance was "Bradybunch." He learned to spell Sugar Smacks before his own name. Recently, he tried to karate-chop his younger sister after she broke his Six Million Dollar Man bionic transport station (she retaliated by bashing him with her Cher doll). His nursery-school teacher reports that he is passive, noncreative, and has almost no attention span; in short, he is very much like his classmates. This fall, he will officially reach the age of reason and begin his formal education. His parents are beginning to discuss their apprehensions—when they are not too busy watching television.

It is only in recent years—with the first TV generation already grown up—that social scientists, psychologists, pediatricians, and educators have begun serious study of the impact of television on the young. According to television survey-taker A.C. Nielsen, children under five watch an average of 23.5 hours of TV a week. Today's typical high-school graduate has logged at least 15 000 hours before the small screen—more time than he has spent on any other activity except sleep. At present levels of advertising and mayhem, he will have been exposed to 350 000 commercials and vicariously participated in 18 000 killings. The conclusion is inescapable: After parents, television has become perhaps the most potent influence on the beliefs, values, and behavior of the young.

Unquestionably, the plug-in picture window has transmitted some benefits. In general, the children of TV enjoy a more sophisticated knowledge of a far larger world. They are likely to possess richer vocabularies, albeit with only a superficial comprehension of what the words mean.

Research on the impact of "Sesame Street" has established measurable gains in the cognitive skills of many pre-schoolers.

Nonetheless, the overwhelming body of evidence—drawn from more than 2300 studies and reports—is decidedly negative. Michael Rothenberg, a child psychiatrist at the University of Washington, has reviewed the 50 most comprehensive studies involving 10 000 children from every possible background. Most showed that viewing violence tends to produce aggressive behavior among the young. "The time is long past due for a major, organized cry of protest from the medical profession," concludes Rothenberg.

An unexpected salvo was sounded last winter when the normally cautious American Medical Association asked ten major corporations to review their policies about sponsoring excessively gory shows. "TV violence is both a mental-health problem and an environmental issue," explained Dr. Richard E. Palmer, president of the AMA. In defense, broadcasting officials maintain that the jury is still out on whether video violence is guilty of producing aggressive behavior. And network schedulers say they are actively reducing the violence dosage.

But televised mayhem is only part of TV's impact. TV has at the very least preempted the traditional development of childhood itself. The time kids spend sitting catatonic before the set has been exacted from such salutary pursuits as reading, outdoor play, even simple, contemplative solitude. Few parents can cope with its tyrannical allure. Recently, Dr. Benjamin Spock took his stepdaughter and granddaughter to New York to see a concert and a Broadway show. But the man who has the prescription for everything from diaper rash to bedwetting had no easy solution for dislodging the kids from their hotel room. "Of all the attractions in New York," recalls Spock, "they seemed to find the TV set the most fascinating."

Small wonder that television has been called "the flickering blue parent." The after-school and early-evening hours used to be a time for "what-did-you-do-today" dialogue. Now the electronic box does most of the talking. Dr. David Pearl of the U.S. National Institute of Mental Health suspects that the tube "has displaced many of the normal interactional processes between parents and children which are essential for maximum development."

Even more worrisome is what television has done to, rather than denied, the tube-weaned population. A series of studies has shown that addiction to TV stifles creative imagination. For example, a University of Southern California research team exposed 250 elementary students to three weeks of intensive viewing. Tests found a marked drop in all forms of creative abilities except verbal skill. Some teachers are encountering children who cannot understand a simple story without visual illustrations. Nursery-school teachers who have observed the pre-TV generation contend that juvenile play is far less imaginative and spontaneous than in the past. "You don't see kids making their own toys out of crummy things like we used to," says University of Virginia psychology professor Stephen Worchel. "You don't see them playing hopscotch, or making up their own games. Everything is suggested to them by television."

Too much TV too early may also instill an attitude of spectatorship, a withdrawal from direct involvement in real-life experiences. "What television basically teaches children is passivity," says Stanford University researcher Paul Kaufman. "It creates the illusion of having been somewhere and done something and seen something, when in fact they've been sitting at home."

Conditioned to see all problems resolved in 30 or 60 minutes, the offspring of TV exhibit a low tolerance for the frustration of learning. Grade-schoolers are quickly turned off by any activity that promises less than instant gratification. "You introduce a new skill, and right away, if it looks hard, they dissolve into tears," laments one first-grade teacher. "They want everything to be easy—like watching the tube."

The debate over the link between TV violence and aggressive behavior in society has had a longer run than "Gunsmoke." Today, however, even zealous network apologists concede that some children, under certain conditions, will imitate antisocial acts seen on the tube. Indeed a study of 100 juvenile offenders commissioned by ABC found that no fewer than 22 confessed to having copied criminal techniques from TV. Behavioral sleuths are also uncovering evidence that the tide of TV carnage increases children's tolerance of violent behavior in others, because they have been conditioned to think of violence as an everyday thing.

And now a word about the sponsors. The hottest battle in this area involves the impact of child-directed commercials on their audience's eating habits. Many of the ads on Saturday and Sunday morning "kidvid" peddle sugarcoated cereals, candy, and chewing gum, hooking children on poor eating habits long before they develop the mental defenses to resist. "This is the most massive educational program to eat junk food in history," charges Sid Wolinsky, an attorney for a San Francisco public-interest group. According to a study by Columbia University psychology professor Thomas Bever, misleading TV ads may also be "permanently distorting children's views of morality, society, and business." From in-depth interviews with 48 youngsters between the ages of 5 and 12, Bever concluded that by the time they reach 12 many find it easier to decide that all commercials lie than to try to determine which are telling the truth.

A few daring parents have counterattacked by simply pulling the plug. Charles Frye, a San Francisco nursery-school teacher and the father of five boys, decided he would not replace his set after it conked out in 1972. Frye's brood rebelled at first, but today 14-year-old Mark fills his afternoon hours with tap dancing lessons, scout meetings, and work in a gas station. Kirk, his 13-year-old brother, plays a lot of basketball and football and recently finished *Watership Down* and all four of the Tolkien hobbit books.

Short of such a draconian measure, some parents are exercising a greater degree of home rule. Two years ago, the administrators of New York's Horace Mann nursery school became distressed over an upsurge of violence in their students' play. Deciding that television was to blame, they dispatched a letter to all parents urging them to curb their children's viewing. "After we sent the letter, we could see a change," recalls principal Eleanor Brussel. "The kids showed better concentration, better comprehension, an ability to think things through."

Clearly, there is no single antidote. For the children of today, and their progeny to come, TV watching will continue to be their most shared—and shaping—experience. Virtually all the experts agree, however, on one palliative. Instead of using TV as an electronic babysitter, parents must try to involve themselves directly in their youngsters' viewing. By watching along with the kids at least occasionally, they can help them evaluate what they see —pointing out the inflated claims of a commercial, perhaps, or criticizing a gratuitously violent scene. "Parents don't have to regard TV as a person who can't be interrupted," says behavioral scientist Charles Corder-Bolz. "If they view one show a night with their kids, and make just one or two comments about it, they can have more impact than the whole program."

Reduced to the essentials, the question for parents no longer is: "Do you know where your children are tonight?" The question has become: "What are they watching—and with whom?"

Suggested Activities

First Reactions

Tip • For suggestions about using your Response Notebook, see page 183 of Resource One.

1. In your Response Notebook, react to one or more essays in this group. For example, you might:

   a) relate an anecdote about an occasion when you made a decision about cheating

   b) reflect on whether Bruce's or Chisholm's evidence is more convincing and why

   c) compose a variety of working thesis statements and determine which is the most worthwhile to pursue

   d) draft a dialogue between two friends arguing about cheating on an exam.

2. In small groups, plan and present a role-play or mime which dramatizes your views about an issue of interest, such as cheating in the classroom or on the playing field, or the effects of television viewing.

Tip • For assistance, see Resource Four on page 189.

3. With a partner, decide which essay is most effectively argued.

Tip • As a class, develop criteria, or refer to page 185.

4. With a partner, reflect on which writer's voice you prefer and consider what you can learn about expressing your own voice from these essayists.

The Writing Folder

Tip • You may wish to discuss your progress with a partner as you revise, edit, and polish your work, or you may prefer to leave your work in first-draft form. Resource Two, which begins on page 181, will help you with this process.

5. After brainstorming ideas for writing in small groups, draft a formal argumentative essay about a topic of interest. Remember to use verifiable evidence.

Tip • You might begin working in small groups to compose a list of controversial quotations and proverbs around which to build writing topics. For example:

- **Cheaters never prosper**.
- **We must make the world honest before we can honestly say to our children that honesty is the best policy.** *G.B. Shaw*
- **The vast wasteland of TV is not interested in producing a better mousetrap but in producing a worse mouse.** *Laurence C. Coughlin*

Media Extensions

Tip • *Resource Five, which begins on page 190, may be of help with your media assignment.*

6. Make a videotape based on one of the above activities or an activity of your own that portrays information. You might want to view the film *This Is a Recorded Message* (NFB).

7. Compile a photostory with a collage of photographs from the best of early American situation comedies. The storyline and accompanying written text should argue a thesis about these comedies.

Independent Learning

Tip • *Resource One, which begins on page 178, may help you devise and complete your project.*

8. Argue a case about bias in news coverage. You might select one event and follow its coverage on radio and television and in the press. Log your work with each medium. Present your findings in a speech, an audio or videotape, or an essay.

9. Assemble an attractively packaged anthology that focuses on a form of betrayal, such as cheating, hypocrisy, or dishonesty, and its effects. Include approximately twelve items, including poems, song lyrics, and brief excerpts from essays, short stories, and novels. Illustrate your anthology with photographs, drawings, and cartoons. Write an introduction and conclusion about the theme, and a brief explanation of each work.

Connections

10. Attend a play which dramatizes one of the issues presented in the three essays in this section.

NOTE: *For additional activities, see "Responding to the Essay". (page 174).*

PERSUADING YOUR AUDIENCE

Let's suppose your cousins are buying a pet. You want to persuade them that your dog, Chimo, is a better buy than, say, your friend's dog, Emilio. You might proceed in two ways. First, you'd use facts about both breeds to convince your cousins that a cocker spaniel is the better choice. Then, you'd appeal to their emotions with anecdotes about your dog's lovable traits.

Persuasion is a form of exposition which convinces the audience of a claim, or thesis, through apppeals to both the heart and the head. Factual information and emotional appeals entice the audience to act. Persuasion differs from argumentation in the degree to which emotion enters into the discussion. Appeals to the emotions are often constructed through highly connotative and figurative language and rhetorical devices that affect the senses.

Before reading the sample persuasive essays and student response essay, you may want to consider the writing variables (see page 183) and discuss this pattern's characteristics.

The Persuasive Essay

Purpose	To persuade your audience to act
Audience	Various
Tone	Various; often subjective, impassioned, inspired
Mood	Various; often moved, energized, impassioned
Language	Formal through informal; impersonal through colloquial; appeals to senses and emotions through connotative words and rhetoric
Voice	Generally pronounced and expressive

**Margaret
Laurence**
....

My Final Hour

Talking Points

*1. Under what circumstances, if ever, is war justified? You might
discuss the impact of media portrayals of war in such films as* Platoon
and Born on the Fourth of July. (*See also* A Writer in the Nuclear
Age: A Conversation with Margaret Laurence *[NFB]*).

*2. Do you think Canada's role in the 1991 Gulf War was ethically and
politically correct?*

*3. What sentiments about war do both classic poems and contempo-
rary songs convey?*

My generation was the first in human history to come into young adulthood
knowing that the human race now had the dreadful ability to destroy all life
on earth and possibly the earth itself. Only later did we realize the full extent
of the destruction of life, a continuing destruction passed on to the then-
unborn children of survivors, but we *did* know that after Hiroshima, August
6, 1945, the world would never be the same again. The annihilation caused
by the first atomic bombs was unthinkable, but it had happened. Also, we
had taken it for granted that through wars, through disasters, yet would the
earth endure forever. It was clear to many of us in 1945 that this was no
longer to be taken for granted. We have lived with that thought ever since,
and have yet borne our children, lived our lives, done our work. The will to
survive and to pass on important caring to future generations is very strong.
But today we have to realize that the bombs used at Hiroshima and Nagasaki
were *small* bombs, compared to today's nuclear weapons.

I ask you to think of the Holocaust in Europe, when the Nazis murdered a
very great part of all the Jewish communities. That horror, surely, must *never*
be forgotten. No amount of mourning will *ever* be enough for those millions
of children, women, and men whose lives were torn from them by the group
of de-humanized humans who had taken power in Hitler's Germany. Are we
to remember the Holocaust and the horrors of Hiroshima and Nagasaki and
yet remain silent when we hear today about a "winnable" nuclear war or a
"limited" nuclear war? I think not.

Our lives and the lives of all generations as yet unborn are being threatened, as never before, by the increasing possibility of a nuclear war. I believe that the question of disarmament is the most pressing practical, moral, and spiritual issue of our times. I'm not talking about abstractions. I'm talking about my life and your life and my kids' lives and the lives of people everywhere. If we value our own lives, and the lives of our children and all children everywhere, if we honour both the past and the future, then we must do everything in our power to work non-violently for peace. These beliefs are not only an integral part of my social and moral stance but of my religious faith as well. Human society now possesses the terrible ability to destroy all life on earth, and our planet itself. Can anyone who has ever marvelled at the miracle of creation—who has ever borne or fathered a beloved child, who has ever looked closely at a tree or a plant or a river—fail to feel concerned and indeed anguished, every single day, at this thought?

A central disagreement, of course, exists between those who think that more and yet more nuclear arms will ensure that nuclear arms will never be used, and those of us who believe that the proliferation of nuclear weapons brings us closer all the time to the actuality of nuclear war—a war that no side could possibly win; a war that would be so devastating that we cannot begin to imagine the horror. Whatever we are being told about a "limited" or a "winnable" nuclear war, the fact remains that such a war could destroy all that we, as humankind, have aspired to, have achieved. It could destroy the future, not only of the world's peoples but of all creatures that share our planet with us.

As America and Russia develop more and more nuclear arms, so the other will inevitably respond in kind. Nuclear arms have long since ceased to be a "deterrent," if indeed they were ever so, and have become by their very existence a monstrous threat. Daily, the chances are increasing for a nuclear war to break out by accident, by a failure of the intricate and not totally reliable control and warning systems on either side, or simply by human panic and a mutual mistrust between the superpowers.

It is precisely this failure of the imagination on the part of militarists and leaders that is so dangerous today, the failure to visualize what a nuclear holocaust would mean, the apparent inability to imagine the scorched and charred bodies of children . . . our children or children of Russian parents or parents anywhere, and to know, by an extension of imagination, that *all* children are our children. The jargon of the militarists is a distortion and a twisting of language, of our human ability to communicate. Language itself becomes the vehicle of concealment and deception. Such words as "overkill" and "megadeath" do not convey in any sense at all what would really happen—the dead, mutilated, and dying suffering humans screaming for help with no medical help available, no water, no relief at all for the unbearable pain of millions of humans except finally the dark relief of death for all. Any shelters that the few might reach would in time turn into tombs. Civil defence plans are a sham. In a nuclear war there would be nowhere to hide, and nowhere except a dead and contaminated world to emerge back into.

I profoundly believe that we must proclaim that *this must not happen*.

Yes, but what about the Russians? If we try to persuade our government to refuse Cruise missile testing, aren't we playing into the hands of the bad guys? Won't the Soviet Union, as soon as they have clear superiority in nuclear arms, blow us all to hell without a second's thought? I do not think so. Isn't it necessary to have more and ever more nuclear weapons in the hands of the Americans so that we can feel *safe*? I do not think so. Let me make it clear that I hold no brief for the present Russian system of government. I hold no brief for *any* system of government that is repressive and cruel, and this includes those far-right regimes in countries such as El Salvador, to whom the U.S.A. is determinedly giving so much military aid. The U.S.A. and Russia, the two superpowers, must, I believe, co-exist in this world, even if there are some terrible things wrong in *both* systems, and *there are*. Russia suffered horribly in World War II, whereas war has not been fought on American soil since the Civil War. I cannot believe that the Russian leaders are all that anxious to begin nuclear war in which the Soviet Union would be, if not totally annihilated, then certainly decimated beyond any hope of recovery.

Quite frankly, I can't believe that Russia any longer has hopes of a world revolution. I can believe, though, that the Russian people, the ordinary people who love their children just as much as I love mine, are frightened, just as I am frightened, just as a very large proportion of the American people are frightened and are expressing that fear and outrage. The American people are indeed our cousins, and a very great many of them, young and old, are saying virtually the same things as I am saying here.

Do we care so little about our children? Do we honour life so little that we will not speak out? I believe we do care, passionately and profoundly. Indeed, one thing that gives me hope is that so many of our churches and synagogues, so many people of all faiths, of all professions and trades, of all ages, are speaking out against the arms race and the descent into madness. *Physicians for Social Responsibility*, active in this country as well as in America and elsewhere, are telling us what human damage would be done, and how impossible any thought of medical aid would be in a nuclear war. Interchurch groups such as *Project Ploughshares* are making strong representations to our government, as are labour unions, academics, and indeed and perhaps most importantly, women and men everywhere, in every walk of life. This is true in so very many places in the world today.

The money spent on arms, including nuclear arms, continues to mount. Recently I read that $550 billion dollars are being spent, world-wide, yearly, on arms. An even more recent estimate puts it at $600 billion dollars. That sum is so great we cannot really comprehend it. But we *can* comprehend that for the cost of *one* Trident nuclear submarine, malaria could be wiped out from the world. Think of that for one minute. I think of the people in the world who are suffering from thirst, from starvation, from preventable diseases, from ceaseless fighting, and the brutality of oppressive regimes. I think, too, of the growing number of unemployed people in our own land. I think of the Reagan program in America—more and yet more money spent on nuclear arms; less and less spent on social programs and help to the poor and the disabled.

I have to speak about how I feel as a writer. I don't like calling myself "an artist," but I guess I am, and would join with my tribal sisters and brothers in many ways. I believe that as a writer . . . an artist, if you will . . . I have a responsibility, a moral responsibility, to work against the nuclear arms race, to work for a recognition on the part of governments and military leaders that nuclear weapons must never be used and must systematically be reduced. Throughout human history, artists have affirmed and celebrated life. Whether we work in words, in music, in painting, in film, in bronze or stone or whatever our medium may be, the artist affirms the value of life itself and of our only home, the planet Earth. Art mirrors and ponders the pain and joy of our experience as human beings. In many parts of the world, and over many centuries, artists have risked and even given their own lives to portray the society around them as they perceived it, and to speak out against injustices. Since the most ancient times, artists have passed on to succeeding generations the tales, the histories, the songs, the sagas, the skills of their trade. Can we conceive of a world in which there would be no succeeding generations? A world in which all the powerful works of the human imagination would be destroyed, would never again be seen or listened to or experienced? We must conceive that this is now a possibility, and one not too far in our uncertain future, either. We must not, as artists, or so I feel, stand by and passively allow this to happen. The death of the individual is the end which we will all some day meet, but in the knowledge that our children and their children will live, that *someone's* children will go on, and that the great works of humankind will endure in art, in recorded history, in medicine, in the sciences and philosophies and technologies that our species has developed with devotion and a sense of vocation through-out the ages. The individual is the leaf on the tree. The leaves fall but the tree endures. New leaves are born. This concept has been the mainstay of our species from time immemorial. Now the tree itself is threatened. All art is a product of the human imagination. It is, deeply, an honouring of the past, a perception of the present in one way or another, and a looking towards the future. Whatever the medium of any particular artist, art is reaching out, an attempt to communicate those things which most concern us seriously in our sojourn here on earth. Artists, the real ones, the committed ones, have always sought, sometimes in ways prophetic and beyond their own times, to clarify and proclaim and enhance life, not to obscure and demean and destroy it. Even the so-called literature of despair is not really that at all. Despair is total silence, total withdrawal. Art, by its very nature of necessary expression, is an act of faith, an acknowledgement of the profound mystery at the core of life.

As a writer, therefore, I feel I have a responsibility. Not to write pamphlets, not to write didactic fiction. That would be, in many ways, a betrayal of how I feel about my work. But my responsibility seems to me to be to write as truthfully as I can, about human individuals and their dilemmas, to honour them as living, suffering, and sometimes joyful people. My responsibility also must extend into my life as a citizen of my own land and ultimately of the world.

I do not claim to have done this well. There are no personal victories in those areas. The individual, here, becomes part of a community and only as a part of that community can one person ever be effective and true to herself or himself. There has to be the resolve not to give up, and to join with all others who believe that life itself is more important than our own individual lives, important though these certainly are.

So, if this were indeed my Final Hour, these would be my words to you. I would not claim to pass on any secret of life, for there is none, or any wisdom except the passionate plea of caring. In your dedication to your own life's work, whatever it may be, live as though you had forever, for no amount of careful and devoted doing is too great in carrying out that work to which you have set your hands. Cultivate in your work and your life the art of patience, and come to terms with your inevitable human limitations, while striving also to extend the boundaries of your understanding, your knowledge, and your compassion. These words are easily said; they are not easily lived. Learn from those who are older than you are; learn from your contemporaries; and never cease to learn from children. Try to feel, in your heart's core, the reality of others. This is the most painful thing in the world, probably, and the most necessary. In times of personal adversity, know that you are not alone. Know that although in the eternal scheme of things you are small, you are also unique and irreplaceable, as are all your fellow humans everywhere in the world. Know that your commitment is above all to life itself. Your own life and work and friendships and loves will come to an end, because one day you will die, and whatever happens after that, or if anything happens at all, it will not be on this earth. But life and work and friendship and love will go on, in others, your inheritors. The struggle for peace and for social justice will go on—provided that our earth survives and that caring humans still live. It is up to you, now, to do all that you can, and that means a commitment, at this perilous moment in our human history, to ensure that life itself *will* go on.

In closing, I want to quote one verse from that mighty book . . . more like a vast library . . . that Dr. Northrop Frye calls "The Great Code," and which has so shaped, sometimes so ambiguously, the imagination, the art, and the many facets of faith in our world. This verse is from Deuteronomy, Chapter 30:

"I have set before you life and death, blessing and cursing; therefore choose life, that both thou and thy seed may live."

Brenda
Chow
· · · · · · · ·

SEIZE THE DAY

Student Response Essay to
Margaret Laurence's "My Final Hour"

Talking Points

1. What social and political issues most concern you? View a film such as Pies *(NFB), or discuss a feature film such as* Children of a Lesser God *or* My Left Foot.

2. Do you feel your generation faces greater problems than those that challenged your parents' and grandparents' generations? Justify.

3. Consider several healthy strategies to deal with the pressures of daily life.

"You don't have to watch this if you don't want to," the teacher says.

This is a filmstrip on the Second World War. The projection screen is broken, but the slides hint at shapes on the blackboard; some of the terror still remains. I see gaunt shadows of Jesuit Germans, their eyes sunken, hopeless. It is horrible, yet riveting. As she listens to a brief commentary on the nuclear devastation of Hiroshima and Nagasaki, the girl next to me winces and bows her head. The room is silent for a moment before the narrator picks up the skein of historical fact and drones on about Hitler and fascism.

These memories come back to me as I read Margaret Laurence's poignant speech, "My Final Hour." But I can't help but ponder the different concerns of her generation and mine. If I'd been a child of World War II, I might focus more on the possibility of nuclear war. If I'd seen the devastation of Hiroshima and Nagasaki perhaps I'd have lobbeyed for the nuclear freeze movement.

But that was then. The possibility of nuclear war hovered relentlessly on the periphery. Everyone had an opinion about nuclear armament and the ethics of using such a force on a helpless Japanese nation. People like Margaret Laurence saw their safe, narrow path into the future devastated by the atomic bomb.

That was then.

To today's teenagers, nuclear war is not a day-to-day reality. After all, the atomic bomb has been around for some fifty years, and nothing "final" has eventuated. Yes, the meltdown at the Chernobyl nuclear plant did happen. When radiation undulated gently above our world, we paid attention. For fleeting moments I wondered about the countless deformed bodies, packaged in lead coffins, that might grace anonymous plots. But then it was old news; the moment passes and I turn back to a recalcitrant trig identity. Why? The longer we anticipate an event and the more an event is postponed, the more our ardour cools.

Now, it's the 1990s and our concerns lie elsewhere. War is "out" and peace is "in," Operation Desert Storm notwithstanding. Oat bran, cellular phones, and faxes are the rage. Working out and being rich is what it's all about, we're told. Saving the environment and combatting AIDS, urban gang violence, and crack addiction are today's front-page news. French Canadians are fighting for special privileges and the Oka Indians battle for basic rights. And what of my generation? We're just fighting to survive.

Survive? Yes, our battle is the here-and-now of everyday survival. In this fast-paced global village, technology bombards us with propaganda and information overload. Our air and water are polluted, our streets overrun with drug-crazed maniacs and people spreading AIDS. What is nuclear war compared to the threat of everyday living?

But survival for us means more than just staying alive. We want to do it in style. Now that not only B.A.s but M.B.A.s and L.L.D.s are a dime a dozen, it's necessary to prove oneself more capable than the next person. Since the average teenager wants—dare I say expects—a well-paid, satisfying job, the pressure is on to achieve high grades, enter the best university, and compete for prestigious positions.

Take Jennifer, for example. She wants to study occupational therapy, a frighteningly competitive field. Even though her grade average is in the nineties, she constantly pushes herself to improve. What with applying for just about every scholarship available and engaging in extracurricular activities to embellish her resumé, Jennifer rarely leaves school before six. And then she completes four hours of homework.

Now, Margaret Laurence might well have asked, How do the Jennifers of my generation feel about nuclear war? Abruptly, one day, I asked her.

"What?" Jen stares at me blankly.

"Nuclear war. Do you . . . think about it ever?" Hesitation.

"Well, no."

"Do you worry about the environment?" Less of a pause.

"Not exactly. I recycle."

"What does worry you, then?"

"Physics. I don't understand it."

Or take Lynda, the yearbook editor. She doesn't think about homework, parties, or life beyond high school. Her single-minded obsession is the yearbook—whether the ditzy sub-editor came through with the layout, whether page thirty-four is colour or not. When I query her about nuclear war, she mutters distractedly: "My God, we've only got fourteen pages ready!"

How can my generation so blindly assume this classic pose of the ostrich's head in the sand, you may ask. What is a yearbook compared to nuclear devastation? Well, I detect a new fatalism—perhaps cynicism—among us these days. The offbeat English teacher, Mr. Keating, of the cult movie *Dead Poets Society*, succinctly sums up the contemporary teenager's motto. "Seize the day." Tomorrow may never come. But if it does, and we must assume the burdens of Real Life, we must do so armed for personal survival, not as sixties flower children, naïvely scattering sunshine and roses upon the world.

It's not that we assume nuclear war could never come. We know the earth may be destroyed. We know about nuclear stockpiling. We know we could wake up one morning with the glorious flames of the mushroom-cloud spelling our demise. We know all this, as did Margaret Laurence. It's old news, this nuclear war issue. And because we know all about it, because we were born with the deed already done, we're innured to its impact. We're almost resigned to whatever happens.

Yet we fight on valiantly against the diseases, the anomalies, and the prejudices of this turn-of-the century world. Though I doubt that in the great, grand scheme of the universe our actions figure extravagantly, I am incensed with the injustice of it all. For we're fighting the mistakes, the excesses, the banalities of another generation, Margaret Laurence. And when it all gets to be too much, we climb back into our private bubbles where nuclear war holds little sway. It's physics, it's the yearbook, it's our resumé that we battle.

Ronald G.
Calhoun
and Anne
Doncaster
············

SHOULD ANIMALS BE USED IN MEDICAL RESEARCH: THE PROS AND CONS

Talking Points

1. Do animals have moral rights? Against what criteria does one weigh the rights of one species over another? You might read poems such as "The Animals in That Country" (Margaret Atwood), "Northern Water Thrush" (D.G. Jones), or "The Predator" (Irving Layton).

2. Should our federal government legislate the use of animals for medical testing? Debate.

3. How might the depiction of animals in children's stories, films, and cartoons affect an individual's position on this issue? For example, view the classic program "Jeremy, the Bear" or discuss the films Black Beauty *or* Lassie.

Last spring, a band of animal-rights activists invited the media to a sit-in at the University of Toronto faculty of medicine. Their target was experiments that they called cruel to animals. Such tactics challenge one of the central tenets of medical research: that animals must be used to combat human disease.

PRO (Ronald G. Calhoun)
Do countless thousands of Canadians have the right to the healthy lives they now enjoy? Do future generations have the basic human right to even greater freedom from disease? These questions command attention now that a few vocal radicals are threatening us all by trashing laboratories, intimidating researchers, and seducing the media. Their attempt to compromise our freedom from the pain and helplessness of disease must be seen as it is—political, self-serving, and narrowly focused.

Human good requires experimentation on lower animals in a humane and, yes, loving environment. The extension of the average human life span from 42 years at the turn of the century to 72-plus today, while partly because of nutrition, results largely from animal research. Heart disease, cancer, cystic fibrosis, polio, diabetes, glaucoma, multiple sclerosis, diphtheria, anemia . . . treatments for all these and more owe much to animal experiments. Without them, we would have little hope for a cure for AIDS. Virtually every Canadian alive today has already benefited—and so, incidentally, have our pets and farm animals.

Animal rightists, who owe their own good health to the very research they attack, urge researchers to rely totally on other methods, such as computer models and tissue cultures. These militants have great conviction but little knowledge of the facts. Not only are the touted alternatives already widely used; they are based upon animal research, and their development was financed by the scientific community, not the war chest of the antivivisectionists.

Some proponents of animal rights have argued that humans are the only scientifically valid subjects for the study of human disease. Nothing could be farther from the truth. For example, the comparatively short life span of rats and mice makes them ideally suited to studies of the aging process, allowing medical researchers to study several generations within a few years.

Dogs have a high incidence of kidney disease, making them natural subjects for kidney research (in fact, so much has been learned about the dog's kidneys that it has benefited more from this research than humans have). Knowledge of the dog's heart physiology led to coronary-bypass techniques, modern cardiopulmonary resuscitation, the cardiac pacemaker, open-heart surgery, and the heart transplant.

Pigs lend themselves to dermatological research because they are relatively hairless and their abdominal skin has an almost human texture. Many drugs and treatments for skin disease have been developed in the pig, including therapy for severe burns—perhaps the most afflicting of human injuries, and among the most difficult to study.

A massive public-education job lies ahead. In 1986, an Ontario government poll found 83 percent of respondents aware that stray dogs and cats, which would otherwise be put to death, go on to serve a higher purpose in medical research. But 42 percent were unaware of the humane treatment these animals receive in labs, and almost as many did not know that, in Ontario, a strict law governs the animals' care. Even so, 68 percent of respondents supported the use of unwanted animals in research.

With their convoluted thinking, the animal-rights radicals assign the same moral worth and privileges to a rodent that they do to a human. But I wonder, if their own survival were at stake, whether they would defer to the rodent. That is precisely what they are asking others to do as they attempt to foist their own standards on the public. Because of their campaign, millions of dollars once earmarked for research must be diverted to security. The time has come for the stakeholders in medical research—every one of us—to protect our rights to good health.

CON (Anne Doncaster)
Every year, Canadian scientists use more than 2 000 000 animals in medical experiments, teaching, and testing. These animals are confined in tiny cages behind closed doors until it is their turn to die. In the scientific literature, the animals are not sentient beings, but the tools of the trade. They are sacrificed not because we have the right, but simply because we have the might.

Researchers use animals in a misguided effort to dodge an ethical dilemma. From a scientific perspective, humans are the only appropriate models for the study of human diseases or injury. A human, after all, is not a rat, a dog, or a monkey. But scientific validity is not the primary consideration. Public morality, quite properly, would not permit noxious experiments to be performed upon humans.

So animals are subjected to such procedures as induced disease and injury, invasive surgery, electric shock, poisoning, burns and genetic manipulation. Some are given addictions to alcohol or drugs; others are deprived of food, water, and social and environmental stimulation.

The fate of these animals is left entirely in the hands of the researchers. Most countries using large numbers of animals in research have national legislation to protect them, but only three Canadian provinces have laws on the treatment of laboratory animals and, in any case, these laws are inadequate. Elsewhere, there is only a voluntary system that operates under the misnomer "Canadian Council on Animal Care" (CCAC). Although CCAC's many levels of peer review can sound impressive to the uninitiated, each level is dominated by members of the research community, and the deliberations of the committees are confidential. For laboratory animals, the researchers are judge, jury, and executioner—a blatant conflict of interest.

But discussions of the proper use of animals ignore the basic tenet of the animal-rights movement: that the use of animals is morally wrong. Philosophers have failed to find a justification for it. To legitimize our current double standard of morality, they would have to identify morally relevant characteristics that humans possess and animals lack.

Supporters of animal research argue that animals, but not humans, can be used in experiments because humans are more intelligent. But if intelligence is the criterion on which we determine moral worth and exclude humans from experimentation, we immediately encounter a dilemma. Some humans, the severely brain damaged, are less intelligent than many animals. Experiments on the less intelligent humans would rightly lead to a public outcry. It is therefore logically and morally inconsistent for researchers to experiment upon the more intelligent animals.

A similar dilemma remains when researchers substitute other criteria for distinguishing humans from animals, such as self-awareness, moral behavior, or the capacity to participate in a social contract. All of these are missing in some humans and present in some animals. The unavoidable conclusion is that painful or harmful experiments upon animals are as morally unacceptable as they would be if performed upon humans.

The research industry claims that much good comes from animal research. Yet, this blind insistence that the ends justify the means has already been exposed as an excuse for unconscionable cruelty. During World War II, highly respected German and Japanese scientists justified experiments on prisoners on the grounds that their countries' own soldiers benefited. The subjects were considered subhuman.

I have seen some Canadian labs, and their resemblance to concentration camps is striking. Whatever we might be gaining from this abuse of animals, we are losing something far more important—compassion, honor, and decency.

Suggested Activities

First Reactions

Tip • For suggestions about using your Response Notebook, see page 183 of Resource One.

1. Express your feelings about one ethical issue raised by Laurence, Chow, Calhoun, or Doncaster. You might draft a poem, song, or paragraph in your Response Notebook.

2. With a partner, select words and phrases in Laurence's essay which appeal to your eye and ear.

Tip • Look for sound appeal (repetition, alliteration, euphony, and cacophony) and visual appeal (imagery, colour, and shape). You might draft a shape poem with these phrases; or you might consider adding sight and sound appeal to enliven a recent piece of your writing.

3. With a partner, rank the persuasiveness of each essay in this group. Compose a criteria checklist, or consider:

   a) emotional commitment and intensity
   b) the balance of fact and opinion
   c) the degree to which you are moved to act
   d) tips you can apply to your persuasive writing.

The Writing Folder

Tip • You may wish to discuss your progress with a partner as you revise, edit, and polish your work, or you may prefer to leave your work in first-draft form. Resource Two, which begins on page 181, will help you with this process.

4. With a partner, compose resolutions or thesis statements about ethical issues for oral or written debate. Then write a speech or one side of a debate persuading the audience to act upon your position.

Media Extensions

Tip • Resource Five, which begins on page 190, may be of help with your media assignment.

5. Devise a print or television advertisement which persuades the audience to adopt your views on animal use in medical research. You might first view a film such as the NFB's *Street Kids* or *Return to Dresden*.

6. Prepare a collage, photo essay, or videotape which persuades the audience to act upon your feelings about a local or national issue. The text should enhance your visual presentation.

Independent Study

Tip • *Resource One may help you devise and complete your project.*

7. Research the anti-war protest songs of the 1960s which criticized the Vietnam War. Collect an annotated anthology of exemplary work and include a preface and conclusion. You might also illustrate the song lyrics with photographs.

8. Assemble an anthology of songs, poems, short stories, essays, photographs, and drawings which persuade your audience to rectify a social wrong. Include a preface, conclusion, and brief explanation of each item's relevance.

Connections

9. Invite a speaker from an animal rights or nuclear disarmament group to visit your class. Compile clear questions for discussion prior to the speaker's appearance.

10. Attend a play, film, or art or photography exhibition which explores a social or political issue. Compile a review for your writing folder.

NOTE: *For additional questions, see "Responding to the Essay" (page 174).*

Part Two

PERSPECTIVES

STUDENT RESPONSES

The essays in this section range from the playful to the scholarly, and are the work of both senior students and professionals. Like our student reviewers, a sample of whose reactions to some of the essays are below, you'll probably want to write, discuss, debate, and reflect upon your responses. Some suggestions for focusing your responses to these essays can be found on pages 174-175.

Kalle Radage on "The Melancholy of Anatomy" (page 67)
"This essay made me laugh."

Leigh Murtha on "Rape on Campus" (page 93)
"Scary! It would be interesting to discuss and hear what the males think about this."

Andrea Chisholm on "When Men Refuse to Grow Up" (page 98)
"This essay would be a smart choice to read with *Catcher in the Rye*."

Mike McGregor on "How to Spot Rock Types" (page 116)
"It's funny and leads to good class discussion."

Sam Blythe on "Grim Fairy Tales and Gory Stories" (page 137)
"This essay has an intriguing thesis. Book banning is an important topic for us to consider."

Andy Sinclair on "The Strange Case of the English Language" (page 141)
"I thought about language in a different way."

Kris Janssen on "X-Rated Boob-Tube" (page 147)
"You can't change people by changing the product."

Margaret Atwood

....

BREAD

Your sister . . . is starving, her belly is bloated, flies land on her eyes.

Imagine a piece of bread. You don't have to imagine it, it's right here in the kitchen, on the bread board, in its plastic bag, lying beside the bread knife. The bread knife is an old one you picked up at an auction; it has the word BREAD carved into the wooden handle. You open the bag, pull back the wrapper, cut yourself a slice. You put butter on it, then peanut butter, then honey, and you fold it over. Some of the honey runs out onto your fingers and you lick it off. It takes you about a minute to eat the bread. This bread happens to be brown, but there is also white bread, in the refrigerator, and a heel of the rye you got last week, round as a full stomach then, now going mouldy. Occasionally you make bread. You think of it as something relaxing to do with your hands.

Imagine a famine. Now imagine a piece of bread. Both of these things are real but you happen to be in the same room with only one of them. Put yourself into a different room, that's what the mind is for. You are now lying on a thin mattress in a hot room. The walls are made of dried earth and your sister, who is younger than you are, is in the room with you. She is starving, her belly is bloated, flies land on her eyes; you brush them off with your hand. You have a cloth too, filthy but damp, and you press it to her lips and forehead. The piece of bread is the bread you've been saving, for days it seems. You are as hungry as she is, but not yet as weak. How long does this take? When will someone come with more bread? You think of going out to see if you might find something that could be eaten, but outside the streets are infested with scavengers and the stink of corpses is everywhere.

Should you share the bread or give the whole piece to your sister? Should you eat the piece of bread yourself? After all, you have a better chance of living, you're stronger. How long does it take to decide?

Imagine a prison. There is something you know that you have not yet told. Those in control of the prison know that you know. So do those not in control. If you tell, thirty or forty or a hundred of your friends, your comrades, will be caught and will die. If you refuse to tell, tonight will be like last night. They always choose the night. You don't think about the night, however, but about the piece of bread they offered you. How long does it take? The piece of bread was brown and fresh and reminded you of sunlight falling across a wooden floor. It reminded you of a bowl, a yellow bowl that was once in your home. It held apples and pears; it stood on a table you can also remember. It's not the hunger or the pain that is killing you but the absence of the yellow bowl. If you could only hold the bowl in your hands, right here, you could withstand anything, you tell yourself. The bread they offered you is subversive, it's treacherous, it does not mean life.

There were once two sisters. One was rich and had no children, the other had five children and was a widow, so poor that she no longer had any food left. She went to her sister and asked her for a mouthful of bread. "My children are dying," she said. The rich sister said, "I do not have enough for myself," and drove her away from the door. Then the husband of the rich sister came home and wanted to cut himself a piece of bread; but when he made the first cut, out flowed red blood.

Everyone knew what that meant.

This is a traditional German fairy tale.

The loaf of bread I have conjured for you floats about a foot above your kitchen table. The table is normal, there are no trap doors in it. A blue tea towel floats beneath the bread, and there are no strings attaching the cloth to the bread to the ceiling or the table to the cloth, you've proved it by passing your hand above and below. You didn't touch the bread though. What stopped you? You don't want to know whether the bread is real or whether it's just a hallucination I've somehow duped you into seeing. There's no doubt that you can see the bread, you can even smell it, it smells like yeast, and it looks solid enough, solid as your own arm. But can you trust it? Can you eat it? You don't want to know, imagine that.

Russell
Baker
·········

THE MELANCHOLY OF ANATOMY

The garden-design man is no more fit for modern urban living than a spade is to go up against an intercontinental ballistic missile.

City life started me thinking about toes. Somebody had stepped on five of mine in a crowded place, and it occurred to me that for city people toes were a mistake. In fact, major parts of the human design are a mistake for city living.

Things that must have seemed very sensible when the architect was designing an anatomy meant to live in a garden wearing nothing but its own pelt seem like hopeless blunders in an organism compelled to dwell among hordes, drink gin and worry about who's gaining on it from behind. I do not fault the creating architect for miscalculating the destiny of man. How could anyone have guessed that man would prefer to quit contemplating lilies and peacocks for life on the subway?

Yet, it is time to rethink the design from head to toes for the garden-design man is no more fit for modern urban living than a spade is to go up against an intercontinental ballistic missile.

The skull might be a good place to start. At present, it houses nothing but an absurd clump of hair—and sometimes not very much of that. For man in a garden, hair might be a reasonable appurtenance; it gives him something to twine dandelion chains in during spring evenings. In the city, however, its chief function is to release dandruff, which makes males loathsome to the women they desire and exposes women to the humiliation of lectures from their husbands on correct tonsorial sanitation.

Besides being a troublemaker, hair occupies the one place on the body that is most easily shampooed. And what does urban man need shampooed most urgently? His lungs. Everyone who lives in the city ought to wash his lungs at least twice a week. The sensible place to locate lungs is on the surface of the head, a location now occupied by the idle and mischievous hair.

Afflicted with the anatomy of Garden Man, we now have the lungs locked inside a prison of ribs; as a result, we can avoid their befoulment only by not breathing. A reasonable design change would require only a transfer of body parts. The lungs would go to the present location of the hair, while the hair would be sealed inside the ribs, where no one would have to see what it was up to.

This might even make it possible for tobacco addicts to smoke again without terror, since it is entirely possible that smoking may destroy dandruff.

Whether all the toes could be disposed of I am reluctant to guess. True, their most palpable function in city life is to be stepped on by other peoples' feet, but some such vulnerable protuberances may be necessary, for reasons known only to anatomists. In any case, there is surely no reason to have ten toes to do the job. The creating architect was remarkably generous in passing out the toes. When we consider that he thought two kidneys, two eyes, two ears were enough to handle far more interesting work than the toes are called upon to perform, it seems possible that he was simply padding out the construction with left-over materials.

My guess is that one or two toes per foot would be more than adequate to do whatever toes are supposed to do. It would certainly reduce the number of toes vulnerable to assault in crowded intersections.

The architectural generosity in toes did not extend to the liver, regrettably, perhaps because it was assumed that the Garden Man would spend so much time planting dandelions in his hair he would have little time left over for trips to the martini pitcher. A reasonable calculation for a garden environment, but dangerous if constructing a man who is in terror because he's been breathing the air, because he's been riding the subway, and desperate because, lacking eyes in the back of his head, he can't see who is gaining on him from behind.

For Urban Man, one liver is not enough, especially since the liver, being made of notoriously inferior materials, is subject to frequent breakdowns. Instead of ten toes, he needs two livers. Or better yet, no liver at all, but another kind of alcohol-processing system which can easily be worked on in case of factory recalls

A sensible solution here would be to use the ears. Originally designed to keep dandelion chains from slipping down around the neck, they have lost all purpose in a society that strangles itself with neckties, bandannas, and chains of mineral and are, moreover, marvelously accessible for repair and replacement if ravaged by sour mash.

Aesthetes may protest that a man with lungs in his head and livers behind his cheekbones makes a disagreeable spectacle. Considering the variety of styles that New York Man affects in public, however, I believe we can safely conclude that nobody will notice anything even slightly amiss.

June
Callwood
....

Why Canada Has To Beat Its
Literacy Problem

When you can't read, it's like being in prison.

Carole Boudrias shudders when she remembers the time she almost swallowed Drano because she thought it was Bromo. Even more painful to recall is the time she mistook adult pain-killers for the child-size dose and made her feverish child much sicker.

"When you can't read," she explains, "it's like being in prison. You can't travel very far from where you live because you can't read street signs. You have to shop for food but you don't know what's in most of the packages. You stick to the ones in a glass jar or with a picture on the label. You can't look for bargains because you can't understand a sign that says "Reduced." I would ask the clerk where is something and the clerk would say, aisle five. I'd pretend that I was confused so they'd lead me right to the shelf."

Carole Boudrias is able to read now, at last. She's a 33-year-old single parent who lives with her five children in a handsome townhouse on Toronto's harbourfront and holds a steady job. But her struggle with illiteracy is all too vivid in her memory. "You can't get a job," she says earnestly. "You can't open a bank account. You have to depend on other people. You feel you don't belong. You can't help your children. You can't help yourself."

Six years ago when her oldest child started school, the boy floundered. Because he had been raised in a household without books, print was strange to him. He would point to a word in his reader, that classic, endearingly silly *Dick and Jane*, and ask his mother what it was. She was as baffled as he, so he'd check with his teacher the next day and that evening would proudly read the new word to his mother. She began to absorb the shape of the words he identified. She found she could recognize them even days later.

That was astonishing. As a child she had been labelled mentally retarded and confined to "opportunity classes" where reading wasn't taught. She grew up believing that she wasn't intelligent enough to learn. Nevertheless, she *was* learning. The vocabulary of words she could read in her son's reader was growing. She began to think maybe the experts were wrong. Then, one miraculous day, she realized she was learning to read even faster than her son was.

"My son was my first teacher," she grins. She had never allowed herself to believe that it was possible that she could learn to read. She hadn't even tried: no one whose life is made up of poverty and failed relationships is ready to take on, voluntarily, the potential for another defeat, another kick in the self-esteem. She hesitated a long time but the evidence was persuasive— she was beginning to read. Her welfare worker had always been kind, so she summoned the nerve to ask her where she could find help.

That led her to Beat the Street, a program that helps people who are illiterate for all the reasons that befall sad children: unrecognized learning disabilities, emotional stress, too many schools, scorn and belittling, terror, bad teachers. She was linked with a volunteer tutor and they came to admire each other deeply.

"Now I can read, I can read books, anything. I can write. In English *and* French."

Carole Boudrias has written a book, *The Struggle for Survival*, which tells of her tortured childhood lacerated with incest and violence, and her triumphant recovery from illiteracy. Last summer she was the poet laureate of the annual golf tournament hosted by Peter Gzowski, the beloved and respected heart of CBC Radio's *Morningside*. He has befriended the cause of literacy in Canada and over the past four years has raised a quarter of a million dollars for Frontier College, one of the first organizations in the country to tackle the problem of illiteracy.

"Learning to read," Carole Boudrias says quietly, "was like a second birth, this time with my eyes open. Before I could read, I was a blind person."

Canada has nearly five million adult citizens who are described as functionally illiterate, which means that they can recognize a few words, such as washroom signs and exits, but they can't read dense print at all. They can't decipher directions, for instance, or application forms, or warnings on labels. The world of newspapers, posters, advertising, books, menus, banking, recipes, and instructions-for-assembly that literate people take for granted is barred to them; they live a life of bluff, anxiety, embarrassment, and isolation.

A good many Canadians are as profoundly illiterate as Carole Boudrias was. People who meet illiterate adults are struck by the similarity of their textural experience. All of them liken the inability to read and write with being disabled or chained in a prison. Edwin Newman, a U.S. broadcaster who writes about language, calls illiteracy "death in life."

The sense of being caged and blinded is not morbid fantasy. People who can't read may be able to walk freely but they can't go far. Subway stops rarely have pictures to guide them and the destinations bannered across the front of buses and streetcars are meaningless. If they ask for directions, well-intentioned people tell them, "Go along Main Street to Elm and turn left."

Consequently, they must travel by taxi or stay home, though they usually are the poorest of the poor.

Almost every job, even simple manual labour such as street-cleaning, requires an ability to read. Personnel managers don't take kindly to people who can't fill out an application, or when asked, can't spell their own addresses.

The divide between the literate and illiterate has never been wider. In this half of the century North America has become a world of forms and documents and instructions, written warnings, posted rules, leaflets, and vital information circulated in brochures. Two generations ago, illiteracy was prevalent but not such a great disadvantage. Someone functionally illiterate could fake it through an entire lifetime and still hold a good job. Employment skills were acquired by watching someone else; apprenticeship was the accepted teacher, not two years in a community college.

Today inability to read is a ticket to social segregation and economic oblivion. A poignant example is the skilled house-painter who turned up one day in the crowded quarters of the East End Literacy Program in Toronto. He said he wanted to read. The counsellor asked him, as all applicants are asked, what he wanted to read. "Directions on paint cans," he answered promptly. "I'm losing jobs. I can't read how to mix the colours."

Many who are illiterate can't read numbers. When they are paid, they don't know if they are being cheated. Because she couldn't fill out bank deposit slips, Carole Boudrias used to cash her welfare cheque in a storefront outlet which clips poor people sharply for no-frills service. To pay for goods, she would hold out a handful of money and let the cashier take what was needed—and perhaps more, she never knew. Once she would have been short-changed $50 she could ill afford if a stranger who witnessed the transaction hadn't protested.

The common emotional characteristic of people who can't read is depression and self-dislike. All feel at fault for their situation: with few exceptions, they went through school with bright little girls exactly their age who leaped to their feet to recite and smart little boys who did multiplication in their heads. Everyone else in the world, it seemed, could learn with ease; for them, even C-A-T looked a meaningless scribble. Teachers called them stupid; worse, so did other children.

"Stupid" may just be the cruellest word in the language. It consumes confidence, on which the ability to learn relies. Seven-year-olds having trouble with reading will frolic at recess with an edge of glee; 11-year-olds who can't read have bitter faces and scarred souls.

Loss of hope for oneself is a descent into desolation without end. It causes men to rage in fury and women to wound themselves. People who can't read come to view themselves as worthless junk, and many feel they must grab what they can out of life and run. Canada's prisons are full of young men who can't read. The Elizabeth Fry Society estimates that close to 90 percent of the women in Kingston's infamous prison for women are illiterate.

Because Canada has five million people who can't read, the political shape of the country and the priorities of governments are not influenced greatly by the needs of the poor. Since illiterates are effectively disenfranchised, the political agenda is written by the more powerful. Candidates rarely find it advantageous to uphold the causes that matter most to Canada's illiterates— an end to homelessness and the need for food banks, welfare payments that meet the poverty line, and better educational and job-training opportunities. Few votes would follow any politician with such a crusade. The electorate that can't read won't be there to ruffle the complacent on election day.

Their silence costs this country severely. Education is free in Canada because it was recognized that democracy isn't healthy unless all citizens understand current events and issues. Five million Canadians can't do that. Voters, most of them literate, choose candidates who help their interests; those who don't vote, many of them illiterate, by default get a government that does not need to know they exist.

The result is a kind of apartheid. The government has lopsided representation, which results in decisions which further alienate and discourage the unrepresented. The gap between the haves and have-nots in Canada is already greater than at any time in this century, and widening. Urban apartment houses are the work places of crack dealers, the streets are increasingly unsafe, and households have installed electronic security systems. The poor, if asked, would have better answers than guard dogs. The best, most lasting responses to crime and addiction and violence are literacy programs, coupled with job training and full employment.

Schools are in disgrace, with a failure rate of fully one-third of all high-school students. A soup company with such a record would be out of business in a day. The educational system has managed to exacerbate the class differences which are developing in this country. Canada's millions of illiterates went through school the required number of years, give or take time-out for truancy, illness, running away from abuse, and confinement in detention homes. These human discards, identified promptly in the first years of elementary schools, will ever after drift around disconsolately. They are surplus people, spare parts for which society has no use. Unless there is a war.

Carole Boudrias is working on a project, Moms in Motion, to help young mothers to get off welfare rolls. She says to them, "What do you want?" They reply, "To go back to school."

Another chance. Five million Canadians need another chance. Maybe they can become literate, maybe they can become healed and whole. What a lovely goal for the 1990s.

**Rod
Cohen**
········

SEXISM IN ROCK-AND-ROLL LYRICS

***Very often rock lyrics are degrading and/or malicious towards
women.***

Rock-and-roll can be summed up with accuracy by the title of a James
Brown song, "It's a Man's, Man's World." Very often rock lyrics are degrading
and/or malicious towards women and, like all other forms of media abuse
to the female gender, are generally overlooked. In fact, sexist attitudes are
used to sell the music.

There are many reasons why the lyrics of pop music are not criticized by
the fans, critics, rock journalists, and disc jockeys. Peer pressure ensures
that, even if rock fans have doubts about the validity of what they hear, they
will keep those doubts to themselves. However, many listeners may be just
as sexist as the musicians and disc jockeys who refuse to play these records
might lose their jobs.

Just as in the motion pictures, many "super stars" have developed in rock-
and-roll. The Beatles, the Rolling Stones, the Who, Bob Dylan, and Jimi
Hendrix all have reached stardom and their records will sell for generations
to come. Such success does not mean necessarily that these performers
were blatantly sexist in their climb to stardom. Some stars, however, have
abused females through their male-chauvinist writing. For instance, the
Rolling Stones, considered by most to be the quintessential rock band, have
constantly exhibited sexism throughout their eighteen-year career.

One might think that as society supposedly gets more liberal, there would
be a trend towards equality of the sexes in the lyrics, but such is not the case.
In fact, rock lyrics have, in some cases, become more blatantly anti-woman.
"Hits," well-known songs, and songs that fill out albums can all contain
strongly sexist content.

Why are rock artists praised and endorsed by the paying public with little
reaction to this lyrical violence against women? There are a number of
possibilities, most of a sociological nature, which suggest an unspoken
agreement by fans to accept these attitudes. Most fans will argue that the
music is the message, not the words: "I couldn't care less what they are
saying; it is the beat, the music, the guitars I am listening to." Still, the writers
are debasing women and getting rich in the process.

The Rolling Stones' "Under My Thumb" is a classic example of a sexist rock lyric. The song is about a man who appears to have been "dominated" by his female mate. It goes on to describe how he has turned the situation around; he is now in full control. There is, of course, no mention of her feelings, needs, or wants in the relationship. The line "it's down to me" displays the speaker's "macho" desire to dominate his woman. Other lines confirm his "control" and assert that that is how it *should be*. Here is a prime example of the sexist double standard:

> Under my thumb, her eyes are
> kept to herself,
> Under my thumb, well I can still
> look at someone else.

He gloats over the control he possesses. The women becomes a "squirm dog," who has had her day and who has changed her way *for him*. His disassociating her from intelligence and independence takes place in lyrics that refer to her as a "Siamese cat of a girl." This line is not so bad in itself except that the Stones follow it with "the sweetest PET in the world." The woman has lost all identity and is now his pet. And this particular song, written by Mick Jagger and Keith Richard in 1965, is a "classic" piece of rock-and-roll.

John Lennon's "Run For Your Life" is about a man singing of his feelings for his "girlfriend" but his love is rather difficult to comprehend. The song portrays male "piggishness" and possessiveness. It begins by calling for sympathy; if the girl does him *wrong* then he is finished. There is no idea of a mutual understanding between two adults. Then Lennon threatens the woman: if she does not do what he wants, then *he* will be lost. Instead of working out the problem, he places the responsibility for his sanity on her shoulders. In other words, he blames her for *his* lack of control. He confesses that he is "a wicked guy with a jealous mind" but he does not criticize himself for this. She has to accept the way he is or else. Next he says that he cannot spend his life waiting for her to realize and accept that he is inconsiderate, selfish, and chauvinistic and that she should be content to become his possession. He refers to his "lady" as "little girl," a degrading term for anyone who should be his equal, and commands her to be like an ostrich, to admit her guilt and shame for doing him wrong. The song does not make clear in the end whether the pair remain together or not, but either way the song is a final confirmation of his control and superiority, because, even after the relationship is over, she must still be concerned with his wellbeing and not live a life of her own. Lennon is a unique case, though, because under the influence of Yoko Ono, he admitted his sexism and guilt about his relationships with women. However, his ingrained sexism was something which, at the time of "Run For Your Life," he was himself not able to notice.

The chauvinism Lennon displayed in this song was and still *is* considered a normal attitude. Anything different exhibits "deviance and radicalism" opposing the normal societal beliefs.

"Heavy Metal" rock is, however, historically the worst offender. It is a very loud and aggressive musical style, with lyrics rarely mentioning anything but fornication and "women hatred."

"Sweet Talker" by Whitesnake is one long putdown of women; it consists of very bland, stereotypical statements about women: ". . . by the way you walk . . ."; "you give it away by the way you talk"; ". . . long legs and a black girl sway." Such lines say nothing except that we are supposed to possess the writer's ideas about women. Line 5 mentions "giving away her school-girl name." In other words, whatever her educational level, this girl is a sexual tease. The only role such women have is to satisfy the singer's sexual desires and fantasies. The chorus also makes anti-women statements to finish off the song. The phrase "bad daughter" is another derogatory comment about females. There is no indication of a relationship, or even acquaintance, with the female in question. Thus the line is just a hateful stab at women in general. The song ends with a senseless comparison of a woman to a canine awaiting fertilization.

The Australian band AC/DC could claim the right to wear the crown of women-hatred. They sing crudely of fornication and put down women with unadulterated crassness. Their song "The Jack" begins in classic fashion with the woman giving herself to the singer for no apparent reason. He then degrades her by relating her consent to her "promiscuity." Then he makes her cry and scream. He thinks he is the "victim" of her past, her supposed lie to him about her "purity," and the "shame" *he* will bear as a result of her reputation. . . .

"Squeeler" is another example of AC/DC's attitude toward women. The singer again finds a sexually inexperienced woman and imagines that he will initiate her into a supposedly very warm and beautiful experience. He builds a picture of "breaking in" the unsuspecting female to her life as "slave" to her sexually potent male. Instead of using warmth, sensitivity, and love, he is violent in his *rape* of the woman to the point of ". . . fixing her good," so that she will never again enjoy the beauty of a true sexual relationship. This song is the most violent and vicious writing I have ever found in all my readings of rock-song lyrics (and I use the term "lyric" hesitatingly). The song finishes with a decree of dominance that makes clear the necessity of women's battle to be equals on a planet that is controlled by many uncaring and prejudiced males.

Van Halen's "Bottoms Up" exemplifies the plasticine, inhumane image of women put forward by a great number of rock bands. The singer goes to a night club for the evening, to have fun, to sing and to dance, and he chooses a "babe" whom he would like to share in his enjoyment of the festivities of the evening. But, later, he becomes like a commander ordering his crew to "set up all the pretty babes" in the position he would most appreciate: "Bottoms Up." Again, as in other lyrics, there is no feedback from the recipients of his yearnings; they are like chess pieces to be set up for his entertainment and use (or abuse). The women here have no personhood or identity. The song is sexist, tasteless, and demeaning, but typical of too many lyrics in rock.

This study shows the humiliation and degradation of women in the lyrics of rock music. Such lyrics are not representative of the entire world of rock music but do represent a very large element that is often ignored even by enlightened listeners. Perhaps, if all critics were sensitive, responsible, and non-sexist, and if all disc jockeys made critical comments on the blatantly sexist content of such music, more people would look past the talented guitar playing, the impressive production methods, and the accomplished vocals and realize that such music is nothing more than a mass-media attack on women.

Fortunately, John Lennon provided a contrast to such sexism and hatred:

I use to be cruel to my woman,
I beat her and kept her apart from
the things that she loved.
Man, I was mean,
but I've changed my scene,
and I'm doing the best I can.

Andrew
Coletto
....
Student
Essay

RISING ABOVE THE TURMOIL

The Ice Hawks team was an unforgettable cast of characters who personified the word "diversity."

Hockey! It's a game I've adored ever since I was a small boy. It's my consuming passion. Without hockey, I wouldn't be the same person.

For almost twelve years I've religiously played this great Canadian game. There have been countless teams and countless coaches and countless teammates, all providing warm memories. But none are more vivid than the memories of the 1989-90 Ice Hawks.

The Ice Hawks team was an unforgettable cast of characters who personified the word "diversity." We boasted our share of flashy goal scorers, role-players, grinders, prima donnas, and practical jokers. Each player contributed to make our team what it was—a thrill to watch.

Opposing opinions, dissension, turmoil—we had them all. Indeed, our collective egos could have swamped the entire playing field of Yankee Stadium. If you looked up "conflict" in a dictionary, you'd likely discover our team's photograph underneath the word. But despite each player's proud ego, when game time rolled around the conflicts and turbulence were left behind in the dressing room.

Time and time again during our roller-coaster 1989-90 season, I observed this phenomenon. Even when times were tough, even when we skidded down a long and agonizing losing streak, even when a cloud of tension instigated finger-pointing and back-stabbing, we rose above the turmoil to play inspired hockey. There's one example I remember particularly well, after our team dropped its sixth consecutive game. We were leading the game 4-2 at the beginning of the third period. But after two periods of solid play, we folded up like a cheap tent. The puck was veritably dancing around our listless defencemen. In the final minutes of the game, the opposing team scored to cut our lead to one goal. My eyes locked onto the score clock ticking away at the rink's far side; I begged it to tick faster and end our suffering. The suffering, however, was only beginning.

The frozen black disk reached the opposing team's pointman stationed alone in the slot. Cocking his stick, he prepared to hammer home the tying goal. Our team resembled six clumsy, beached whales, helplessly gasping and flopping around. No one so much as breathed on the pointman as he calmly unleashed a wrist shot that would clink off the crossbar into the net behind our helpless netminder to tie the game. "This goalie here should sue you guys for lack of support," our coach, Mr. Crumb, would later fume.

After the goal, we all groaned and slumped in utter disappointment; eleven helmets sank to the floor. Coach Crumb stood in a frozen rage, eyeballing the rink's rafters, as if in conference with the gods. Finally gazing out onto the ice, he shook his head in wordless disgust.

"Sixty seconds remaining," bellowed the timekeeper. In those sixty seconds our entire bench sat poised in despair. Our players seemed to stand idly by and watch as the opposition peppered our goaltender with shots, finally scoring the game-winning goal with only eight seconds to go. We felt hopeless, pathetic. The opposition's bench exploded in jubilation while our team shuffled off the ice like a herd of water buffalo searching for a pasture.

Wordlessly, our team filed down the hall, systematically undressed, and prepared to escape. Even Matt "Worm" Baites, our team jester, cracked no quips. Staring into the thick black tape wrapped around his stick blade he hunched motionless in shame. This stick was, after all, the very same stick that had fired a puck off the right goal post at a time when we desperately needed an insurance goal. Even our clutch scorer had choked.

Confused and disappointed, many of the guys looked to our captain for encouragement and inspiration. But Danny sat silently staring at the wall. I'll never forget it. Was he wondering if playing for the Hawks was worth it? I felt sorry for Danny, the guy with the biggest heart on the team, the guy with the most character and the greatest determination to win. Even at times when we were losing by a hopelessly wide margin, he always refused to quit. But on that bitterly cold February night, his spirits sagged. I was frightened, frightened because when the player with the most spirit and character cannot summon optimism, the team's future looks gloomy.

Silence loomed for a good ten minutes. But then Coach Crumb thundered through the door. He was an imposing figure, to say the least; about 45, he weighed over 200 pounds and his voice boomed, much the same way a ship's fog horn resounds. Coach Crumb was a paradox—your worst nightmare one minute and your best friend the next. He expected us to show up both mentally and physically prepared—no passengers. If someone was just going through the motions, Crumb would immediately set him straight. I liked Coach Crumb because he had the guts to tell you what he thought. No mind games. All fire and brimstone, he'd rage and fume when he was angry, but when you made a good play he'd slide up to your ear, whisper an inspiring word, and pat you on the back. No doubt he came from the old school of coaching—no nonsense, 100 percent business.

After our crushing defeat, however, Crumb lost his self-control. He blew into the room like a raging thunderstorm, hollering and kicking hockey gear around. Fuming over our listless, chicken-hearted play, he questioned the ability of every team member. Wayne "The Natural" Noonan was the particular centre of his wrath today. The player with the most talent was mired in a season-long slump. Some said it was caused by a back injury suffered on the construction site of a summer job. But others speculated that it was the amount of time he spent with his new girlfriend instead of working out with the team that was hurting his play. And so it was Wayne who bore the brunt of the coach's rage. But as Crumb tore into him, Wayne stared between his skates as if no one was talking to him. When our coach succeeded in alienating the team's most talented player, I began to wonder if the Hawks could ever be a winning team again.

Coach Crumb warned us that our team was destined for dramatic changes. Claiming his patience was exhausted, he said that *he* was going to pull us out of our slump since we couldn't—or wouldn't—do it ourselves.

At the time, we didn't pay much attention to his threat. But the next night, Crumb came into the dressing room before the game and announced a surprising three-player deal that traded Wayne for two big wingers. We were stunned. The coach's expression was colder than an iceberg. He turned and left the dressing room without a backward glance. Had he looked back, he would have seen sixteen gaping mouths. His message was loud and clear: play hard or you're gone.

And we all took in that message. That night we stormed onto the ice and steamrolled the opposition. Our inspired play showed our true character. We didn't bury our heads, mope, or feel sorry for ourselves. Instead, we were hungry for a victory and we crushed our opponents. That victory triggered a winning streak that would see us win fourteen consecutive games. Once again, we showed that we could rise above the turmoil and tension and make the thrilling dash towards the league finals. And no one was prouder than Coach Crumb.

*John
Haslett
Cuff*

·········

TELEVISION NEWS

Network news goes out of its way to present a pageantry of officials . . . making official statements about official things.

In spite of all its technological advantages over print, the globe-girdling speed of satellites, and the instantaneous "live" pictures made possible through advances in electronic news gathering (ENG), television news is rarely immediate and always the slave of format, of sterile rituals dictated by a commercial agenda that supersedes every other concern. And the chief result, paradoxically, of television's technological superiority and popular ascendance over print is the reduction of information, the preshrinking of news to serve both the corporate and political elites.

Any cursory look at several competing evening newscasts quickly reveals their sameness, most differing only in the individuals who report and read the news. Most obvious is their reliance on the planned and staged event, whether engineered by a single-issue interest group or the politicians who perform so opportunistically and cynically to its uncritical, unblinking eye.

Michael Arlen, *The New Yorker's* television critic, summed it up this way in an interview with author Joyce Nelson (*The Perfect Machine: TV in the Nuclear Age*): "Basically, I think network news is almost entirely a news of important people talking to other important people, or about important people. It's a news of institutional events. It is bureaucratic. By and large, network news goes out of its way to present a pageantry of officials everywhere making official statements about official things."

The biggest staple of the television news agenda is the news conference. And whether it is called (always in time to accommodate the evening newscast) by a prime minister or president, an eco-activist or native dissident, it almost always consists of a prepared statement, followed by prepared answers to prepared questions. All media are equally guilty of playing along in this game and to some extent have little choice. But they do have a choice as to what they do with this "information" and, most important, what context they place it in.

The underlying paradox of the news business is that all of the players—newspapers, radio, and television—are competing, yet are largely content to have the same story, the same information and, in the case of TV, the same pictures. But print journalists have (generally) more room to tell the story and can therefore embellish it and provide more context and information. TV newscasts, however, are very rigidly planned and timed in advance, every story allotted only a fraction of the space and time it might require.

Above all, of course, the "pictures" are paramount. However, the pictures are numbingly similar night after night: a head of state getting in and out of a car, surrounded by reporters, besieged on the steps of some official building or posed at a lectern in front of an obedient, orderly group of newshounds. And all of these reporters will then run off and file the same story.

Then the 6 o'clock newscast, the 10 o'clock, the 11 o'clock, the next morning's and the next afternoon's newscasts will usually run the same pictures and the same story over and over—on every channel. There is, judging by what we see on the tube, no news until another news conference is called. The rest of the newscast is then filled with similar official pronouncements from around the world, occasional accidents or disasters and often with what Eric Malling of "W5" has called "the whine of the week": stories that are usually described as "gripping or compelling," human interest items of some kind that titillate the viewer but add nothing to his or her store of information or knowledge.

Regardless of the culpability of all media, TV news must bear the brunt of criticism because it is the single most-relied-on source of news and information. Its influence and power to tell a story and impart important information is simply unrivalled; therefore, it bears an enormous responsibility for the "health" of the public, of the democracy it serves.

Somehow it must find a way to escape the tyranny of its hidebound formulas and a way to use its resources so that reporters are given the time and incentive to dig deeper for news, for stories, and for the ideas and context that will make each report more useful and substantial. Do we really need 200 reporters covering every bland, self-serving political announcement? Wouldn't their time really be better spent foraging elsewhere in those huge, complex bureaucracies (political and corporate) that increasingly rule and homogenize our lives? Isn't it time that TV news used its state-of-the-art resources to lead us into the new century with ideas and stories that help us to make sense of the world's complexities instead of, as it currently does, reinforcing our sense of helplessness and bolstering the status quo by enshrining its most numbingly vacuous utterances in every newscast?

Robertson
Davies
. . . .

A FEW KIND WORDS FOR
SUPERSTITION

**Superstition . . . is linked to man's yearning to know his fate,
and to have some hand in deciding it.**

In grave discussions of "the renaissance of the irrational" in our time,
superstition does not figure largely as a serious challenge to reason or
science. Parapsychology, UFOs, miracle cures, transcendental meditation,
and all the paths to instant enlightenment are condemned, but superstition
is merely deplored. Is it because it has an unacknowledged hold on so many
of us?

Few people will admit to being superstitious; it implies naïveté or ignorance. But I live in the middle of a large university, and I see superstition in
its four manifestations, alive and flourishing among people who are indis-
putably rational and learned.

You did not know that superstition takes four forms? Theologians assure
us that it does. First is what they call Vain Observances, such as not walking
under a ladder, and that kind of thing. Yet I saw a deeply learned professor of
anthropology, who had spilled some salt, throwing a pinch of it over his left
shoulder; when I asked him why, he replied, with a wink, that it was "to hit
the Devil in the eye." I did not question him further about his belief in the
Devil: but I noticed that he did not smile until I asked him what he was
doing.

The second form is Divination, or consulting oracles. Another learned
professor I know, who would scorn to settle a problem by tossing a coin
(which is a humble appeal to Fate to declare itself), told me quite seriously
that he had resolved a matter related to university affairs by consulting the *I
Ching*. And why not? There are thousands of people on this continent who
appeal to the *I Ching*, and their general level of education seems to absolve
them of superstition. Almost, but not quite. The *I Ching*, to the embarrassment of rationalists, often gives excellent advice.

The third form is Idolatry, and universities can show plenty of that. If you
have ever supervised a large examination room, you know how many jujus,
lucky coins, and other bringers of luck are placed on the desks of the
candidates. Modest idolatry, but what else can you call it?

The fourth form is Improper Worship of the True God. A while ago, I learned that every day, for several days, a $2 bill (in Canada we have $2 bills, regarded by some people as unlucky) had been tucked under a candlestick on the altar of a college chapel. Investigation revealed that an engineering student, worried about a girl, thought that bribery of the Deity might help. When I talked with him, he did not think he was pricing God cheap, because he could afford no more. A reasonable argument, but perhaps God was proud that week, for the scientific oracle went against him.

Superstition seems to run, a submerged river of crude religion, below the surface of human consciousness. It has done so for as long as we have any chronicle of human behaviour, and although I cannot prove it, I doubt if it is more prevalent today than it has always been. Superstition, the theologians tell us, comes from the Latin *supersisto*, meaning to stand in terror of the Deity. Most people keep their terror within bounds, but they cannot root it out, nor do they seem to want to do so.

The more the teaching of formal religion declines, or takes a sociological form, the less God appears to great numbers of people as a God of Love, resuming his older form of a watchful, minatory power, to be placated and cajoled. Superstition makes its appearance, apparently unbidden, very early in life, when children fear that stepping on cracks in the sidewalk will bring ill fortune. It may persist even among the greatly learned and devout, as in the case of Dr. Samuel Johnson, who felt it necessary to touch posts that he passed in the street. The psychoanalysts have their explanation, but calling a superstition a compulsion neurosis does not banish it.

Many superstitions are so widespread and so old that they must have risen from a depth of the human mind that is indifferent to race or creed. Orthodox Jews place a charm on their doorposts; so do (or did) the Chinese. Some peoples of Middle Europe believe that when a man sneezes, his soul, for that moment, is absent from his body, and they hasten to bless him lest the soul be seized by the Devil. How did the Melanesians come by the same idea? Superstition seems to have a link with some body of belief that far antedates the religions we know—religions which have no place for such comforting little ceremonies and charities.

People who like disagreeable historical comparisons recall that when Rome was in decline, superstition proliferated wildly, and that something of the same sort is happening in our Western world today. They point to the popularity of astrology, and it is true that sober newspapers that would scorn to deal in love philters carry astrology columns and the fashion magazines count them among their most popular features. But when has astrology not been popular? No use saying science discredits it. When has the heart of man given a damn for science?

Superstition in general is linked to man's yearning to know his fate, and to have some hand in deciding it. When my mother was a child, she innocently joined her Roman Catholic friends in killing spiders on July 11, until she learned that this was done to ensure heavy rain the day following, the anniversary of the Battle of the Boyne, when the Orangemen would hold their parade. I knew an Italian, a good scientist, who watched every morning before leaving his house, so that the first person he met would not be a priest or a nun, as this would certainly bring bad luck.

I am not one to stand aloof from the rest of humanity in this matter, for when I was a university student, a gypsy woman with a child in her arms used to appear every year at examination time, and ask a shilling of anyone who touched the Lucky Baby; that swarthy infant cost me four shillings altogether, and I never failed an examination. Of course, I did it merely for the joke—or so I thought then. Now, I am humbler.

Edward
Dolnick
....

THE PEOPLE WITHIN

I remember being in the third grade . . . and I remember going back after Christmas break, and the next thing I knew it was fall, around October, and I was in the fifth grade.

Julia Wilson* keeps a clock in every room of her house. When she looks at her watch, she checks not only the time but the date, to make sure that she has not somehow lost an entire chunk of her life.

Julia is, in novelist Kurt Vonnegut's phrase, "unstuck in time." "Since I was three or four," she says, "I've lost time. I remember being in third grade, for instance, and I remember going back after Christmas break, and the next thing I knew it was fall, around October, and I was in the fifth grade."

Recounting the story now, two decades later, there is bewilderment and not-quite-subdued panic in her voice. "I knew who my teacher should have been, and I wasn't in her classroom," she says. "Everyone was working on a report, and I had no idea what I was supposed to be doing.

"I remember another time, eleven or twelve years ago," she recalls. "I was sitting in a kind of scummy bar, the kind of place I don't frequent. And I was talking to this guy. I had no idea who he was, but he seemed to know me a whole lot better than I knew him. It was, 'Whoa, get me out of here.' Believe me, this is not a relaxing way to live."

The fear of falling down one of those memory holes has become a preoccupation. "I might go home today and find out that my daughter, who is nine, graduated from high school last week," she says. "Can you imagine living your life that way?"

Julia is only now finding out how she loses time, and why. Her story is so strange that she herself is alternately fascinated and appalled by it. Julia has multiple personalities: she harbours within herself scores of alter egos. Some are aware of one another; some are not. One speaks Italian; another is mute. Some are friendly; still others are murderously angry with Julia and leave signed notes threatening to cut and burn her.

For centuries, doctors have written up case histories that sound uncannily like Julia's. But it was only in 1980 that the bible of psychiatry, the *Diagnostic*

---

*Not her real name.

and Statistical Manual of Mental Disorders, first recognized multiple personality as a legitimate illness.

The condition is still far from the medical mainstream. Part of the problem is that it is too glitzy for its own good, too easy to write off as more suited to Hollywood and Geraldo Rivera than to serious clinicians and scientists: in a single human being, we are told, there might be both female and male personalities, right-handers and left-handers, personalities allergic to chocolate and others unaffected by it.

Just as the symptoms strain credulity, the cause, too, is almost beyond imagining. Nearly always, people who develop multiple personality were subjected to horrifying abuse as children. Therapists recount one case after another of children tortured—for years—by parents, or siblings, or cults. The abuse is typically far worse than "ordinary" child abuse: these children were cut or burned or raped, repeatedly, and had no place they could seek refuge.

Almost every therapist who has diagnosed a multiple personality was blinded at first by skepticism or ignorance. Robert Benjamin, M.D., a Philadelphia psychiatrist, recalls a woman he had been treating ten months for depression: "Every now and again, she'd have slashed wrists. I'd ask how that happened, and she'd say, 'I don't know.'

" 'What do you mean, you don't know?'

" 'Well,' she'd say, 'I don't know. I certainly wouldn't do something like that. I'm a proper schoolteacher. And by the way, I find these strange clothes in my closet, outfits I wouldn't be caught dead in, and there are cigarette ashes in my car.'

" 'What's so strange about that?'

" 'I don't smoke,' she'd say. And I'd get phone calls from her, and she'd say. 'I'm on the Pennsylvania Turnpike halfway to Pittsburgh, and I don't know what I'm doing here.'

"And then a couple of weeks later," Dr. Benjamin goes on, "a young woman walked into my office who looked like my patient, except she was dressed like a streetwalker, with a cigarette hanging out of her mouth. I knew my patient didn't smoke, and then I had my brilliant diagnostic moment. She looked at me and said, 'Well, dummy, have you figured out what's going on yet?' "

He was so slow to catch on, Dr. Benjamin says, because he'd had drummed into him the old medical saying, "If you hear hoofbeats, think horses, not zebras." But, precisely because the disorder is exotic, the diagnosis remains controversial. Even the harshest critics concede that *some* people have multiple personalities, but they insist that bedazzled therapists incorrectly slap the label on every confused patient who comes through the door.

Before 1980, when the condition made it into the psychiatrists' handbook, the total number of cases ever reported was about 200; the number of *current* cases in North America is about 6000, according to one expert. Does that support the fad theory? Or does it reflect a new awareness that a real disorder was long overlooked, that sometimes what sounds like a horse really is a zebra?

Julia is 33, an articulate, college-educated woman. She is pretty, with delicate features and dark blond hair pinned up on top of her head. She seems nervous, though no more skittish than many people; this is a woman you would be glad to sit next to on the bus or chat with in line for a movie.

We met at the office of her therapist, Anne Riley. Julia and I were at either end of a brown corduroy couch, with Riley in a chair in front of us. Julia sat smoking and drinking one Diet Coke after another, trying to convey to me some sense of what her days are like.

Listening to her was like reading a novel whose pages had been scattered by the wind and then hastily gathered up—the individual sections were clear and compelling, but chunks were missing and the rest hard to put in order. What was most disorienting was her feeling of not knowing firsthand about her own life. She is continually obliged to play detective.

"Sometimes I can figure out who's been 'out,'" she said. "Obviously, if I find myself curled up in a closet and crying, that's a pretty good indication it's somebody fairly young—but most of the time I just don't know what the hell's been going on. The little ones tend to do things with their hair. Sometimes I have braids or pigtails and I think, *Patty*. If my hair is cut shorter, I know one of the guys has been out."

She recounted such stories with a kind of gallows humour, but occasionally her tone grew darker. "This gets into scary stuff," she said at one point. "I have some old scars, they've always been there, and I don't know where they came from."

Riley asked for details. "I can remember my father having razor blades," Julia said. "I remember once feeling like I was getting cut, but I'm real detached from it." Her voice had become quieter, slowing and drifting almost to a murmur.

She was silent for a moment and changed posture slightly. It was subtle and far from histrionic—she pulled a bit closer to the edge of the couch, turning slightly from me, drawing her legs under her a bit more closely, and holding both hands to her mouth. Several seconds went by.

"Who's here?" Riley asked.

A tiny voice. "Elizabeth."

"Were you listening?"

"Yeah." Long pause. "We got cut a lot, if that's what you're asking."

"You remember your dad cutting you?"

Julia shifted posture, stretching her legs out toward the coffee table and picking up her cigarettes. "He's not *my* dad," she spit out venomously. The voice was slightly deeper than Julia's, the tone far more belligerent.

"Who's there? George?" asked the therapist.

"Yeah." George is 33, the same age as Julia, and tough. A male.

"Can you explain what it's like for you, George, being a guy?" Riley asked. "Whose body is it?"

"I don't think about it too much. I'm real glad I'm a guy. If somebody messes with me, I can hurt them more than a girl can."

George paused. "He" seemed jumpy. "People [Julia's personalities] are kind of close today. There's lots of us around."

Riley continued asking questions, but in the parade of names and references I lost track of which personality was speaking. Then something panicked Julia. She whipped her head toward me, wide-eyed like a cornered doe, and leapt off the couch we had been sharing.

Riley recognized a personality named Sandi, a bright but terrified 4-year-old. A minute or two passed, and Sandi seemed more at ease. "Want me to write my name?" she asked timidly.

After a few minutes more, Sandi ventured back to the couch to show me her writing. Riley told her that it was time to speak with Julia again.

I was taking notes, not watching, and I missed the switch. But there, sharing the couch with me again, was Julia. She seemed a bit befuddled, the way someone does when you wake her, but she knew me and Riley and where she was. "You've been gone a couple of hours," the therapist said. "Do you remember? No? Let me tell you what happened."

Frank Putnam, M.D., a psychiatrist at the National Institute of Mental Health and perhaps the leading authority on multiple personality, lists three rules of thumb: the more abuse the patient endured, the more personalities; the younger the patient when another personality first appeared, the more personalities; the more personalities, the longer the time needed in therapy.

Personalities, he explains, often see themselves as different in age, appearance, and gender—somewhat the way a woman with anorexia sees her skinny body as grotesquely fat. They seem unable to grasp that they share one body. Julia finds notes in her home, written in different handwriting and signed by various of her personalities: "I hate Julia so much. I want her to suffer. I'll cut her when I can. You can count on it."

A multiple may have as few as two and as many as hundreds of personalities. The average number is 13. Sybil, the woman portrayed in the movie by the same name, had 16; Eve, according to her autobiography, did not have "three faces," but 22. Anne Riley says Julia has close to 100 personalities. Multiples can sometimes control switches between personalities, particularly once they have become aware of their alter egos through therapy. Some switches are akin to flashbacks—panic reactions triggered by a particular memory or sight or sound. Other switches are protective, as if one personality had bowed out to someone better able to cope.

Surprisingly, many people with multiple personality do fairly well in the workaday world. "There's a lot going on beneath the surface, but if it's so far beneath that it's not perceived, then for all practical purposes things are going along smoothly," says psychiatrist Richard Kluft, M.D., of the Institute of Pennsylvania Hospital. A stranger would be unlikely to notice anything amiss. Spouses or children often think something is very strange but have no explanation for what they see. "Once you've described the diagnosis to the family," says Dr. Putnam, "they call up for a week rattling off incident after incident that suddenly make sense."

One multiple in six has earned a graduate degree. Some work as nurses, social workers, judges, even psychiatrists. Julia, who is not working now, was a drug-abuse and alcoholism counselor for a time. In many cases the personalities "agree" to cooperate, striking such deals as that the "children" will stay home and the "grown-ups" go to work.

In fact, personalities typically have specific roles and responsibilities. Some deal with sex, some with anger, some with child rearing. Others are "internal administrators," deciding which personalities are allowed "out," which have access to various bits of information, and which are responsible for memories of trauma. Often, it is the administrator who holds down the person's job. The administrators, Dr. Putnam says, come across as cold, distant, an authoritarian, intentionally aloof to keep anyone from coming close enough to find out about the other selves.

All multiples have a "host"—the personality they most often present to the world outside the workplace. The host usually does not know about the other selves, though there is often one personality who does. Julia is the host, and her memory is pocked with holes, while Elizabeth, the first of Julia's personalities I met, knows everyone. Elizabeth once put together a list for Anne Riley headed Inside People. It filled a sheet of notebook paper and read like the cast of a large play: Susan, 4, very timid; Joanne, 12, outgoing, deals with school; and so on. A few have last names, too, and some have only labels, such as "Noise."

Nearly all multiples have child personalities, like Julia's Sandi, frozen in time at the age that some trauma occurred. Most have a protector personality, often a male if the patient is female, as in the case of Julia's George, who emerges in response to threats of danger. The threat could be real—a mugger —or it could be mistaken—a stranger innocently approaching to ask for directions.

Many multiples have a persecutor personality who is at war with them. Julia's threatening notes are written by persecutors. The danger is real. Most people with multiple personality attempt suicide or mutilate themselves. Julia has "come to" to find herself bleeding from rows of self-inflicted razor wounds. "Multiples seem to teeter continuously on the brink of disaster," Dr. Putnam says.

Strangely enough, some personalities seem to differ physically. For example, in a survey of 92 therapists who had treated a total of 100 multiple personality cases, nearly half the therapists had patients whose personalties responded differently to the same medication. One fourth had patients whose personalities had different allergic symptoms.

"I once treated a man who in almost all his personalities, except one called Tommy, was allergic to citric acid," recalls Bennett G. Graun, M.D., of Rush-Presbyterian-St. Luke's Medical Center in Chicago. "If Tommy drank orange or grapefruit juice and stayed 'out' for a couple of hours, there would be no allergic reaction. But if Tommy drank the juice and went 'in' five minutes later, whichever other personality that would next emerge would begin itching and breaking out in fluid-filled blisters. And if Tommy came back, the itching went away, though the blisters remained."

Dr. Putnam believes these physical differences may not be as inexplicable as they seem. "People look at the brain scans of multiples' personalities and say, 'See, they are so different they're like different people,'" he says. He draws a long, exasperating breath. "It's not true. They're not different people —they're the same person in different behavioural states. What makes multiples different is that they move between states so suddenly. Normal people might show similar abrupt physiological shifts, if you could catch them at the right time." An example: you're calmly listening to your car stereo when a tractor-trailer cuts in front of you on the freeway; you jam on your brakes and your blood pressure and adrenaline skyrocket.

But *why* all the personalities? "Their basic coping strategy has been 'divide and conquer,'" Dr. Putnam says. "They cope with the pain and horror of the abuse they suffered by dividing it up into little pieces and storing it in such a way that it's hard to put back together and remember."

Multiple personality disorder is an extreme form of what psychiatrists call dissociation. The term refers to a kind of "spacing out," a failure to incorporate experiences into one's consciousness. At one end of the spectrum are experiences as common and innocuous as daydreaming or "highway hypnosis," where you arrive home from work with only the vaguest memory of making the drive. At the other extreme lie multiple personality and amnesia.

Dissociation is a well-known reaction to trauma. In multiple personality cases, the trauma is most often child abuse that is far more sadistic and bizarre than usual. According to Julia's therapist, Anne Riley, both Julia's mother and father, and a brother, abused her physically and sexually for many years. Riley doesn't go into the details but admits, "I don't consider that I've led a sheltered life—for six years I was a Washington, D.C., cop, specializing in child abuse—but I had no inkling that anything like this existed."

Age is a key to multiple personality. The trauma at its root occurs during a window of vulnerability that extends to about age 12. One proposed explanation of why age makes a difference is that it takes time for infants and children to develop an integrated personality. They have fairly distinct moods and behaviours and make abrupt changes from one to another—a happy baby drops his rattle and instantly begins howling in misery. "We all come into the world with the potential to become multiples," Dr. Putnam suggests, "But with halfway decent parenting, we learn to smooth the transitions and develop an integrated self. These people don't get a chance to do that."

Some therapists believe that the incidence of the disorder has been widely exaggerated. They propose a simple explanation—faddism—and a more complex one: they say the multiple personality diagnosis represents self-deception on the part of both patient and therapist. "We're all different people in different situations," says Eugene E. Levitt, Ph.D., and clinical psychologist at the Indiana University School of Medicine. "You're one person with your wife, an entirely different person with your mother, still another person with your boss.

"A person may be unaware that he turns different facets of his personality to different people," Levitt says. "The man who comes home and domineers over his wife doesn't realize, or doesn't want to realize, that he cringes before his boss."

The goal of therapy, Levitt says, is to help patients discover and face up to the sides of their characters that they would rather deny. But some therapists may address the various parts of their patients' personalities as if each were a separate person. And this can unwittingly encourage patients to believe there are independent "personalities" that are beyond their control. Levitt also points out that the overwhelming majority of therapists have never encountered a multiple personality while a few diagnose such cases regularly.

Under any circumstances, the diagnosis can be hard to make because people with multiple personality work so hard to cover up. Patients wander through the mental health system for an average of seven years before being accurately diagnosed. On the way, they pick up one label after another—schizophrenic, depressive, manic depressive.

During her teens Julia saw a psychiatrist for depression. "He just told me that all teenagers have their issues and that I came from a very upstanding family," she says. She tried to commit suicide at 15, by swallowing sleeping pills. She steered clear of the mental health system after that but was finally diagnosed about five years ago after she checked herself into a hospital, hallucinating that she was being chased by neon-orange spiders. A resident made the diagnosis when, in the middle of an interview, Julia suddenly said,

"I can tell you some things about what's going on. I'm Patty."

Most cases, like Julia's, are diagnosed at around age 30. It's not clear why things go wrong then. It may be that the person becomes more conscious of episodes of lost time; it may be that the multiple's defense system erodes when he or she is finally safe, away from abusive parents. In many cases, some new trauma precipitates a breakdown.

For both patients and therapists, treatment is a long and harrowing ordeal. The first hurdle is that patients with multiple personality all had their trust violated when they were young and are therefore wary of confiding in any authority figure. They have had a lifetime's practice in keeping secrets from themselves and others, and that practice is hard to change. And the treatment itself is painful; the key, says Dr. Putnam, is to exhume, relive, and accept the original trauma, and that obliges the patient to confront terrifying and deeply hidden memories.

Patients usually have two or three sessions a week of therapy, for three years or more. The goal is to transfer traumatic memories across the amnesiac boundaries separating the personalities, to make the pain more bearable by sharing it. If that happens, the separate personalities can fuse together. But nothing is simple. Often when the therapist thinks he or she has met all the personalities, new ones seem to emerge, as if from hiding. And once they are fused, more therapy is needed to develop some way other than "splitting" to cope with problems.

The prognosis for multiple personality is fairly encouraging. Dr. Kluft, one of the most esteemed therapists in the field, has reported a success rate of 90 percent in a group of 52 patients. He calls treatment successful if the patient shows no signs of multiple personality in the two years following the end of therapy.

Julia has been seeing Riley for two and a half years and talks about the prospect of integrating her various personalities wistfully but without much hope. "In my better moments I say, 'You should be damned proud you've survived—don't let the bastards win now,'" she says. "But my idea of myself is very disjointed and that's really frightening.

"I don't have a history," she goes on. "Not just for the bad things, but for the accomplishments, too. I was in the National Honour Society in high school, and I had a very good college record, but I don't have any sense of pride, any feeling that I did it."

She talks as if she is at the mercy of someone with a remote-control channel-changer who keeps zapping her out of one scene and into another. "If I could just lose less time," she says plaintively. "If I could just have—I hate the word—normal reactions to things.

"Do you know my idea of heaven? A little room with no doors and no windows and an endless supply of cigarettes and Diet Coke and ice."

No more surprises, ever.

Ric
Dolphin
· · · · · · · · · ·

RAPE ON CAMPUS

Surveys put the number of campus rapes in the United States at about 6000 a year.

McGill University's Zeta Psi fraternity, based in a three-storey brick house near the campus in downtown Montreal, was holding one of the parties for which it has become famous. The Sept. 22 occasion was in honour of McGill's female rugby team, which was initiating 20 of its rookies. As part of their initiation, the young women were required to obtain male signatures on their stomachs. At 8 p.m., they arrived at the packed Zeta House, where they were offered beer. The male rugby team had 25 of its initiates pay a naked visit to the party. Later, a 19-year-old rookie member of the female rugby team told a reporter for the campus newspaper, *The McGill Daily*, that she was sexually assaulted by three men while as many as 10 others looked on. At the time, she was in an apartment in a coach house behind the frat house.

Last week, while Montreal police continued the investigation into the complaint against three Zeta members, feminist organizations on campuses across North America voiced alarm at what they say is a striking increase in campus sexual assaults. Surveys put the number of campus rapes in the United States at about 6000 a year—roughly two for every college in the country. And only 10 percent of those, according to officials at the Rape Treatment Centre in Santa Monica, Calif., are reported to authorities. A recent poll of 698 American colleges by the newspaper *USA Today* showed that only 38 percent of the female students interviewed felt safe walking home alone on campus after dark. At a candlelight vigil two weeks ago at the University of Illinois, at Champaign, where a series of sexual attacks have alarmed female students, coed Laurel MacLaren said, "Making women sex objects is closely tied to the degradation of women, which ultimately can lead to rape."

A few days before the vigil, the University of Mississippi suspended the charter of the Sigma Alpha Epsilon fraternity on its Oxford campus for violating the university's alcohol policy, after a freshman Chi Omega sorority pledge said that she was driven to a field, beaten, then raped by a Sigma member. At Florida State University in Tallahassee, three fraternity men were charged last April with the sexual battery of an 18-year-old freshman coed at a fraternity party, after carrying her to a neighbouring frat house so that it would appear she had been assaulted there. And last month, five students at Frankfort's Kentucky State University, including four members of the football team, were charged with the first-degree rape, sodomy, and unlawful imprisonment of a female student in a men's dormitory.

In Canada, there are few signs to suggest that the incidence of campus rape is reaching those alarming proportions. But aside from the McGill incident, there have also been five official reports of sexual assault at Ontario's University of Guelph since Jan. 1, after eight in 1987. Two of this year's assaults involved attacks on women walking on campus, while the other three involved men allegedly entering unlocked female residence rooms and fondling the occupants. Now, some women at the university are protesting against the handling of the assaults by campus police. Maureen Evans, 22, news editor of Guelph's student newspaper, *The Ontarion*, labelled campus police "chauvinistic" for categorizing the incidents as minor and for suggesting that the victims should have kept their doors locked. For her part, Kathryn Edgecombe, coordinator of Guelph University's Women's Resource Centre, criticized campus police for only reluctantly releasing statistics on sexual assaults when she wanted them to prepare a study last year.

At the same time, sexual assaults by off-campus intruders have become a concern at some universities. Another concern among women on campus is the phenomenon known as "date rape"—situations in which men force sex on women at the end of a date. Said Ruth Gillings, a staff worker at one of Vancouver's rape crisis centres: "Eighty percent of our calls are acquaintance rape, by a date, a husband, co-student, or colleague at work." Many reports of rape by a stranger go to the police, not the crisis centre, she said. "Women who are raped by someone they know are afraid to report to the police, so they come to us," added Gillings. "But it's hard to know if rape is on the increase or if women are just reporting it more."

Indeed, the number of reported sexual assaults in Canada has increased by 87 percent in the past five years—to 22 369 in 1987 from 11 932 in 1983. Experts in the field say that it is not clear whether the figures reflect more sexual assaults or the fact that women are more likely to report them. "It probably has more to do with a change of attitude," said Nathan Pollock, a coordinator of clinical psychology at Toronto's Clarke Institute of Psychiatry. "The status of women has been elevated in society. Rape used to be seen as a woman's lot in life. Now it is a violation."

Meanwhile at McGill, where the Zeta Psi fraternity has suspended three of its members pending the results of the police investigation, reports of the incident shocked the McGill campus. "If this complaint is true," said dean of students Irwin Gopnik, "it is reprehensible, and we will not tolerate this behaviour." But if feminist critics are right, some old campus institutions will have to change.

Henry G.
Felsen
··········

WHEN DOES A BOY BECOME A MAN?

When the time comes that you no longer feel the necessity to prove to me ... or to yourself that you are a man—you will have become one.

Last Saturday you and I disagreed on how late you should be allowed to stay out. When I refused to extend your curfew, you complained that I was not treating you like an adult. This has become your standard answer whenever you can't have your own way. But what you really mean is that I don't go along with your idea of what constitutes adulthood.

Let me put it this way: I do not pretend you are a grown man because you are a 16-year-old boy. I am not as you are deceived by a few similarities of plumage, diet, and song into identifying you as a genuine adult. You may be as big and strong and capable as many adults (and you probably argue better than most!), but only a child would maintain—and sincerely believe—that his manhood can be measured by the lateness of the hour his father permits him to stay out at night.

Recently I attended an assembly of teen-agers that was addressed by a grown man. He seemed to believe that the way to get the audience on his side was to pretend that he was one of them. He jittered and jiggled, and made odd faces, spoke disdainfully about adults, and laboured to use a great deal of what he thought was current teen-age slang.

Later, I heard the kids talk with amusement and contempt about his efforts to appear as one of them by imitating what he thought was teen-age behaviour. It was obvious from their comments that the speaker would have commanded more respect and attention if he had appeared as a grown man and not as a caricature of a boy. All he did was make more obvious the gulf of years that lay between him and his audience.

The kids could see how silly it was for an adult to pretend he was a boy, but they could not see the same thing in reverse. After the assembly I saw teen-age boys swaggering down the street with forbidden cigarettes in their mouths, manfully cursing as they swaggered. Others roared away in their cars, belligerently demonstrating their "right" to the streets. I saw little teen-age girls teetering along on spike heels in tight dresses, with extravagantly styled and dyed hair. All this, I am sure, because they believed they could impress the world with their maturity if they imitated behaviour that, to them, appeared to be adult.

All this reminded me of a fable I used to read aloud when you were little, about the donkey who longed to be a lion. The donkey, if you recall, covered himself with a lion's skin, crept in among the lions, and lay down quietly among them. When the lions took no notice of him, and seemingly accepted him as one of them, the donkey was filled with joy and confidence. It seemed to him that he had actually become a lion, and he thought of donkeys with contempt. All went well until evening, when the lions began their customary evening roaring. The little donkey, completely fooled by his own disguise, lifted his head and roared with them. What came out, of course, was a donkey's bray. Whereupon the lions fell upon him and devoured him.

The moral applies equally to boys and men. Human victims of self-deception are likely to be devoured by the lions of reality.

If the extremes of behaviour among teen-agers represented nothing more than a little natural daydreaming and imitation, they could be overlooked. But the danger in them—as in your attitude toward how late you stay out—is that they look like real lion skins, and are so employed.

I can understand why you and your friends are eager to become adults, and to enjoy the freedoms, privileges, and even the bad habits that are denied to you as children. What you fail to see is that these freedoms and privileges are routine and minor by-products of being an adult. They are not, as many of you believe, the components of genuine maturity.

Look around a typical American town. Ninety percent of the people who could stay up all night are in bed by ten. Ninety percent of the people who have the legal right to smoke wish they were able to give up the habit. Ninety percent of the people who have the right to buy and drink all the liquor they want are sober. Ninety percent of the grown single men and women, who have the opportunity to be as sexually casual as they wish, are looking for a mate with whom to settle down. What it all adds up to is the fact that the huge majority of men and women are mature. And yet children seem to believe that the way to prove themselves adult is to imitate the unstable, destructive, irresponsible minority.

It is possible for children to convince themselves and each other that disobedience, late hours, smoking, drinking, sexual experiments, and the rest actually transform them into adults. When this happens they often begin to despise their own contemporaries and the tasks that are appropriate to their age. They often come to resent not only parental direction and control, but to resist and resent school, and avoid normal teen-age activities and patterns. The boy who believes that a deep voice and bad habits have made him manly wants to quit school, get a job, buy a car, and "be a real man." The girl who has talked and acted and dressed her way out of being her age believes that getting married at once will result in her being an instant woman.

Several days ago, our newspaper interviewed a group of teen-agers on what they thought it meant to be adult. Some of the boys seemed to envision maturity as a time when they would be big enough to be irresponsible without having to account to anyone for their behaviour. One girl of seventeen wanted to get married right away so she could escape her parents, be an adult, and be in a position where "nobody can tell me what to do."

I felt sorry for these boys whose goal in life was to be failures as men. I felt sorry for the girl who didn't seem to understand that the absence of orders did not mean the absence of duties; that the reason no one seems to tell adults what to do is that they do what has to be done without being told.

It is a sad thing when children renounce their own generation and try to sneak into maturity as though it were a border to be crossed under cover of darkness. They do not become free and equal citizens of the adult world. They become half-formed semi-adults who are as out of place in the adult world as they thought they were in the child's. They are the young, untrained, uneducated, unprepared, and inept people who have trouble finding and keeping the worst jobs, whose hasty escape-marriages fall apart at the first tremor, whose babies often become public charges. They try to flee the restraints of being adults as once they fled the restraints of being children. Only now there is nowhere to run. They are the donkeys who are so taken in by their lion costumes that they attempt to roar and are devoured when, in fact, they bray.

You complain that I do not treat you like an adult. My reply is, I would rather treat you like what you are. And at sixteen, you are a boy and you belong in a boy's world, accepting a boy's responsibilities, dreaming a boy's dreams, learning a boy's freedoms, appreciating your boyish years. Being a successful boy is the best guarantee in the world that you will be a successful man.

In a few years, time and experience will make you an adult. When it does, I will treat you like an adult. It will be impossible for me to do otherwise. I don't know when that time will come, or when you will discover that it has. But I can give you one clue. When the time comes that you no longer feel the necessity to prove to me, to your friends, to the world, or to yourself that you are a man—you will have become one.

Judith
Finlayson
············

WHEN MEN REFUSE TO GROW UP

***I've watched the Holden Caulfield complex acted out in the
lives of men and . . . it reveals a malignancy at the heart of
our society.***

Like McDonald's to the taste of America, *The Catcher in the Rye* is a novel that
has influenced several generations of young minds. In fact, a recent *Esquire*
story celebrating its 30th birthday pointed out that the book is second only
to *Of Mice and Men* as the most frequently taught novel in public school. It
still sells a phenomenal 20 to 30 000 copies a month. This helps to explain
why all my life I've been meeting men who tell me they're Holden Caulfield.

Why Holden? In his own words, he's probably "the biggest sex maniac
you ever saw," an "exhibitionist" who all too easily behaves "like a prize
horse's ass." It's hardly an irresistible combination. Still, Holden does have a
kind of innocent appeal. Seen lovingly through the eyes of his creator, he's an
adolescent individualist who refuses to conform to his social role.

To some extent, Holden's good eye for hypocrisy redeems his asinine
behaviour. But over the years, I've watched the Holden Caulfield complex
acted out in the lives of men and I've become alarmed at the implications.
Carefully scrutinized, it reveals a malignancy at the heart of our society.

For instance: in October, *Esquire* ran a story on Doug Kenney, the "comic
genius" who gave us *National Lampoon* and *Animal House*. His brilliance
made him a millionaire six times over and yet, at the age of 34, he walked off
a cliff in Hawaii. "He was deciding whether he wanted to be an adult."

At the time of his suicide, Kenney was making plans to marry, although the
story pointed out that emotionally "he had never left high school." In his
imagination, adolescence was *Paradise Lost*. Another friend made the defini-
tive connection: "Doug Kenney was Holden Caulfield, the *Catcher in the
Rye*."

For better or for worse, the literature we read shapes our imagination. So it
should surprise no one that an analysis of American literature reveals an
intimate acquaintance with death and violence, juxtaposed against a longing for innocence symbolized by sexual purity. In his monumental work,

---

NOTE: Also read "Watch Out for the Lure of Holden" by Alan Stewart on page 167.

Love and Death in the American Novel, critic Leslie Fiedler points out that a deep undercurrent in American literature is a terror of adult sexuality combined with a pathological obsession with death.

It's a tradition into which Holden Caulfield all too neatly fits. He lives in the shadow of his younger brother Allie's untimely death, and although obsessed by sex as an imaginary pursuit, he's so alarmed by the reality that he even botches an attempt with a prostitute. Placing this within a critical perspective, Fiedler concludes, "the flight from sexuality leads to a literature about children written for the consumption of adults. But the reading of that literature has turned those adults in their own inmost images of themselves into children."

Fiedler sees Holden Caulfield—and likely Doug Kenney if he had the chance—as a twentieth-century version of Huckleberry Finn. Huck's flight on the raft, like Holden's from school, is a declaration of maleness and an archetypal image for the emotional life of American men. Floating down the river, they're "on the lam from the female symbols of civilization" and adult sexual love.

But this inability to move beyond boyhood can have disastrous results. As Fiedler points out, Holden Caulfield "comes to the dead end of an ineffectual revolt in a breakdown." Doug Kenney committed suicide, proving that life imitates art, often in alarming ways.

Perhaps even more alarming was the revelation that when Mark David Chapman shot John Lennon, a copy of *The Catcher in the Rye* was in his pocket. After he was sentenced, Chapman read aloud the passage where Holden sees himself standing on the edge of a cliff catching children who might otherwise fall over the side. Did Doug Kenney jump with the wild hope that Holden was waiting to save him? It doesn't matter. What does matter is the tragic lesson of *The Catcher in the Rye* and its social implications. The failure to love as an adult results in death, both imagined and real.

I AM A NATIVE OF NORTH AMERICA

It is hard for me to understand a culture that spends more on wars and weapons to kill than it does on education and welfare to help and develop.

In the course of my lifetime I have lived in two distinct cultures. I was born into a culture that lived in communal houses. My grandfather's house was eighty feet long. It was called a smoke house, and it stood down by the beach along the inlet. All my grandfather's sons and their families lived in this large dwelling. Their sleeping apartments were separated by blankets made of bull rush reeds, but one open fire in the middle served the cooking needs of all. In houses like these, throughout the tribe, people learned to live with one another; learned to serve one another; learned to respect the rights of one another. And children shared the thoughts of the adult world and found themselves surrounded by aunts and uncles and cousins who loved them and did not threaten them. My father was born in such a house and learned from infancy how to love people and be at home with them.

And beyond this acceptance of one another there was a deep respect for everything in nature that surrounded them. My father loved the earth and all its creatures. The earth was his second mother. The earth and everything it contained was a gift from See-see-am . . . and the way to thank this great spirit was to use his gifts with respect.

I remember, as a little boy, fishing with him up Indian River and I can still see him as the sun rose above the mountain top in the early morning . . . I can see him standing by the water's edge with his arms raised above his head while he softly moaned . . . "Thank you, thank you." It left a deep impression on my young mind.

And I shall never forget his disappointment when once he caught me gaffing for fish "just for the fun of it." "My Son" he said, "the Great Spirit gave you those fish to be your brothers, to feed you when you are hungry. You must respect them. You must not kill them just for the fun of it."

This then was the culture I was born into and for some years the only one I really knew or tasted. This is why I find it hard to accept many of the things I see around me.

I see people living in smoke houses hundreds of times bigger than the one

I knew. But the people in one apartment do not even know the people in the next and care less about them.

It is also difficult for me to understand the deep hate that exists among people. It is hard to understand a culture that justifies the killing of millions in past wars, and is at this very moment preparing bombs to kill even greater numbers. It is hard for me to understand a culture that spends more on wars and weapons to kill than it does on education and welfare to help and develop.

It is hard for me to understand a culture that not only hates and fights his brothers but even attacks nature and abuses her. I see my white brothers going about blotting out nature from his cities. I see him strip the hills bare, leaving ugly wounds on the face of mountains. I see him tearing things from the bosom of mother earth as though she were a monster, who refused to share her treasures with him. I see him throw poison in the waters, indifferent to the life he kills there; and he chokes the air with deadly fumes.

My white brother does many things well for he is more clever than my people but I wonder if he knows how to love well. I wonder if he has ever really learned to love at all. Perhaps he only loves the things that are his own but never learned to love the things that are outside and beyond him. And this is, of course, not love at all, for man must love all creation or he will love none of it. Man must love fully or he will become the lowest of the animals. It is the power to love that makes him the greatest of them all . . . for he alone of all animals is capable of love.

Love is something you and I must have. We must have it because our spirit feeds upon it. We must have it because without it we become weak and faint. Without love our self-esteem weakens. Without it our courage fails. Without love we can no longer look out confidently at the world. Instead we turn inwardly and begin to feed upon our own personalities and little by little we destroy ourselves.

You and I need the strength and joy that comes from knowing that we are loved. With it we are creative. With it we march tirelessly. With it, and with it alone, we are able to sacrifice for others.

There have been times when we all wanted so desperately to feel a reassuring hand upon us . . . there have been lonely times when we so wanted a strong arm around us . . . I cannot tell you how deeply I miss my wife's presence when I return from a trip. Her love was my greatest joy, my strength, my greatest blessing.

I am afraid my culture has little to offer yours. But my culture did prize friendship and companionship. It did not look on privacy as a thing to be clung to, for privacy builds up walls and walls promote distrust. My culture lived in big family communities, and from infancy people learned to live with others.

My culture did not prize the hoarding of private possessions, in fact, to hoard was a shameful thing to do among my people. The Indian looked on all things in nature as belonging to him and he expected to share them with others and to take only what he needed.

Everyone likes to give as well as receive. No one wishes only to receive all the time. We have taken much from your culture . . . I wish you had taken something from our culture . . . for there were some beautiful and good things in it.

Soon it will be too late to know my culture, for integration is upon us and soon we will have no values but yours. Already many of our young people have forgotten the old ways. And many have been shamed of their Indian ways by scorn and ridicule. My culture is like a wounded deer that has crawled away into the forest to bleed and die alone.

The only thing that can truly help us is genuine love. You must truly love us, be patient with us and share with us. And we must love you—with a genuine love that forgives and forgets . . . a love that forgives the terrible sufferings your culture brought ours when it swept over us like a wave crashing along a beach . . . with a love that forgets and lifts up its head and sees in your eyes an answering love of trust and acceptance.

This is brotherhood . . . anything less is not worthy of the name.

I have spoken.

Elizabeth
Glaser
and Laura
Palmer
·············

In The Absence Of Angels

**As a member of a family struggling with AIDS, I learned
that few wanted to help enough to change a system that had
become strangled by red tape.**

*A decade ago, before the nation awakened to the daily nightmare that is AIDS,
Elizabeth Glaser was infected with the virus through a tainted blood transfusion.
She did not know that she had passed the virus on to her two children until her
daughter, Ariel, developed the disease at age 4. For more than three years, Eliza-
beth, 43, and her husband, director Paul Michael Glaser, 47, the former star of the
TV series "Starsky and Hutch," kept their painful ordeal private.*

*Then in 1989, just after the first anniversary of Ariel's death, the Glasers went
public with their story upon learning that a tabloid was about to expose their
tragedy in an unauthorized feature. Since then, Elizabeth and writer Laura Palmer
have collaborated on* In the Absence of Angels, *an inspiring account of the Glaser
family's struggles and triumphs. . . . "After we found out that my family was HIV-
positive," says Elizabeth, "it was clear that I would have to grow as a person more
than I had ever imagined in order to find a way to cope. I wanted to let America see
how painful it is to be a family battling AIDS and how hard it is to deal with the
isolation and discrimination that comes through ignorance."*

*The book is more than an anguished account of a mother's loss; it is a testament
to one woman's brave refusal to surrender. "If reading my story can help open hearts
to people who are battling this disease," says Elizabeth, "then maybe other families
will have an easier time." Here is a selection from* In the Absence of Angels.

May 1981
There were no words, no sounds, everything was obliterated by a single
focus, getting to the hospital. It was as though I were motionless and the
scenery was being pulled past me.

When I arrived at Cedars-Sinai Medical Center, my husband, Paul, rushed
over, and I could see the fear in his face. I was six months pregnant and had
started bleeding. My baby wasn't due for 11 more weeks.

I was diagnosed as having placenta previa, which meant the placenta was growing across my cervix. All we could do was pray that I would stop bleeding, because my child was probably too small to live outside my body. I lay there, day after day, with Paul by my side, waiting.

On the sixth day, I was sent home and told to stay in bed for the rest of my pregnancy. I was so afraid that I did less than whatever the doctor said I could. Each day was a victory, the next, a challenge.

Finally, on Aug. 4, 1981, Ariel Glaser was delivered by cesarean section. She was three and a half weeks early and weighed five pounds, two ounces, but I didn't care. When I looked into her eyes for the first time, I was amazed that this miracle was mine. Our fears were gone.

I was trying to tell the doctor how glad I was that it was over, when I heard the anesthesiologist saying that something was wrong. I couldn't breathe. I haemorrhaged. I was gasping for air. My doctor pushed on my stomach and I could feel the warm blood gushing out. I was too horrified to even scream. What was happening to me?

The transfusions began. I watched the dark red blood drip out of the squat plastic bag, flow through an IV tube and into a vein in my arm. I was transfused with seven pints. After the doctors packed me with cotton I finally stopped bleeding.

It wasn't until I saw my baby daughter again that the weariness and terror began to drift away, to be replaced with an instinctive love. She *was* beautiful, and we had both survived. It was over. I finally fell asleep, thinking about the wonderful life the three of us had to look forward to.

Three weeks later I saw an article about a new virus called AIDS. I called my obstetrician immediately. "I just read an article in the paper about AIDS, a virus that may be transmitted by blood transfusions. I just got seven pints!"

"Oh, Elizabeth," he said, "you've been through a difficult ordeal, but it's behind you. Relax and enjoy your baby. Your nightmare is over. AIDS isn't ever going to have anything to do with you."

June 1975

I had pork chops, not passion, on my mind when I met Paul 15 years ago. I was coming home from a session with my therapist and determined to defrost two chops and have supper by myself.

I had, in fact, just spent 50 minutes explaining why I didn't need a man. Then, while waiting for the light to change at the intersection of Santa Monica and Beverly Boulevards, I looked at the car next to me. "Oh, my God, that is the cutest guy I have ever seen," I thought. I smiled. He smiled. The light changed.

I turned right. He turned right. I glanced into the rearview mirror and he signaled me over with his arm. I was anxious and jittery as I pulled over. He stepped out of his car and walked toward me. I rolled down my window and he said, "Okay, let me see your driver's license." I looked at him and laughed. He was droll and disarming.

"What are you doing for dinner?" he asked. Thinking of therapy, I told him I was going home and making pork chops. "Wouldn't you rather go out for Chinese food?" "Yes," I said without missing a beat. One therapy session thrown out the window.

We went to Al Fong's in Beverly Hills. It was dark and the food was dreadful. Midway through the moo shu pork I asked Paul what he did. He said, "I'm an actor." I was so disappointed. I had lived in Los Angeles long enough to know that being an actor meant absolutely nothing. "Are you working?" I asked politely. "Actually, I am. I'm in a show that's just been picked up by a network. It'll be on ABC in the fall." "What's it called?" "'Starsky and Hutch.' It's a cop show about two detectives. I play Starsky."

I knew that night that even though he was an actor, this was the man for me. I was 27 and in love. When I looked at Paul I saw happily-ever-after. In September I moved into the one-room bungalow in the Hollywood Hills he shared with a dog named Max.

Paul didn't even have a television. We watched the debut of "Starsky and Hutch" with David Soul, the actor who played Hutch, at the home of David's agent. Everyone, including the stars, felt the show would be cancelled in eight weeks. By Thanksgiving, it was the hottest show on TV, and Paul and David were as famous as rock stars.

Paul and I were both stunned by his instant celebrity status. For years, he had worked steadily, doing everything from Shakespeare to soaps. "Starsky" was not how he imagined becoming famous. There was a lot of adjusting to do. The simple joy of taking a walk on the beach in our jeans and sweatshirts came to a halt. Until you went out in public with Paul, you had no sense of how overwhelming, demanding, and ridiculous being a celebrity was.

During the years that "Starsky" was on the air, we never got involved in the social side of Hollywood. We saved our money, knowing that actors usually have lean times, and wanted to be prepared for that. The price I paid for Paul's celebrity was invisibility. Hollywood people would nod and smile when I would say I was a teacher or, later, an exhibits director at the Children's Museum. I had to find ways to accept that; one solution was to make a life of my own that was independent and strong.

I definitely knew I wanted to be married and have children. I had had a wonderful childhood and was looking forward to starting a family of my own. But Paul's childhood had been more complicated, and marriage and family were scary to him. Paul and I talked it through, and he finally agreed that we'd get married when we were ready to have children.

Three months after our wedding in August 1980, I was pregnant. All the goodness in the world seemed to be ours. In nine months I would have what I had always wanted most, a child of my own with a man that I loved.

When Ari was about a year and a half old, we began looking for a larger house. Paul and I wanted more children, and I was trying to get pregnant again. From the moment I walked into the sprawling Mediterranean house in Santa Monica, I knew this was the home for my family. Our children would grow up and go to college, and then Glaser children would come home with Glaser grandchildren.

Everything seemed to be going well. I had gotten pregnant and had miscarried, but was pregnant once more. And on Oct. 25, 1984, I delivered a beautiful son we named Jake.

In the spring of 1985 Paul was offered the job of directing his first feature film, *Band of the Hand*. The film was being shot in Miami, so we packed up the family and rented a house on the beach for the three-month shoot.

From Miami I took the children to visit my parents, who were living in Puerto Rico. We had just returned from that trip when Ari, who was then 4, started to have stomach aches and cramps. She was in a great deal of pain. We consulted a pediatrician who said that she had probably picked up a bug in Puerto Rico. When Ari didn't get better, I went to another doctor who suggested a stomach specialist. He had Ari hospitalized for more tests. The doctors said they had no idea what was wrong with Ariel, but for the next three days they watched her as if she might die. Once again I saw her life as precarious. I could feel all my dreams and plans start to crumble. My many fears began to return. Without even knowing what was wrong, I was fighting for Ari's life all over again.

By the time we left Florida in November Ariel was stronger, but not well. Doctors there said that she suffered from a blood disorder that usually leads to kidney failure. There was more colour in her face and lips, but she still had bouts of diarrhea and would wake up in pain. Over the next few months we were doing test after test, trying to diagnose the underlying cause of Ari's illness. Paul and I had told Ari there was something funny with her blood and that was the reason she was so frequently tired. We told her that the doctors were going to find a way to make her better.

As time went by and things still didn't improve, Ariel was tested for all sorts of unusual diseases including lupus and leukemia. There was also talk of doing a liver and kidney biopsy, but that was postponed. When each test came back negative, I felt we had won another diagnostic round. But Ari's doctor, Richard Fine, wasn't as cheerful. He knew what we didn't—that Ari's diarrhea and low helper T-cells count [an important part of the immune system that fights infection] were symptoms of AIDS.

I don't think I was any more anxious about an AIDS test than I was about anything else. Just as her doctors had ruled out lupus and leukemia, they'd rule out AIDS. We took her in to be tested.

When the phone rang the next day, Paul answered it and after he hung up he said, "They've got to run it again. It's shown some kind of positivity. It's probably a mistake and we'll know in two days." The two days slowly passed. Richard Fine called that morning in late May. "The test has come back positive. You all have to come in tomorrow to be tested."

Ari had been diagnosed. Ari's illness now had a name. Ariel had AIDS. I remember walking into the bathroom and screaming as loud as I could. Ari and Jake must have been out of the house because I would never have fallen apart in front of them. Paul walked into the bathroom, but we couldn't touch. We couldn't even look at each other. He turned and walked out. I was still crying. He walked back in. He said, "You have to pull yourself together." I thought, "Why? My life is over. The most important thing in my life—my daughter—is going to die."

I became more and more hysterical. Finally, Paul sat down by me on the edge of the tub and just said, "We don't know. You have to get control for Ari and Jake, Elizabeth. You have to—now *do it*."

From that moment on I had no choice but to become intentionally schizophrenic. What I felt was one thing, and what I presented to my children and to the rest of the outside world was another.

The next morning we were all tested. Richard Fine called back later. "We have to run the tests on Elizabeth and Jake again," he said, and by then we knew what that meant. We had tested positive.

Paul and I went back to UCLA and sat numbly in Dr. Fine's office with him and Dr. Richard Stiehm, the pediatric immunologist who would become Ari's doctor. They explained that there had been a lot of infected blood at Cedars-Sinai Medical Center in the early years of the epidemic because it is located on the edge of West Hollywood, which has a large gay population.

Dr. Stiehm said he thought I had been infected through my blood transfusion and had passed the virus on to Ari during breast feeding and to Jake in utero.

Paul and I sat there. In our worst nightmares, we could never have imagined the devastation of that office visit. Our entire world had been crushed. Ari, Jake, and I might all die. It was too much to comprehend. Still, today, it is too much to comprehend.

They said that Ari should start on gamma globulin treatment right away to shore up her immune system. She could get the infusions at the UCLA clinic once every three weeks, by sitting for four hours with an IV in her arm. Dr. Stiehm strongly recommended that we shouldn't tell anyone about our diagnosis because the experiences of other families with AIDS had not been positive. "The world is not ready for your family," was how he put it.

Nevertheless, he said we needed to either tell her nursery school or take her out of it. The Centers for Disease Control guidelines, at that time, said that a child with AIDS should not be in nursery school without first getting permission from the school. It was surreal. Along with this hideous medical diagnosis came instructions on how we needed to handle the rest of the world.

Dr. Stiehm told me that I could test positive and carry the AIDS virus without being symptomatic or showing any signs of the disease. In other words, there was a big difference between being HIV-positive and having full-blown AIDS. Although Jake had tested positive, his other tests were all normal.

I told Dr. Stiehm that I could not live without telling my friends. They had been following Ari's illness since Miami, and their support and concern had been crucially important. Paul and I decided we had two choices. We could tell some friends or we could pick up, sell our house, and begin our life all over again someplace else. The life we had known was over. I had to stay strong so I could save my children. Our first steps were perhaps the hardest.

Paul and I decided to confide in only a handful of friends. I told my women friends in person, one by one, and made each of them promise not to tell anyone except their husbands. For some, whose children were playmates of Ari and Jake, finding out that we had AIDS was like finding out that for years their children had been in imminent danger. Most of our friends wanted to stand beside us, but they also wanted assurances that there was no risk to their children. In May of 1986, answers were in short supply and there were no guarantees.

At first, no one would allow their children to come and play at our house. Some friends refused to let my kids come to their homes at all. Some said their children could continue to play with mine, but only at the park. Some dropped out of our lives.

The day after I told my yoga teacher about our diagnosis she called to tell me that she never wanted to see me again. We asked a therapist to see if a child psychiatrist would work with Ari when and if we felt it was appropriate. I was later told that psychiatrists would not see my child, because they were afraid if word leaked they would lose too many other patients.

People were responding so fearfully that I started to feel dangerous myself. The doctors said there was no reason for fear, but that meant nothing because our neighbours and our friends were not doctors. Every time I went to the supermarket, I envisioned everyone slowly and silently moving away as if they had just seen a rattlesnake. It would be nine months before the Surgeon General would appear on television to say flat out that you can't get AIDS from saliva or kissing. And with that information, our lives slowly regained some normalcy.

When we told people, we forced them to enlist in a conspiracy of silence.

The quality of our lives now hinged on the ability of our friends to keep quiet. Were word to get out, we knew we would be treated like plague victims for no reason. All of us were very afraid and confused.

What could have stopped the fear and hysteria was strong leadership from the Reagan administration. But in those early years of the epidemic, that leadership was absent. AIDS may one day cost me my life, but community reaction right away cost me the right to live the rest of my life the way I choose. That was my first fight.

It was a time that would almost be unimaginable if we hadn't lived it. It is what all families battling AIDS had to face then. You are told that you and your children may die. You are told that there are no answers now. And then as you are struggling not to completely fall apart, you realize that very few people are going to reach out to help or comfort you. We felt so alone. We wished for an angel who would help us get through it all. But at that time it seemed we had no angels watching over us.

July 1986
One of the telephone calls I dreaded most was to Crossroads Elementary School, where Ari had been accepted. Both Paul and I desperately wanted her to start kindergarten that fall. It was one of the few direct links we had to the future, and it meant so much to Ari. Paul Cummins, the school's headmaster, had no idea why I'd walked into his office. He seemed both confident and relaxed. I took a deep breath before I began.

"We were planning on having our daughter, Ariel, start kindergarten here in September," I said. "But I just found out that she, my son, and I are all infected with the AIDS virus." I started to cry. I was sure he would send me away and tell me to find another school. Paul Cummins walked over and put his arms around me. "You are part of our family," he said. "We want you here." He held me as I cried. I left his office feeling both relief and joy. As long as I could see that not every door was going to be closed to us, I could hope.

Ari had spent just one week at Crossroads when Cummins met with the Glasers to explain that the school's board was about to draft an AIDS policy. He was concerned that Ari's presence in the school might jeopardize its passage. So Ari was uprooted and transferred to a nearby public school that already had an AIDS policy, where she remained until the following year, after the Crossroads board had agreed to admit children with AIDS. Says Elizabeth: "It was another hard lesson in how little could be taken for granted."

While I was fighting my battles, Paul was coming to grips with his own private war—a battlefield on which he might lose all those he loved. It was a difficult struggle for him then and it still is now. He worked as much as he could, as that gave him the strength to keep going. Sometimes it is hard for me to believe that my life is real, but trying to imagine being Paul is even more difficult.

Ariel was doing well. Each morning I would sit with her and pick out the hair ribbons she would want to wear. We would stand in front of the bathroom mirror and I would brush her hair 100 times to make it shine. As her hair glistened, silent tears would fill my eyes and my heart would break, knowing that I might lose her. It became impossible for me to ever feel really happy, without feeling achingly sad.

That autumn, I kept wishing for things that never seemed to happen. I wished Ari would be invited to someone's house for a sleepover. I wished one of Jake's friends would invite him for a play date. It would be lovely if Paul and I were invited to a dinner party.

At that point in our lives, coping with fear was far worse than coping with AIDS. The fear of rejection or exposure was with us at all times. Most people have nightmares when they sleep, but when you are a family facing AIDS, the nightmare begins fresh each day. Sleep is the only time when I feel just like everyone else. Often I wake up in the morning having forgotten for an instant about AIDS, but that lasts for only a blink of an eye.

In the fall of 1986, the doctors still had no answers. Naively, I thought we were ahead of the game. Since none of us was sick or deteriorating, I felt that maybe if we could just stay strong, doctors would find a cure. Ari was already five years old, while most children with AIDS died by the time they were two.

I felt I had every right to be angry. But what good was it going to do? Would it make Ari well? Would it make Jake live longer? I couldn't stop myself from being angry, but I could keep that anger from being trapped inside my body. I would think of a room with two doors. If the anger came in one door, I tried to be sure there was always another door so the anger would get out.

I had to learn to forgive. I had to forgive the blood donor. I had to forgive the doctors, the hospitals, the schools, and I had to forgive fate. I had to forgive God, if there is one, and I had to forgive my friends, who had to forgive me. Right away Paul saw that we would have to forgive everyone, that we would have to let the anger pass right through us. He helped me to learn this. It was bitterly hard. Anger is a poison that will seep into your system and want to stay.

But I still get angry. Sometimes when I am alone in my car I scream, "If you are there, God, I hate you! I hate you for letting Ari get sick. And I hate you because I don't really think you are there." My throat hurts when I'm done, but I usually feel calmer.

I would feel a painful jealousy whenever I saw people who seemed to have normal lives and healthy children. I would feel an excruciating envy toward strangers and my friends who could have what I never could. And then I would feel very, very sorry for myself.

I learned to let go of all of these emotions that depleted me. I am never going to be able to have what other people have. At some point you begin to accept that this is your life. I've learned that you often have no say in what happens to you, but you can choose how you bear the consequences.

Paul had finished directing *Running Man* in the spring [of 1987], and we had decided we would make our annual summer trip to Maine. We were swimming, boating, hiking, or picking wild blueberries on Pleasant Mountain. At night we would make a fire and toast marshmallows. Simple and intense delight. But Ari started to seem weak, and I sensed for the first time that she was beginning to fail. Her appetite diminished and she complained of stomach pain. In past summers she had always been eager to go in the canoe and be by the water, but now that eagerness was gone. As a mother, I knew instinctively that I was losing her.

I called Dick Stiehm in Los Angeles.

"We've got to get AZT now," I said. "She's starting to fail." In 1987, AZT was the only treatment that seemed to be effective against AIDS.

"It's not ready for children," he replied.

"What do you mean? It's ready for me!" Although I hadn't needed to start taking it yet, I knew it was available.

"AZT hasn't been approved for pediatric use. It's just not ready."

"We've got to find a way to get it and use it."

"Elizabeth," he said, "we don't even know the dose to give her. We can't just experiment. It could kill her."

"When will it be ready?"

"In the fall."

I took a deep breath and prayed that we could hold on until then.

By the time we got home, Ari was thinner and weaker, but Dr. Stiehm felt she would still be able to start school. She had her heart set on beginning first grade. It didn't work. Although Ariel looked beautiful with her shiny hair and luminous blue eyes, she frequently had outbursts of ghastly pain. She was a valiant fighter but was only able to finish two weeks of first grade.

As the pain increased, Ari and I became more and more like one person. In her worst moments, my eyes would start to fill with tears and I would say, "Oh, Ari, I wish I could take all your pain into my body. I wish I could make it all go away." She would look right into my eyes and very slowly answer, "But you can't, Mom." We both knew it was true.

We would cherish the good moments more than ever. Paul would take Ari to the end of the block to feed the pigeons, and at night he would lie beside her in bed and make up wonderful fanciful stories.

In the fall parents started getting curious about Ari's long absence from school. Rumors were raging and several parents asked the school's director if Ariel Glaser had AIDS. Each time we found out that someone was asking, our anxiety soared. Paul and I still felt the risk of going public clearly overshadowed any gains. As awful as it had been for us to shoulder the massive weight of the secret for the previous year and a half, we dreaded even more the risk that our child might experience any of the hysterical fear that still surrounded AIDS in many parts of the country.

Paul and I had stopped going out, except with the few who were pledged to secrecy. Our friends worked as hard to protect our privacy as we did. At night, Paul and I would climb into bed exhausted by the strain of just being us. If we talked about our fears, we felt overwhelmed. If we talked about our hopes, it felt like pie-in-the-sky dreaming. So usually, we didn't talk at all.

Some nights I would just lie there and think how trapped Paul must feel. How hard it was to live with us and how impossible it would be to leave. If he walked away, everyone would think he was such a "bad" guy. But I knew he must have wanted to run away at times. Part of me would have wanted that. But he never said it, we never shared what we were thinking. It was too scary. On a good night we would fall asleep in each other's arms.

Ari was getting weaker and weaker. We had been waiting for AZT all that year and each month it wasn't ready. Paul and I were silently praying that something would change the course of our lives, working hard to keep optimistic.

Shortly before Thanksgiving 1987, Ari was hospitalized with acute pancreatitis. She was released after four weeks but had to continue being fed through an elaborate intravenous system, which Paul and Elizabeth mastered so that they could care for their daughter at home. Ari began taking AZT orally right before Christmas, but the drug had no positive effect.

Through January of 1988 Ari became more confined. By February she stopped walking completely. We didn't know why. The doctors had no answers. I carried her everywhere. She was unable to speak, but we both remembered the words that had already been said. We would still go for long walks. I would put her in the stroller cushioning her with pillows and wrapping a blanket over her legs. Despite the pain and the weariness that she always felt, she never failed to respond to the beauty around her.

In March 1988, nearly two years after our initial diagnosis, the guillotine fell. Ariel got pneumonia and we were back at UCLA again. We learned that her brain had severely atrophied. The doctors said it was irreversible. It was one of the central nervous system complications of AIDS that is quite common in children, though not in adults.

After four days, Dick Stiehm solemnly sat us down and told us that Ari had probably 48 hours to live. She was breathing weakly, but what none of us knew then was that she hadn't given up.

It was not until the doctors told us that there was absolutely no hope that I confronted the possibility of Ari's death for the first time. I sat with a friend and lit one cigarette after another. I was shaking and not yet able to talk. "No one cares if we all die from AIDS," I said. "Something is very wrong. I have to get to the President."

It was in that moment of honest desperation that I realized I could no longer sit quietly in Santa Monica. A mother's job is to save her child; it's a basic animal instinct. But I was failing. I had to do more.

Propelled by anger and frustration, Elizabeth considered ways to take a more active role in AIDS issues without compromising her family's privacy. Ariel survived the pneumonia, yet her health seemed ever more fragile. The day the Glasers brought their daughter home from the hospital, Elizabeth discussed her intentions with Paul.

Paul was silent for a long time and then with great gentleness he said, "I'll support you in whatever you have to do." I gave my husband a big hug and felt a smile spreading across my face. I knew this was the moment when I was taking that hard first step. I didn't know it at the time, but it was the step that has kept me in motion ever since.

As a member of a family struggling with AIDS, I learned that few wanted to help enough to change a system that had become strangled by red tape. The ones who tried were often ignored because AIDS was something many refused to deal with. Someone had to care enough to be willing to shake things up, but I didn't know who it would be. I realized my country was failing me. The compassion as well as the moral and ethical foundations of our society were being tested, and from my point of view, America had let me down.

Determined to educate herself about AIDS as a national issue, Elizabeth met with physicians, politicians, and friends to plan an assault on policymakers in Washington, D.C. Her first goal was to explain that AIDS affects children differently than adults and then to persuade legislators to make federal funds available, specifically for pediatric AIDS research. During her visit to the capital six weeks later, Elizabeth also met Dr. Phil Pizzo, chief of pediatrics at the National Cancer Institute in Bethesda, Md., who had launched the first federal study of AIDS in children. When he learned that Ari had been taking AZT orally with no favourable results, he recommended that she take the drug intravenously. Dr. Stiehm had already tried to get AZT in this form for several of his patients but had failed because it was still only available for trial testing. Elizabeth returned home and refused to give up until she was able to obtain the intravenous drug for her daughter in May 1988.

I sat in my den, relieved that we had succeeded in getting the drug and furious at the inhumanity of a system that cared more about rules than lives. Did I love my child any more than the mother in Harlem, Miami, or Newark loved her child? Absolutely not. Did Ari deserve a chance any more than their children? No. Every child with AIDS deserves a chance. And what about the children who had no one to speak for them?

Then, three weeks to the day after we started intravenous AZT, I walked into Ariel's room in the morning and she looked up and said, "Good morning, Mom. I love you." I could hardly believe it. Ari was back! The sky had opened up. I had to find Paul. Maybe miracles did happen. Maybe one was going to happen in our house.

Ari continued to improve over the next six weeks. The intravenous AZT was unwinding her cocoon of paralysis, and her 6-year-old self was still underneath. The whole world had started spinning again. In March we were told to prepare for a funeral. By May we had a shot at second grade. If Ari could make it, we were all going to make it.

In June, friends arranged a meeting between Elizabeth and the Reagans at the White House, where she appealed to the President to lead the nation on this urgent issue. Although the Reagans welcomed her warmly, their private concern had no positive impact on public policy. The more Elizabeth learned about the government's indifference to the issue of children with AIDS, the more determined she became to form a private foundation to raise funds for pediatric AIDS research.

July 1988

It was one of those beautiful Los Angeles days when the sun, air, sky, and sea all seem perfect. I asked Ari if she would like to go down to the Santa Monica pier, which has rides and an amusement arcade with cotton candy and stuffed animals for prizes.

Ari and I went on the Ferris wheel together, around and around, waving wildly, queens of the sky and sea. For a moment, I was experiencing the thrilling unadulterated joy of just being a mom. Maybe there was some part of Ariel that knew this was the last day that she was really going to get to be a little girl.

Two weeks later Ari was readmitted to UCLA hospital. Her white blood cell count had fallen too low, and we had to take her off the intravenous AZT. She was having fevers that we couldn't break. But I persistently believed that this was just another crisis that we would somehow survive. I have never been able to accept endings that I don't like. I fight to make life the way I want it to be, and because of that I never believed that Ari was going to die.

We had Ari's seventh birthday party in the hospital, and Dick Stiehm gave her a UCLA T-shirt and told her it was what she would wear on the day she went home. But Ari had regressed greatly. In a few weeks, we had slid back down the mountain we had climbed since June. Her care was intricate and complex, but all I wanted was to take her home.

Three weeks later, on Friday. Aug. 12th, 1988, we were packing up her things. Ari was lying in her bed and I said to her, "We have to see if you can sit in your stroller, honey." And Ari said, "No, Mom, I'm going to walk home." She couldn't move her legs. I looked at her and said, "Give me a break." Ari said simply, "No, Mom, I'm going to walk home." "All right, Ari," I said. "Go for it."

Paul and I continued getting her things together. It was not until the last 10 minutes of her life that I knew she was dying. And then very quickly she was gone. She was never supposed to die. It was too short a time to have had her. Paul wept and I cried. "Noooo!" It was a "no" that wanted to turn back time. It was a "no" to a world that had failed me. Our beautiful daughter had died. Ariel Glaser had been on the earth for seven years and eight days.

That Sunday, the Glasers held a memorial service for Ariel at home, and on Tuesday, Aug. 16, their daughter was buried next to Paul's father at a cemetery in Boston.

We have left Ari's room just as it was when she was alive. Paul and I decided we couldn't imagine changing it. We each find our way into her room at different times and in different ways to tell her we love her. Her door is always open. It's not maudlin it's just life. Ari's room remains though Ari is gone and her spirit fills our hearts.

Peter
Goddard
....

HOW TO SPOT ROCK TYPES

**Social distinctions are as jealously guarded among rockers as
they are at any country club. Often they are just as petty.**

It might appear to the uninitiated or uninvolved that pop music fans, like the
followers of British football, are alike and all equally unruly.

The truth is quite the opposite. There are more factions, sub-factions, and
sub-sub-factions going to this summer's bumper crop of concerts than there
are garrulous sects among Protestants. And as with theological disputes, the
differences between one kind of fan and another, although barely noticeable
to the outsider, can be enormous indeed.

Music has something to do with it, of course. Someone who finds their
heart enraptured by Engelbert Humperdinck is not likely to get much out of
a punk performance at which the singer is graphically describing nine ways
he's going to tear off your face. And vice versa.

The real differences, the kinds that often end up with a collision of fist and
teeth, go beyond the musical. Social distinctions are as jealously guarded
among rockers as they are at any country club. Often they are just as petty. It
is permissible to wear a Black Sabbath T-shirt to an AC/DC concert. To
arrive at the same event wearing a Kenny Rogers T-shirt would be considered hopelessly wimpy, however.

For many of the same reasons, there are certain concerts certain people
should not attend. They may be discovered. Excuses may be needed. If
you're discovered at a hard-core punk event, wall-to-wall in black leather,
by your company's lawyer, for instance, you may have to hastily explain that
it was a disgusting habit picked up in an impoverished youth and you can't
break it.

Better still, whack him with your chain. Then ask him what *he's* doing
there.

To help everyone better identify the various crowds who are going to pop
concerts these days and nights, we've prepared the following collection of
profiles. Study it. It may help you avoid getting lumped in with a loud,
sweaty lot of heavy metal freaks. Or with Engelbert Humperdinck devotees.
Whichever seems worse.

Reggae
There are, in fact, two reggae crowds. The original and basic following for
this danceable roots music from Jamaica is, not surprisingly, made up of
Jamaicans. The other crowd is not made up of Jamaicans—although many in
it wish it were. They are usually white, middle-class, somewhat political,
and very concerned about community. They are, in short, hippies 10 or 15
years down the road. They can tell you everyone who ever played with
singer Peter Tosh and can spell the name of the trio Black Uhuru. What they
often can't do is discern a great reggae song from something that's awful. Just
as often what they're smoking makes the issue fuzzy. They dance at the drop
of a bass note. They eat good, organic natural foods. "Herb" is their favorite
word after "man." They're worried about their health, yet they often look
wan. They are generally harmless and would only want tea, not your 12-
year-old Scotch, should you invite them home. They regularly head to
Jamaica and, with reggae songs in their head, feel they've made a radical
advancement over their parents, who used to head to Jamaica humming
Harry Belafonte songs. They haven't.

New wave
Although occasionally given to dyed hair, shocking colors in shocking
combinations, and/or high-camp styles, the new wave crowd usually looks
like a convention of computer programmers—which it often is. Until
recently it was the fashionable group until it was discovered that the secret
bands the insiders kept talking about—Heaven 17, Haircut 100, Ultra-vox—
were just as boring as all the ratty familiar bands even the most lumpen
outsider knew. Still, this crowd retains some of its social superiority over the
other crowds mainly because no one else can figure out what it's all about.
For the neophyte, a copy of *Wet* magazine, a smattering of German tossed
into the conversation, and complete up-to-the-second knowledge of the
latest technological gimmicks help. Don't worry, though, about being caught
up in a new wave crowd. You'll never know it—and they'll never tell.

Middle of the road
A mysterious and proud race, middle-of-the-roaders can be downright
militant about their sheer, blatant averageness. The most enraged heavy-
metal crowd is no match for a group of Anne Murray fans whom someone
has called "kooky." Wally Crouter, on CFRB radio, is their main man and for
music they tend to listen to Billy Joel, Neil Diamond, Diana Ross (when she's
not being too funky), Carly Simon, and James Taylor—any of the 1960s
singers who, over the years, have come to show their true, middle-of-the-
road colors. This crowd is into health; not a whiff of smoke of any kind
could be smelled at the recent John Denver concert at Maple Leaf Gardens.

They jog, play racket sports, and often eat good, organic natural foods. They're contemporaries of the reggae crowd but lost their sense of commitment about the time mortgage rates started going up. They, too, are generally harmless but should you invite them home, it'll be your 12-year-old Scotch, not tea, they'll be after.

Heavy metal

There's nothing too loud for a heavy-metal crowd. Uriah Heep played at full volume? A train wreck? A dead cat thrown through a plate glass window? Kaaa-rang. More. Gimme more. As you may have guessed, heavy metal is not merely a matter of music but a question of faith—the belief that no excess can ever be too much. Women tend not to be attracted to this. As a result, it's the last completely male bastion this side of the York Club. And in its way, it has clubby rules. There's a uniform—tight jeans, the more worn the better; T-shirt advertising one heavy-metal combo or another; boots; and long hair. And there are certain codes of behavior to follow. If, for instance, you are going to fall down roaring drunk, taking at least one usher with you, only do so after the 15-minute guitar solo, which because of its intensity and sheer repetitiveness, will likely be the only thing you'll remember anyway. One rather caustic critic said that certain heavy-metal crowds weren't exactly comprised of future nuclear physicists. "They couldn't spell 'Jimi Hendrix' if you spotted them the first 10 letter," was the way he put it. This was unfair and not true. For example, no crowd knows more ways of smuggling illicit booze past police into Maple Leaf Gardens.

Jazz

As it is with reggae, there are two jazz crowds. The division here is generational, not racial. The older crowd likes its jazz in bars, is known to take a drink or a dozen while in these bars, and gets misty-eyed when someone mentions such quaint-sounding names as Mezz Mezzrow, Miff Mole, Lucky Millinder, or anything about Kansas City. To this crowd, jazz was—and still is, on occasion—an entertainment. That Earl Hines may be the most gifted pianist in any style in the entire 20th century means less to this crowd than the fact he can swing like a tropical forest before a hurricane.

The new jazz crowd takes it all much more seriously. It rarely gets misty-eyed. Rather, it gets angry when certain names are mentioned: Cecil Taylor or Charlie Mingus or Albert Ayler—men who suffered because they played "black classical music," or what many new jazz fans have come to call jazz. The younger crowd wants the music out of the bars and into the concert halls; it doesn't want to pay concert-hall prices yet.

The old crowd prides itself on being able to name the most obscure sideman and the most obscure record ("Frankie Newton? Didn't he play trumpet with John Kirby back in '40?"). Not the new crowd. It's into theory.

It can tell you which inversion of the dominant ninth pianist McCoy Tyner played just before the augmented sixth. I mean, this crowd takes its jazz *seriously*.

Punks

The most maligned group of them all, the punks went completely out of style a while back, after it was discovered they really didn't want to cut themselves, but were only looking for a better record deal. They're back and back in force, though, at places like Club Domino, off Yonge Street, pale kids in from the suburbs, drenched in leather and beating the stuffing out of each other doing something called slam dancing. Now, slam dancing is jitterbugging for sadists and masochists. Punks and punkettes bob up and down and, when the moment is right, literally slam into one another. And this is where the misunderstanding comes in. Psychologists, sociologists, musicologists, and, in all probability, tree surgeons all think this behavior indicates severe emotional/social/musical or ringworm problems. It indicates nothing of the sort. It is, in fact, fun. And it keeps you in shape, which is more than you can say for bingo.

Funk

The old funk crowd was cool. The new one is aggressively cool. It's not into Marvin Gaye, but Rick James, king of "punk funk" or rhythm and blues with a rocket in the rhythm section. Punk funk is a street style with designer overtones. You should look as if you're perfectly capable of making it behind enemy lines in Iran and at the same time, finish no lower than third in the weekly soul train dance contest. The radio is optional. The "I've-got-you-covered-turkey" look is absolutely essential.

Country

If Nancy Reagan, clothes designer Ralph Lauren, and producers of *Urban Cowboy* had their way, we would all be wearing $300 western boots, drinking Jim Beam bourbon, and, in just about every other way, acting as if we were all good ole boys in the good ole city. But the fake urban-cowboy country crowd went the way of so many other fads and what's left is the real country crowd, which is to say people who look like everyone else but who listen to country music. Well, that's not entirely true. Bring a country music show into town and you're likely to see more pantsuits there than anywhere else. And the belts tend to be more handsome and everyone seems to have a Kodak camera attached to their hands. They are generally harmless—unless you say something untoward about George Jones—and should you invite them home, they won't want your tea or your 12-year-old Scotch. Most likely they will have brought an even better Scotch with them.

Big bands

The older big-band crowd tends to be nostalgic every chance it gets and you can always fob off the latest incarnation of the "Tommy Dorsey Orchestra" on it. The young crowd, the ones who ignored the Beatles for Stan Kenton and have some musical training, is made up of fanatics. There's no other word for them. They know the names of sidemen in bands that decent, common folk didn't know even existed yet. They think rock is trite, punks are ridiculous, jazz is for snobs, and they're ready to fight to prove their point. They have a hungry look about them and they tend to be thin. They look like they couldn't beat up a pillow, but many have secretly trained in karate. A lot of them carry pocket calculators. If they've had musical training, they're that kind of musician who can play anything—a note, fly speck, grease-drop from a Big Mac—that's on paper. They will probably end up ruling the world.

BEAUTY AND THE BEEF

The ingredients of a TV Whopper are, unbelievably, the same as those used in real Whoppers. . . . But like other screen personalities, the Whopper needs a little help from makeup.

When was the last time you opened a carton in a fast-food restaurant to find a hamburger as appetizing as the ones in the TV commercials? Did you ever look past the counter help to catch a glimpse of a juicy hamburger patty, handsomely branded by the grill, sizzling and crackling as it glides over roaring flames, with tender juices sputtering into the fire? On television the burger is a magnificent slab of flame-broiled beef—majestically topped with crisp iceberg lettuce, succulent red tomatoes, tangy onions and plump pickles, all between two halves of a towering sesame-seed bun. But, of course, the real-life Whoppers don't quite measure up.

The ingredients of a TV Whopper are, unbelievably, the same as those used in real Whoppers sold to average consumers. But like other screen personalities, the Whopper needs a little help from makeup.

When making a Burger King commercial, J. Walter Thompson, the company's advertising agency, usually devotes at least one full day to filming "beauty shots" of the food. Burger King supplies the agency with several large boxes of frozen beef patties. But before a patty is sent over the flame broiler, a professionally trained food stylist earning between $500 and $750 a day prepares it for the camera.

The crew typically arrives at 7:00 a.m. and spends two hours setting up lights that will flatter the burger. Then the stylist, aided by two assistants, begins by burning "flame-broiling stripes" into the thawed hamburger patties with a special Madison Avenue branding iron. Because the tool doesn't always leave a rich charcoal-black impression on the patty, the stylist uses a fine paintbrush to darken the singed crevices with a sauce the color of used motor oil. The stylist also sprinkles salt on the patty so when it passes over the flames, natural juices will be encouraged to rise to the meat's surface.

Thus branded, retouched, and juiced, the patties are run back and forth over a conveyor-belt broiler while the director films the little spectacle from a variety of angles. Two dozen people watch from the wings: lighting assistants, prop people, camera assistants, gas specialists, the client, and agency people—producers, writers, art directors. Of course, as the meat is broiled blood rises to the surface in small pools. Since, for the purposes of advertising, bubbling blood is not a desirable special effect, the stylist, like a prissy microsurgical nurse, continually dabs at the burger with a Q-Tip.

Before the patty passes over the flame a second time, the food stylist maneuvers a small electric heater an inch or so above the burger to heat up the natural fatty juices until they begin to steam and sizzle. Otherwise puddles of grease will cover the meat. Sometimes patties are dried out on a bed of paper towels. Before they're sent over the flame broiler again, the stylist relubricates them with a drop of corn oil to guarantee picturesque crackling and sizzling.

If you examine any real Whopper at any Burger King closely, you'll discover flame-broiling stripes only on the top side of the beef patty. Hamburgers are sent through the flame broiler once; they're never flipped over. The commercials imply otherwise. On television a beef patty, fetchingly covered with flame-broiling stripes, travels over the broiler, indicating that the burger has been flipped to sear stripes into the other side.

In any case, the camera crew has just five or ten seconds in the life cycle of a TV Whopper to capture good, sizzling brown beef on film. After that the hamburger starts to shrink rapidly as the water and grease are cooked from it. Filming lasts anywhere from three to eight hours, depending upon the occurrence of a variety of technical problems—heavy smoke, grease accumulating on the camera equipment, the gas specialist's failure to achieve a perfect, preternaturally orange glowing flame. Out of one day's work, and anywhere between 50 and 75 hamburgers, the agency hopes to get five seconds of usable footage. Most of the time the patties are either too raw, bloody, greasy, or small.

Of course, the cooked hamburger patty depicted sitting on a sesame-seed bun in the commercial is a different burger from those towel-dried, steak-sauce-dabbed, corn-oiled specimens that were filmed sliding over the flames. This presentation patty hasn't been flame-broiled at all. It's been branded with the phony flame-broiling marks, retouched with the steak sauce—and then microwaved.

Truth in advertising, however, is maintained, sort of: when you're shown the final product—a completely built hamburger topped with sliced vegetables and condiments—you are seeing the actual quantities of ingredients found on the average real Whopper. On television, though, you're only seeing half of the hamburger—the front half. The lettuce, tomatoes, onions, and pickles have all been shoved to the front of the burger. The stylist has carefully nudged and manicured the ingredients so that they sit just right. The red, ripe tomatoes are flown in fresh from California the morning of the shoot. You might find such tomatoes on your hamburger—if you ordered several hundred Whoppers early in the morning, in Fresno. The lettuce and tomatoes are cut, trimmed, and then piled on top of a cold cooked hamburger patty, and the whole construction is sprayed with a fine mist of glycerine to glisten and shimmer seductively. Finally the hamburger is capped with a painstakingly handcrafted sesame-seed bun. For at least an hour the stylist has been kneeling over the bun like a lens grinder, positioning each sesame seed. He dips a toothpick in Elmer's glue and, using a pair of tweezers, places as many as 300 seeds, one by one, onto a formerly bald bun.

When it's all over, the crew packs up the equipment, and 75 gorgeous-looking hamburgers are dumped in the garbage.

A History Of The Beluga
Whales In The St. Lawrence

There is a lack of . . . effort on the part of . . . government agencies to bring the two conditions needed to ensure the survival of the St. Lawrence beluga: clean water and a protected habitat.

Over the past four years, 58 beluga whales have been found washed up on the shores of the St. Lawrence River. The beluga population of the St. Lawrence, estimated between 350 and 450, is on the verge of disappearing altogether as evidence suggests that their mortality rate is exceeding their birth rate. Industrial discharge, toxic waste dumps, and pesticide run-off, which continued to contaminate the beautiful Great Lakes-St. Lawrence ecosystem, are the major factors preventing the recovery of the endangered beluga.

The St. Lawrence beluga, or white whale (Delphinapterus leucas), lives year round in the area around the confluence of the St. Lawrence and Saguenay Rivers in Québec. This population numbered approximately 5000 in 1885; however, commercial hunting reduced the population to about one-half before ending in the 1940s. A combination of non-commercial hunting, sport-shooting, critical habitat destruction, and pollution succeeded in reducing the population to around 500 by 1975.

Formal protection in 1979 ended all hunting, and in 1983 belugas were accorded an "endangered" status. Despite these protective efforts, belugas now face a new danger from toxic pollutants. Researchers have discovered high levels of organic residues, such as PCBs, myrex, and DDT, in beluga tissue. Of the whales necropsied, 80% had 50 parts per million (ppm) or more of PCBs, and one female was analyzed with an alarming 1725 ppm of PCBs in her milk. Federal standards in both Canada and the U.S. prohibit the sale of fish which contains over 2 ppm PCBs. Not surprisingly, high incidences of diseases readily traceable to severe environmental disturbance have occurred in the beluga, attacking such organs and systems as the liver, skin, blood, stomach, heart, lungs, and bladder. Among the diseases which have been found are: hepatitis, dermatitis, septicaemia, perforated ulcers, pulmonary abscesses, bronchial-pneumonia, and bladder cancer.

The probable cause of bladder cancer is the carcinogen benzo(a)-pyrene or B(a)P, one of the most dangerous of the polycyclic aromatic hydrocarbon (PAH) chemicals. Besides causing cancer, B(a)P breaks down the immunological system in mammals, producing an AIDS-type syndrome.

This chemical is emitted into the atmosphere at a rate of some 60 t a year by the ALCAN aluminum plant on the Saguenay River at Lonquière, Québec. Currently, 73 workers from ALCAN have been diagnosed with the same bladder cancer found in a St. Lawrence beluga. Researchers attribute their cancer to B(a)P. Subsequently, the brain tissue of three beluga were analyzed and all three revealed contamination with B(a)P. Further studies have confirmed that the Saguenay River is contaminated with this same chemical. The ALCAN plant is located only 100 km upstream from beluga critical habitat. Despite the real and demonstrated threat this chemical poses to both human and animal life, no federal or provincial regulations on the emission of B(a)P currently exist in Canada.

There is a lack of coordinated and concentrated effort on the part of federal and provincial government agencies to bring about the two conditions needed to ensure the survival of the St. Lawrence beluga: clean water and a protected habitat. Greenpeace feels that this population could be extinct as soon as the year 2000 unless significant inroads are made to stem the flow of pollution into the waters of the Great Lakes-St. Lawrence ecosystem. The beluga is a symbol of our neglect for the environment. If we can make the St. Lawrence and Saguenay rivers safe for these mammals, then they will also be safe for other wildlife as well as for the human population.

Robert L.
Heilbroner
....

DON'T LET STEREOTYPES WARP
YOUR JUDGMENTS

When we typecast the world . . . we are only revealing the embarrassing facts about the pictures that hang in the gallery of stereotypes in our own heads.

Is a girl called Gloria apt to be better-looking than one called Bertha? Are criminals more likely to be dark than blond? Can you tell a good deal about someone's personality from hearing his voice briefly over the phone? Can a person's nationality be pretty accurately guessed from his photograph? Does the fact that someone wears glasses imply that he is intelligent?

The answer to all these questions is obviously, "No."

Yet, from all the evidence at hand, most of us believe these things. Ask any college boy if he'd rather take his chances with a Gloria or a Bertha, or ask a college girl if she'd rather blinddate a Richard or a Cuthbert. In fact, you don't have to ask: college students in questionnaires have revealed that names conjure up the same images in their minds as they do in yours—and for as little reason.

Look into the favorite suspects of persons who report "suspicious charac-ters" and you will find a large percentage of them to be "swarthy" or "dark and foreign-looking"—despite the testimony of criminologists that crimi-nals do *not* tend to be dark, foreign, or "wild-eyed." Delve into the main asset of a telephone stock swindler and you will find it to be a marvelously confidence-inspiring telephone "personality." And whereas we all think we know what an Italian or a Swede looks like, it is the sad fact that when a group of Nebraska students sought to match faces and nationalities of 15 European countries, they were scored wrong in 93 percent of their identi-fications. Finally, for all the fact that horn-rimmed glasses have now become the standard television sign of an "intellectual," optometrists know that the main thing that distinguishes people with glasses is just bad eyes.

Stereotypes are a kind of gossip about the world, a gossip that makes us prejudge people before we ever lay eyes on them. Hence it is not surprising that stereotypes have something to do with the dark world of prejudice. Explore most prejudices (note that the word means prejudgment) and you will find a cruel stereotype at the core of each one.

For it is the extraordinary fact that once we have typecast the world, we tend to see people in terms of our standardized pictures. In another demonstration of the power of stereotypes to affect our vision, a number of Columbia and Barnard students were shown 30 photographs of pretty but unidentified girls, and asked to rate each in terms of "general liking," "intelligence," "beauty," and so on. Two months later, the same group were shown the same photographs, this time with fictitious Irish, Italian, Jewish, and "American" names attached to the pictures. Right away the ratings changed. Faces which were now seen as representing a national group went down in looks and still farther down in likability, while the "American" girls suddenly looked decidedly prettier and nicer.

Why is it that we stereotype the world in such irrational and harmful fashion? In part, we begin to type-cast people in our childhood years. Early in life, as every parent whose child has watched a TV Western knows, we learn to spot the Good Guys from the Bad Guys. Some years ago, a social psychologist showed very clearly how powerful these stereotypes of childhood vision are. He secretly asked the most popular youngsters in an elementary school to make errors in their morning gym exercises. Afterwards, he asked the class if anyone had noticed any mistakes during gym period. Oh, yes, said the children. But it was the *unpopular* members of the class—the "bad guys"—they remembered as being out of step.

We not only grow up with standardized pictures forming inside of us, but as grown-ups we are constantly having them thrust upon us. Some of them, like the half-joking, half-serious stereotypes of mothers-in-law, or country yokels, or psychiatrists, are dinned into us by the stock jokes we hear and repeat. In fact, without such stereotypes, there would be a lot fewer jokes. Still other stereotypes are perpetuated by the advertisements we read, the movies we see, the books we read.

And finally, we tend to stereotype because it helps us make sense out of a highly confusing world, a world which William James once described as "one great, blooming, buzzing confusion." It is a curious fact that if we don't *know* what we're looking at, we are often quite literally unable to *see* what we're looking at. People who recover their sight after a lifetime of blindness actually cannot at first tell a triangle from a square. A visitor to a factory sees only noisy chaos where the superintendent sees a perfectly synchronized flow of work. As Walter Lippmann has said, "For the most part we do not first see, and then define; we define first, and then we see."

Stereotypes are one way in which we "define" the world in order to see it. They classify the infinite variety of human beings into a convenient handful of "types" towards whom we learn to act in stereotyped fashion. Life would be a wearing process if we had to start from scratch with each and every human contact. Stereotypes economize on our mental effort by covering up the blooming, buzzing confusion with big recognizable cut-outs. They save us the "trouble" of finding out what the world is like—they give it its accustomed look.

Thus the trouble is that stereotypes make us mentally lazy. As S.I. Hayakawa, the authority on semantics, has written: "The danger of stereotypes lies not in their existence, but in the fact that they become for all people some of the time, and for some people all the time, *substitutes for observation.*" Worse yet, stereotypes get in the way of our judgment, even when we do observe the world. Someone who has formed rigid preconceptions of all Latins as "excitable," or all teenagers as "wild," doesn't alter his point of view when he meets a calm and deliberate Genoese, or a serious-minded high-school student. He brushes them aside as "exceptions that prove the rule." And, of course, if he meets someone true to type, he stands triumphantly vindicated. "They're all like that," he proclaims, having encountered an excited Latin, an ill-behaved adolescent.

Hence, quite aside from the injustice which stereotypes do to others, they impoverish ourselves. A person who lumps the world into simple categories, who type-casts all labor leaders as "racketeers," all businessmen as "reactionaries," all Harvard men as "snobs," and all Frenchmen as "sexy," is in danger of becoming a stereotype himself. He loses his capacity to be himself—which is to say, to see the world in his own absolutely unique, inimitable, and independent fashion.

Instead, he votes for the man who fits his standardized picture of what a candidate "should" look like or sound like, buys the goods that someone in his "situation" in life "should" own, lives the life that others define for him. The mark of the stereotype person is that he never surprises us, that we do indeed have him "typed." And no one fits this strait-jacket so perfectly as someone whose opinions about *other people* are fixed and inflexible.

Impoverishing as they are, stereotypes are not easy to get rid of. The world we type-cast may be no better than a Grade B movie, but at least we know what to expect of our stock characters. When we let them act for themselves in the strangely unpredictable way that people do act, who knows but that many of our fondest convictions will be proved wrong?

Nor do we suddenly drop our standardized pictures for a blinding vision of the Truth. Sharp swings of ideas about people often just substitute one stereotype for another. The true process of change is a slow one that adds bits and pieces of reality to the pictures in our heads, until gradually they take on some of the blurriness of life itself. Little by little, we learn not that Jews and Negroes and Catholics and Puerto Ricans are "just like everybody else"—for that, too, is a stereotype—but that each and every one of them is unique, special, different, and individual. Often we do not even know that we have let a stereotype lapse until we hear someone saying, "all so-and-so's are like such-and-such," and we hear ourselves saying, "Well—maybe."

Can we speed the process along? Of course we can.

First, we can become *aware* of the standardized pictures in our heads, in other people's heads, in the world around us.

Second, we can become suspicious of all judgments that we allow exceptions to "prove." There is no more chastening thought than that in the vast intellectual adventure of science, it takes but one tiny exception to topple a whole edifice of ideas.

Third, we can learn to be chary of generalizations about people. As F. Scott Fitzgerald once wrote: "Begin with an individual, and before you know it you have created a type; begin with a type, and you find you have created—nothing."

Most of the time, when we type-cast the world, we are not in fact generalizing about people at all. We are only revealing the embarrassing facts about the pictures that hang in the gallery of stereotypes in our own heads.

Jay
Ingram
·········

THIS CHAPTER IS A YAWNER

**The biggest mystery of all about yawning is its infectiousness.
You see somebody yawn, you yawn yourself.**

You'd think there would be only two important questions to ask about yawning: why do we do it, and why, when one person starts yawning, do others immediately follow? But scientists are much more cautious than that: they want to make sure they know what a yawn *is* first. And it is "a stereotyped and often repetitive motor act characterized by gaping of the mouth and accompanied by a long inspiration followed by a short expiration." That may be a long and accurate definition, but it makes yawning sound like breathing, and other than the fact that they both involve air going in and out, they couldn't feel more dissimilar. One gets the feeling that if that's the definition, then we're still barely out of the starting gates on this one.

How often do we yawn? Students sitting alone in a room for half an hour, pushing a button whenever they start to yawn and releasing it when they finish, have established the length of an average yawn to be six seconds, give or take two seconds. But amazingly, the frequency of yawning varies from only one in half an hour to *seventy-six*. If those seventy-six yawns each lasted six seconds, then that individual spent an entire half-hour yawning, with an average break of only seventeen seconds between yawns.

There's a popular idea that we yawn to get more oxygen to our brains, or conversely, to rid our blood of excess carbon dioxide. The more oxygen in the blood, the more glucose we can burn for energy. Carbon dioxide is a waste product that takes up space in our red blood cells that could be used for oxygen, and it could conceivably build up if we're breathing shallowly for long periods of time. This theory would explain why we yawn when we're tired of sitting in a stuffy overheated lecture hall at three o'clock in the afternoon—not enough fresh air.

But one of the few psychologists researching yawns, Robert Provine at the University of Maryland, has found that changing the levels of carbon dioxide or oxygen seems not to affect yawning. Breathing *pure* oxygen didn't make subjects yawn less, and breathing air high in carbon dioxide didn't make them yawn more. Now it may be that setting this up in a laboratory situation somehow misses a critical factor, but if the cause of yawning were simply the levels of gases in the blood, experiments like this should show some effect. And they don't.

But these experiments don't completely kill the idea that yawning might refresh an oxygen-deprived brain. It's possible that by forcing your mouth wide open as you yawn, and stretching at the same time, you constrict some blood vessels while dilating others, with the net effect of forcing more blood to the brain. More blood means more oxygen, and presumably heightened alertness. It is true that opening your mouth wide is an important part of yawning: volunteers who yawned with clenched teeth reported it to be a highly abnormal experience that did nothing to satisfy the urge to yawn. If you try this yourself you'll see how incredibly unfulfilling it is, and the difficulty of explaining why that should be so just underlines how little yawning is understood. After all, you can still breathe in and out when your teeth are clenched, so it can't be lack of fresh air that leaves you dissatisfied. Maybe it's true that the wide-open stretching of your jaws and the resulting contraction of the facial muscles really do cause changes in blood flow to the brain. But does that mean that instead of yawning, you could just open your mouth as wide as possible for a few seconds, breathe in and out and get the same effects and the same satisfaction? No, it wouldn't be the same.

Medical doctors have collected evidence which suggests that yawning is controlled in a very primitive part of the brain, an area that runs for the most part on automatic pilot, beyond the reach of our conscious mind. Anencephaly is a tragic birth defect in which a newborn is missing most of the brain. Such children (who don't usually live long) have no cerebral hemispheres, the convoluted upper parts of the brain where most of our thinking takes place. But they have no trouble yawning. This must mean that the control of yawning is in one of the few brain parts they have—a lower, more "primitive" area like the medulla oblongata, a structure at the bottom of the brain that's responsible for normal breathing. It seems reasonable that yawning would be pretty well out of reach of your conscious mind; not only can a yawn start without a thought from you, it's also so difficult to stifle one once it's started—a powerful yawn can easily override your conscious efforts to stop it.[1]

This yawning centre must have a complicated set of connections within the brain, because it has to trigger yawns in response to all kinds of different

---

[1] There have also been cases where a patient with an arm paralyzed by a stroke or other brain damage has miraculously moved that paralyzed limb while yawning! They have no control over the movement: The arm just stretches on its own as it would normally do to accompany yawning. This strange occurrence suggests a link between yawning and stretching that completely bypasses the normal voluntary control of movement.

stimuli, ranging from the sight of other people yawning, through fatigue to boredom. In fact the absence of yawning may indicate a problem not with the yawning centre itself, but with another part of the brain to which it is connected. Psychiatrist Hans Lehmann at McGill University noted that he almost never saw mental patients yawn—on the wards, on buses, at public gatherings, or in restaurants. It made perfect sense to Lehmann that these patients, most of whom were schizophrenics, didn't yawn because they were so emotionally flat that they had little interest in what was going on around them. He reasoned that to be bored enough by what's going on around you to yawn, you have to be aware there *is* something going on. These patients were too withdrawn to know what was going on around them, so they couldn't be bored, and didn't yawn. It is said to be a positive sign when some mental patients yawn, because it suggests they're trying to establish contact with reality.

The biggest mystery of all about yawning is its infectiousness. You see somebody yawn, you yawn yourself. This is sometimes explained as coincidence—everyone is yawning at the same time because there's too little air circulation or too little oxygen in the air, and therefore it only appears to be contagious. But as I've already pointed out, experiments have shown that breathing air that's too high in carbon dioxide has no effect on the frequency of yawning. More to the point, you don't even have to be in the same room as the yawner to feel the yawning urge. Students in Robert Provine's lab who watched videotapes of an actor yawned much more often if the actor was yawning than if he were smiling (55 percent versus 24 percent).

Actually you will be prompted to yawn if you just read about yawning. (As you've probably already noticed.) The sound of yawning even provokes blind people to do it. We proved the power of this contagiousness on our program "Quirks and Quarks" in December 1988, when after making a few brief comments on some yawning research, I suggested that any listener who had felt the urge to yawn while I had been talking should write to us. I expected at most a couple of dozen letters (we weren't giving away T-shirts or promising to mention anyone on air), but we were all stunned by the avalanche of letters. The final count was close to three hundred, and the picture that emerged was that of thousands of Canadians yawning uncontrollably at about 12:50 P.M. on December 17, 1988, as they listened to the radio.

Why would we respond to the yawns of others with one of our own? The most popular suggestion is that yawning might be a hangover from our ancestral animal past, something called a "stereotyped action pattern." This is an automatic response to a signal that is common among birds and animals—for example, a frog will lunge hungrily, and unthinkingly, at any small dark moving object—but why would we yawn simply because other humans are yawning? In the early sixties, anthropologist Ashley Montagu, who was one of the believers in the idea that yawning heightened alertness by shunting fresh blood to the brain, speculated that group yawning would, by this mechanism, increase everyone's alertness. On the other hand, in a beautiful example of how any theory fits if you have very little data, an English doctor named Malcolm Weller had recently suggested the exact reverse—that the infectiousness of yawning might have originated as a signal among social animals to go to sleep, not to revive. Weller thinks that if one animal were to signal his weariness by yawning, the pack would imitate him and soon settle for the night.

This picture of our distant ancestors engaging in communal yawning for the good of the group is fine, and if that behaviour became automatic, we might well still be doing it today, long after it had outlived its usefulness. But this is a tricky business, using what anthropologists *think* our ancestors were doing to explain why we do it today.

If our primitive ancestors used yawning as a signal, at what point did we start covering our mouths when we yawn? Obviously it would have been counterproductive for those animals which were signalling each other with their yawns to have been hiding those same yawns with their hands or paws. You can argue that covering the mouth is a recent human cultural invention superimposed on the ancient habit of yawning openly. But by doing so, you're ignoring some intriguing observations of our closest living relatives.

By studying the habits of modern apes and monkeys, scientists believe they can infer some of the ways our ancient ape-like ancestors behaved millions of years ago. Yawning is a social signal among animals like monkeys and baboons, but an aggressive one. Dominant male baboons engage in "threat yawns," a gesture some scientists interpret as being more threatening than a raised eyebrow or a stare. Anthropologist John Handidian spent seven hundred hours watching black apes yawn, and he concluded that the ones doing the yawning are the dominant males: the number one male averaged three yawns an hour, while number four yawned only once every three hours. These apes, and many other related species, have especially long canine teeth which a yawn displays to great advantage.

Some biologists have even reported seeing subordinate animals cover their yawning mouths with their paws, apparently to prevent those yawns from being interpreted as threats they couldn't back up. We claim that we cover our mouths because to do otherwise would be "rude," but maybe that's just our civilized way of saying that it's somehow threatening. An open-mouthed yawn directed at you may not actually be a physical threat, but it can convey an unflattering, even unfriendly message (even without prominent canines).[2] What is really needed here is a study of human groups to see if the dominant individuals don't bother covering their mouths, while the submissive ones do. The Godfather's henchmen always laughed when he did, and stopped laughing when he did. What did they do when he yawned?

And when all the research falls into place, and we know exactly why we yawn, and especially why we yawn when others are yawning, where will the rat data fit in? The rat data? A variety of studies have established that certain drugs will quickly bring on two responses in rats: yawning and erections.

---

[2] Just to add another twist to the story, Robert Provine's research has shown that people will yawn in response to a yawning face with the mouth blanked out—the eyes and forehead are enough to stimulate yawns. So covering your mouth when you yawn does not interfere with its contagiousness.

**Michael
Korda**

....

WHY BE POLITE?

Despite mankind's reputation for violence, most people prefer to avoid confrontation, and avoiding confrontation is what manners are all about.

Almost all of us believe that we live in an age of uncouth manners and that things were better in some previous era. For example, the 18th century in England is known as a period of high refinement in social intercourse. We look back with nostalgia to the soft candlelight, the elaborate courtesies, the hand-kissing—unwilling to confront the brutal reality of a century in which duelling to the death was commonplace, and gentlemen were expected to drink themselves under the table.

Manners change. In our day, it is considered good manners to be clean; indeed, we spend billions of dollars on products designed to keep us "fresh." In the 18th century, by contrast, European standards of cleanliness were shockingly low, and women's extravagant coiffures were often infested with lice.

The changeability of manners makes the whole subject difficult to approach. For example, it was not considered bad manners in the 18th century for a man to wear a hat indoors. He would take it off to greet a lady, but then he'd put it right back on.

The reason for this is perfectly plain. In the first place, the hat had long served as a visible mark of status. In the second place, you couldn't draw a sword easily if you were holding a hat in your hand.

There is a lesson here. For the most part, manners are self-protective devices appropriate to the customs of a particular age. These customs invariably derive from some practical need. Thus, on meeting somebody, we commonly shake right hands—a formal custom of no significance now. But in an age when everybody carried weapons, it was a demonstration that one was prepared to converse without a weapon in one's hand. What we think of as "good manners" was merely a way of saying, "I mean you no harm, if you can show me that your intention is the same."

Caution lies behind manners, wherever we look. In days gone by, a host sipped the wine before serving it, not to check that the wine was all right but to prove to his guests that it wasn't poisoned. A wine steward used his silver server to demonstrate his host's goodwill towards his guests. Silver was thought to neutralize poisons in wine.

Why do we let someone older or more important go through the door first? One theory is that in medieval times it was sensible for the strongest man to leave the castle first, since there was always a possibility he would meet armed opponents or the rebellious peasantry waving pitchforks and scythes. Gradually, a certain honour descended upon this position. It was assumed that the most important person was also the strongest, and even if he wasn't, he could hardly deny it.

Manners are society's way of oiling the machinery. If you don't lubricate relationships, tempers rise and people fight unnecessary battles. Besides, it's worthwhile having good manners, if only so that when you drop them for a moment, everyone knows that you mean business.

People with good manners do better in most situations than those without. Most negotiations, for example, are impossible without good manners, which explains why diplomats are famed for their courtesy. The best lawyers, too, are usually people of exquisite politeness. Beware of the man who never raises his voice and always treats you with courtesy—he is probably going for your jugular.

In the 19th century, most of the great gunfighters of the American West were notorious for their florid good manners, being all too aware that if they let things get out of hand, they would have to draw and shoot. Good manners helped these men survive, since even the best gunfighter could win only so many gunfights before his luck ran out. For the most part, they were not "big-talking men"; they were soft-spoken and courteous. It was said of "Wild Bill" Hickock that the moment he stopped smiling at you, you were dead.

Despite mankind's reputation for violence, most people prefer to avoid confrontation, and avoiding confrontation is what manners are all about. Manners represent the triumph of civilization over barbarism. They are not a demonstration of weakness, but a sign of common sense—mankind's way of saying, "Let's not fight unless we have to." There may be no higher wisdom than that—in diplomacy, in business, in love and marriage, or in the transactions of everyday life.

Aviva
Layton
....

GRIM FAIRY TALES AND GORY STORIES

Children will always be drawn to violence. . . . What we should try to do is steer children away from sterile trash and toward the creative violence we find in works of art. . . .

There has been a mounting crusade against violence lately—violence on the streets and in the subway, violence in hockey, violence in the media. The issue is a relatively clear-cut one. Who in his right mind could possibly condone violence? Recently, however, there has been an outcry against a form of violence in which the issues are most definitely not so clearly defined—violence in children's literature. Within the last few weeks strong objections have been raised against a picture book used in some schools in which a man called Mr. Miacca lies in wait for bad boys, catches them and then proceeds to dine off their various limbs; and also against two reading texts, *Thrust* and *Focus*, used in junior high schools in the Toronto suburb of Etobicoke.

Librarians are getting into the act too. Last week I called my local library (one of the largest and newest in Toronto) to ask if they had a certain picture book based on an Australian aboriginal legend. The librarian supplied me with the title I wanted plus a piece of gratuitous information—namely that the book is "frightening," "disturbing," "menacing," "tasteless." This "frightening" book was, incidentally, unobtainable for well over two weeks. Some child somewhere was obviously having a whale of a time with it.

Could it be that things haven't changed much since those far-off days in 1945 when a librarian of the New York public library refused to give shelf room to E.B. White's *Stuart Little*, having decided that the statement that Stuart Little was born "looking very much like a mouse" would prove too traumatic for the tender sensibilities of Manhattan children? Or when librarians reacted negatively to Maurice Sendak's *Where the Wild Things Are* on the grounds that it would produce similar traumas? This prompted one reviewer to remark, "Boys and girls may have to shield their parents from this book. Parents are very easily frightened."

If we wish to eliminate violence from children's literature, we must eliminate by far the greatest part of children's literature. If we are to give the boot to

Mr. Miacca, then we must immediately purge our libraries of the English folklorist and anthologist Joseph Jacobs from whose famous and well-loved book, *English Folk and Fairy Tales*, *Mr. Miacca* was reprinted. But of course we can't stop there. The aptly named Brothers Grimm must go, as must most of Andrew Lang's fairy books and a large number of Greek and Roman myths. While we are at it, we should severely censor the Osborne collection of early children's books. Many of the books in this famed collection contain tales of sheer terror, both physical and mental, which could have curdled the minds of previous generations of children—and, who knows, probably did. In fact, all fairy tales and myths and legends—Italian, Japanese, Danish, Celtic, Slavic, Asian, Australian, Arabic, Yiddish, French—must be done away with.

I spent an afternoon in the library recently and I was hard put to find a classic children's story without violence. Within the space of a couple of hours I found the following foul deeds described in minute and exquisite detail: victims were flayed alive, buried alive, scalded; they had their throats slit, their bodies dismembered, their mouths stuffed with red-hot embers; they were thrust into ovens, into vats of burning oil, cauldrons of boiling water, tubs of bubbling pitch; parents abandoned their luckless offspring in burning deserts and raging blizzards, ate them alive and dead (after cooking them, that is), committed incest with them, poisoned them, tore out their hearts, their tongues, their nails, gouged out their eyes. Hills opened up and swallowed children whole; horned witches made cakes with blood drawn from sleeping families; monstrous spiders, sea monsters, werewolves, ghosts and goblins leapt out from every page. And this, believe me, is just a partial list.

Why, then, are these stories read? Why have they endured, some for thousands of years, and why do they continue to enchant and fascinate children and adults of all ages? Two stories, one true, the other fiction, describe but do not explain this fascination for and attraction to violence. The true story is told by a British psychoanalyst, Anthony Storr, and it concerns a five-year-old girl who burst into tears at the point in one of the stories in Andrew Lang's *Brown Fairy Book* when a rescue ship appears on the horizon just as the boy-hero is about to be tossed into a cask of bubbling black pitch. The mother, trying to comfort her, assured the little girl that the hero gets saved in time. "But I want him to be thrown into the pitch," sobbed the child. The second story is told by the English short story writer, Saki. Called "Toys of Peace," it is about "enlightened" parents who buy their children a model of a city hall with figures of aldermen, doctors, et cetera, instead of a fort with soldiers and guns. Hours later they come upon their children playing with absorption. They have transformed the city hall into a fort, the aldermen into soldiers, and are having a great time with their "toys of peace."

The truth of the matter is that violence in children's literature is neither good nor bad *in itself*. There is an enormous qualitative difference, for example, in the experience of a child watching a TV program about a man who has slit the throats of his many wives and hung up their corpses in a locked closet and that same small child curled up in an armchair reading *Bluebeard*. What is the nature of this difference? In the former case the violence is vulgar and exploitative. It heightens fear and tensions; it creates anxieties. In the latter case the violence is what I call creative violence. Far from heightening fear and tensions, it alleviates them; far from creating anxieties, it helps resolve them. I mean the violence that has surrounded man since his beginnings—death, decay, and destruction.

Children's inner fantasy lives, like our own, are rampant with sexuality and aggression. Adults usually manage to subdue these forces. Children are far less able to. Creative violence provides an imaginative embodiment of those fears and tensions, a channel through which subconscious desires can find relief. This is why, instinctively, children will always be drawn to violence. We cannot and should not try to legislate it out of existence. What we *should* try to do is steer children away from sterile trash and toward the creative violence we find in works of art in which the chaotic fantasies of the child's mind can be given an order, a shape, a structure.

That librarian I spoke to did not understand what every primitive society recognizes—the importance of acting out in a ritualized art form the anxieties, mysteries, ambiguities, and perplexities which every human being carries within himself. Thus the corroborees, the Australian tribal ceremonies in which an awesome or overwhelming event is acted out in controlled ritual; thus the myths and fairy tales which find their counterpart in every culture in every time. This is why a Mr. Miacca who eats children alive is a familiar and even a reassuring figure. He appears over and over again in myths and fairy tales. His forebear is Cronus who ate his newly born sons for fear they would supplant him. A closer counterpart is the stepmother in *The Juniper Tree* who stewed her stepson and served him to the boy's father who smacked his lips over this tasty meal and exclaimed, "How truly delicious." *The Juniper Tree*, it should be noted, was one of Pamela Travers' favourite childhood stories. It didn't seem to do her too much damage—she grew up to write *Mary Poppins*.

The recurring motif of cannibalism, of being eaten and of eating, is a common fantasy among children. They are, in fact, eaten up many times in the course of an average day—by a smothering mother, an oppressive teacher, an insensitive father, or a rival sibling—and it is folly to assume that the little darlings aren't itching to return the favour. It is the aesthetic embodiment of these secret and unacceptable fantasies which enables the child to free himself from them.

Uncreative violence, on the other hand, vulgarizes these fantasies. Making no demands on the creative imagination, it exploits when it should explore and it throws back to the child, without the refining filter of art, the undigested rawness of his emotions. It is not the demons, the hobgoblins, the hideous unnamed horrors of the dark forest or the bestiality of man which hurt a child's mind. As C.S. Lewis has expressed it, "The dangerous fantasy is always superficially realistic." Thus it is badly written tripe we have to beware of, the relentless vulgarity of, for example, TV sitcoms.

As for the recent fuss over the two school readers, *Thrust* and *Focus* (their names must have been thought up by either a very dense editor or else one with a surpassing sense of irony for they have as much thrust and focus as a couple of limp dandelions), compared to what goes on in a Grimm Fairy Tale, the so-called violent stories read like a mild version of Goody Two-Shoes. What is hideous and unforgivable and infinitely more dangerous and corrupting is the numbing mediocrity which they offer. They are also so hopelessly old-fashioned, Midwestern, small-town American that you can positively smell the stale apple pie when you open the covers. I cannot imagine either book being tolerated in any major city school in the United States.

If parents and educators are going to protest against books such as these, and if they are going to present briefs before royal commissions, then let them do these things for the right reasons. It is the dissemination of mediocrity and vulgarity that does the real violence to the minds of children. May those who are responsible for those two wretched and unutterably silly reading texts being foisted on the poor unsuspecting children of Ontario be gobbled up, in the best tradition of fairy tales, by good old Mr. Miacca. They richly deserve it.

Richard
Lederer
....

THE STRANGE CASE OF THE ENGLISH LANGUAGE

Sometime you have to believe that all English speakers should be committed to an asylum for the verbally insane. In what other language do people drive in a parkway and park in a driveway?

English is the most widely spoken language in the history of our planet, used in some way by at least one out of every seven human beings around the globe. Half of the world's books are written in English, and the majority of international telephone calls are made in English. English is the language of more than 60% of the world's radio programs, many of them beamed, ironically, by the Russians, who know that to win friends and influence nations, they're best off using English. More than 70% of international mail is written and addressed in English, and 80% of all computer text is stored in English. English has acquired the largest vocabulary of all the world's languages, perhaps as many as two million words, and has generated one of the noblest bodies of literature in the annals of the human race.

Nonetheless, it is now time to face the fact that English is a crazy language.

In the crazy English language, the blackbird hen is brown, blackboards can be blue or green, and blackberries are green and then red before they are ripe. Even if blackberries were really black and blueberries really blue, what are strawberries, cranberries, huckleberries, raspberries, boysenberries, and gooseberries supposed to look like?

To add to the insanity, there is no butter in buttermilk, no egg in eggplant, neither worms nor wood in wormwood, neither pine nor apple in pineapple, and no ham in a hamburger. (In fact, if somebody invented a sandwich consisting of a ham patty in a bun, we would have a hard time finding a name for it.) To make matters worse, English muffins weren't invented in England, french fries in France, nor Danish pastries in Denmark. And we discover even more culinary madness in the revelations that sweetmeat is made from fruit, while sweetbread, which isn't sweet, is made from meat.

In this unrealistic English tongue, greyhounds aren't always grey (or gray); panda bears and koala bears aren't bears (they're marsupials); a woodchuck is a groundhog, which is not a hog; a horned toad is a lizard; glow worms are fireflies, but fireflies aren't flies (they're beetles); ladybugs and lightning bugs are also beetles (and to propagate, a significant proportion of ladybugs must be male); a guinea pig is neither a pig nor from Guinea (it's a South American rodent); and a titmouse is neither mammal or mammaried.

Language is like the air we breathe. It's invisible, inescapable, indispensable, and we take it for granted. But when we take the time to explore the paradoxes and vagaries of English, we find that hot dogs can be cold, darkrooms can be lit, homework can be done in school, nightmares can take place in broad daylight while morning sickness and daydreaming can take place at night, midwives can be men, hours—especially happy hours and rush hours—can last longer than 60 minutes, quicksand works *very* slowly, boxing rings are square, silverware can be made of plastic and tablecloths of paper, most telephones are dialed by being punched (or pushed?), and many bathrooms don't have baths in them. In fact, a dog can go to the bathroom under a tree—no bath, no room; it's still going to the bathroom. And doesn't it seem at least a little bizarre that we go to the bathroom in order to go to the bathroom?

Why is it that a woman can man a station but a man can't woman one, that a man can father a movement but a woman can't mother one, and that a king rules a kingdom but a queen doesn't rule a queendom? How did all those Renaissance men reproduce when there doesn't seem to have been any Renaissance women?

A writer is someone who writes, and a stinger is something that stings. But fingers don't fing, grocers don't groce, hammers don't ham, and humdingers don't humding. If the plural of *tooth* is *teeth*, shouldn't the plural of *booth* be *beeth*? One goose, two geese—so one moose, two meese? If people ring a bell today and rang a bell yesterday, why don't we say that they flang a ball? If they wrote a letter, perhaps they also bote their tongue. If the teacher taught, why isn't it also true that the preacher praught? Why is it that the sun shone yesterday while I shined my shoes, that I treaded water and then trod on soil, and that I flew out to see a World Series game in which my favorite player flied out?

If we conceive a conception and receive at a reception, why don't we grieve a greption and believe a beleption? If a horsehair mat is made from the hair of horses and a camel's hairbrush from the hair of camels, from what is a mohair coat made? If a vegetarian eats vegetables, what does a humanitarian eat? If a firefighter fights fire, what does a freedom fighter fight? If a weightlifter lifts weights, what does a shoplifter lift? If *pro* and *con* are opposites, is congress the opposite of progress?

Sometime you have to believe that all English speakers should be committed to an asylum for the verbally insane. In what other language do people drive in a parkway and park in a driveway? In what other language do people recite at a play and play at a recital? In what other language do privates eat in the general mess and generals eat in the private mess? In what other language do people ship by truck and send cargo by ship? In what other language can your nose run and your feet smell?

How can a slim chance and a fat chance be the same and a bad licking and a good licking be the same, while a wise man and a wise guy are opposites? How can sharp speech and blunt speech be the same and *quite a lot* and *quite a few* the same, while *overlook* and *oversee* are opposites? How can the weather be hot as hell one day and cold as hell the next?

If *button* and *unbutton* and *tie* and *untie* are opposites, why are *loosen* and *unloosen* and *ravel* and *unravel* the same? If *bad* is the opposite of *good, hard* the opposite of *soft*, and *up* the opposite of *down*, why are *badly* and *goodly, hardly* and *softly*, and *upright* and *downright* not opposite pairs? If harmless actions are the opposite of harmful actions, why are shameless and shameful behaviour the same and pricey objects less expensive than priceless ones? If appropriate and inappropriate remarks and passable and impassable mountain trails are opposites, why are flammable and inflammable materials, heritable and inheritable property, and passive and impassive people, the same and valuable objects less treasured than invaluable ones? If *uplift* is the same as *lift up*, why are *upset* and *set up* opposite in meaning? Why are *pertinent* and *impertinent, canny* and *uncanny*, and *famous* and *infamous* neither opposites nor the same? How can *raise* and *raze* and *reckless* and *wreckless* be opposites when each pair contains the same sound?

Why is it that when the sun or the moon or the stars are out, they are visible, but when lights are out, they are invisible, and that when I wind up my watch, I start it, but when I wind up this essay I shall end it?

English is a crazy language.

How can expressions like "I'm mad about my flat," "No foot ball coaches allowed," and "I'll come by in the morning and knock you up" convey such different messages in two countries that purport to speak English?

How can it be easier to assent than to dissent but harder to ascend than to descend? Why is it that a man with hair on his head has more hair than a man with hairs on his head; that if you decide to be bad forever, you choose to be bad for good; and that if you choose to wear only your left shoe then your left one is right and your right one is left? Right?

Smaller wonder that we English users are constantly standing meaning on its head. Let's look at a number of familiar English words and phrases that turn out to mean the opposite of or something very different from what we think they mean:

I could care less. *I couldn't care less* is the clearer, more accurate version. Why do so many people delete the negative from this statement? Because they are afraid that the *n't . . . less* combination will make for a double negative, which is a no-no.

I really miss not seeing you. Whenever people say this to me, I feel like saying, "All right, I'll leave!" Here speakers throw in a gratuitous negative— *not*—even though *I really miss seeing you* is what they want to say.

The movie kept me literally glued to my seat. The chances of our buttocks being literally epoxied to a seat are about as small as the chances of our literally rolling in the aisles while watching a funny movie or literally drowning in tears while watching a sad one. We actually mean *The movie kept me figuratively glued to my seat*—but who needs *figuratively*, anyway? If we must resort to a cliché, *The movie kept me glued to my seat* is the clearest, most sensible way of expressing our emotions.

A nonstop flight. Never get on one of these. You'll never get down.

A near miss. *A near miss* is, in reality, a collision. A close call is actually *a near hit*.

My idea fell between the cracks. If something *fell between the cracks*, didn't it land on the planks or the concrete? Shouldn't that be *My idea fell into the cracks*?

I'll follow you to the ends of the earth. Let the word go out to the four corners of the Earth that ever since Columbus we have known that the earth doesn't have any ends. . . . .

Daylight saving time. Not a single second of daylight is saved by this ploy.

A hot-water heater. Why heat hot water?

A hot cup of coffee. Who cares if the cup is hot? Surely we mean *a cup of hot coffee*. . . .

Doughnut holes. Aren't these little treats really *doughnut balls*? The holes are what's left in the original doughnut. (And if a candy cane is shaped like a cane, why isn't a doughnut shaped like a nut?)

I want to have my cake and eat it too. Shouldn't this timeworn cliché be *I want to eat my cake and have it too*? Isn't the logical sequence that one hopes to eat the cake and then still possess it?

The announcement was made by a nameless official. Just about everybody has a name, even officials. Surely what is meant is *The announcement was made by an unnamed official*.

Preplan, preboard, preheat, and prerecord. Aren't people who do this simply planning, boarding, heating, and recording? Who needs the pretentious prefix?

Put on your shoes and socks. This is an exceedingly difficult maneuver. Most of us put on our socks first, then our shoes.

A hit-and-run play. If you know your baseball, you know the sequence constitutes a run-and-hit play.

The bus goes back and forth between the terminal and the airport. Again we find mass confusion about the order of events. You have to go forth before you can go back.

Underwater and underground. Things that we claim are *underwater* and *underground* are obviously surrounded by, not under, the water and ground.

I got caught in one of the biggest traffic bottlenecks of the year. The bigger the bottleneck, the more freely the contents of the bottle flow through it. To be true to the metaphor, we should say, *I got caught in one of the smallest bottlenecks of the year.*

I lucked out. To *luck out* sounds as if you're out of luck. Don't you mean, *I lucked in?*

Because we writers of English seem to have our heads screwed on backward, we constantly misperceive our bodies, often saying just the opposite of what we mean:

Watch your head. I keep seeing this sign on low doorways, but I haven't figured out how to follow the instructions. Trying to watch your head is like trying to bite your teeth.

They're head over heels in love. That's nice, but all of us do almost everything *head over heels.* If we are trying to create an image of people doing cartwheels and somersaults, why don't we say, *They're heels over head in love?*

Put your best foot forward. Now, let's see . . . We have a good foot, a better foot, but we don't have a third—and best—foot. It's our better foot that we want to put forward. "Put your best foot forward" is akin to "May the best team win." Usually there are only two teams in the contest.

Keep a stiff upper lip. When we are disappointed or afraid, which lip do we try to control? The lower lip, of course, is the one we are trying to keep from quivering.

I'm speaking tongue in cheek. So how can anyone understand you?

They do things behind my back. You want they should do things in front of your back? . . .

English is weird.

In the rigid expressions that wear tonal grooves in the record of our language, *beck* can appear only with *call*, *cranny* with *nook*, *hue* with *cry*, *main* with *might*, *fettle* only with *fine*, *aback* with *taken*, *caboodle* with *kit*, and *spic* and *span* only with each other. Why must all shrifts be short, all lucre filthy, all bystanders innocent, and all bedfellows strange? I'm convinced that some shrifts are lengthy and that some lucre is squeaky clean, and I've certainly met guilty bystanders and perfectly normal bedfellows.

Why is it that only swoops are fell? Sure, the verbivorous William Shakespeare invented the expression "one fell swoop," but why can't strokes, swings, acts, and the like also be fell? Why are we allowed to vent our spleens but never our kidneys or livers? Why must it be only our minds that are boggled, and never our eyes or our hearts? Why can't eyes and jars be ajar, as well as doors? Why must aspersions always be cast and never hurled or lobbed?

Doesn't it seem just a little loopy that we can make amends but never just one amend; that no matter how carefully we comb through the annals of history, we can never discover just one annal; that we can never pull a shenanigan, be in a doldrum, or get a jitter, a willy, a delirium tremen, a jimjum, or a heebie-jeebie; and that, sifting through the wreckage of a disaster, we can never find just one smithereen? Indeed, this whole business of plurals that don't have matching singulars reminds me to ask this burning linguistic question, one that has puzzled scholars for decades: If you have a bunch of odds and ends and you get rid or sell off all but one of them, what do you call that doohickey with which you're left?

What do you make of the fact that we can talk about certain things and ideas only when they are absent? Once they appear, our blessed English doesn't allow us to describe them. Have you ever run into someone who was combobulated, sheveled, gruntled, chalant, plussed, ruly, gainly, maculate, pecunious, or peccable? Have you ever met a sung hero or experienced requited love? I know people who are no spring chickens, but where, pray tell, are the people who *are* spring chickens? Where are the people who actually *would* hurt a fly? All the time I meet people who *are* my cup of tea, and whom I *would* touch with a ten-foot pole, but I cannot talk about them in English—and that *is* a laughing matter.

If the truth be told, all languages are a little crazy. As Walt Whitman might proclaim, they contradict themselves. That's because language is invented, not discovered, by boys and girls and men and women, not computers. As such, language reflects the creativity and fearful asymmetry of the human race, which, of course, isn't really a race at all. That's why *six, seven, eight,* and *nine* change to *sixty, seventy, eighty,* and *ninety,* but *two, three, four,* and *five* do not become *twoty, threety, fourty,* and *fivety.* That's why we can turn lights off and on but not out and in. That's why we wear a pair of pants but, except on very cold days, never a pair of shirts. That's why we can open up the floor, climb the walls, raise the roof, pick up the house, and bring down the house.

In his essay "The Awful German Language," Mark Twain spoofs the confusion engendered by German gender by translating literally from a conversation in a German Sunday school book: "Gretchen. Wilhelm, where is the turnip? *Wilhelm.* She has gone to the kitchen. *Gretchen.* Where is the accomplished and beautiful English maiden? *Wilhelm.* It has gone to the opera." Twain continues: "A tree is male, its buds are female, its leaves are neuter; horses are sexless, dogs are male, cats are female—tomcats included."

Still, you have to marvel at the unique lunacy of the English language, in which your house can simultaneously burn up and burn down, in which you fill in a form by filling out a form, in which you add up a column of figures by adding them down, in which your alarm clock goes off by going on, in which you are inoculated for measles by being inoculated against measles, and in which you first chop a tree down—and then you chop it up.

Nilavanh
Limsakoune
··············
Student
Essay

X-Rated Boob Tube

Rather than enlightening the audience, television serves to more deeply entrench discomfort about sex and contributes to continued ignorance in society about love, sex, and responsibility.

"Cheers," "Who's the Boss," "Night Court," "The Golden Girls." . . . What is the connection between these prime-time television shows? You guessed it! SEX. Television sex.

Researcher Diana Workman, a health education and family planning specialist in California, conducted an intensive analysis of ten prime-time television shows that led to some uncomfortable conclusions about television sex.

Her report, titled "What You See Is What You Think" published in *Media and Values*, a Canadian-based magazine, reveals that there is a tremendous amount of sexual activity and innuendo on television, and also finds that there has been a steady increase in sexual explicitness since the 1970s.

How much sex are we watching on prime-time shows? According to Workman, we are constantly being bombarded with physical, verbal, and implied acts or references to sex. Her studies reveal the frequency of many types of sexual behaviour.

• "Touching behaviours," including kissing, hugging, and other affectionate touching were presented at the rate of 24.5 acts per hour;
• "Suggestions and innuendo" involving flirtatious behaviour appeared at the rate of 16.5 times per hour;
• Sexual intercourse was suggested 2.5 times per hour;
• A range of "discouraged sexual practices" such as sadomasochism and exhibitionism were suggested at a rate of 6.2 times per hour;
• On the other hand, educational information about sex was infrequently presented, occurring at a rate of 1.6 times per hour.

"There's a lot of sex for adolescents who watch, on average, five-and-a-half to eight hours of television every day," says Jane Brown and Kim Walsh in the report on media and sex.

"Sex is promoted in the media, but not promoted responsibly," explains Linda Shortt, a health education specialist.

Researchers Kim Bloomfield and Diana Workman found that sex and sexual issues are usually presented in an exploitive way, rather than a loving way.

Jane Brown says that "all too often the information teens are seeking most is just what they're not finding: Sex that is loving and meaningful rather than exploitive or violent."

In her report, Workman explains that "tender, loving sexual behaviour is rarely portrayed between people in committed relationships. Instead, sexual references are presented in a context that makes even normal sexual practices appear extreme. Relationships on recent shows like "thirtysomething" have made loving sex between committed couples more common.

"In contrast, most of the few references to intercourse we observed were made among friends, co-workers, and strangers . . . more problematic were the large number of sexual references to a variety of sexual practices besides intercourse."

Bloomfield and Workman discovered that prime-time sitcom shows such as "Night Court," "Golden Girls," "Cheers," and "Moonlighting" refer with relative frequency to masturbation, voyeurism, transvestitism, transsexualism, homosexuality, sadomasochism, oral sex, prostitution, and pornography.

Dan Fielding, seen weekly on "Night Court," features the largest number of sexual references of this type. He is portrayed as a sexually frustrated, sex-starved attorney who searches relentlessly for sexual partners. In one scene, he is bound and gagged in a closet, implying a sadomasochistic encounter. He is frequently involved in "risky sex" in countless episodes.

"The problem with television sex is that sex is often portrayed as trouble free, something you don't need to plan for or worry about . . . they [teens] get lulled into thinking that sex on television will be the same way for them in real life," says Shortt.

Another problem that concerns Bloomfield and Workman was the lack of discussions dealing with birth control, sex education, sexually transmitted diseases, unintended pregnancies, and contraception.

Their research revealed that television pregnancies are apt to end in miscarriages and stillbirths, leaving the characters unchanged by the experience. Even more common are sexual relationships untroubled by worries about pregnancy and sexually transmitted diseases, even though safe sex, contraception, and sex education are rarely discussed.

"Rather than enlightening the audience, television serves to more deeply entrench discomfort about sex and contributes to continued ignorance in society about love, sex, and responsibility," Workman explains in *Media and Values*, a quarterly resource magazine for media awareness.

Shortt says that "People are uncomfortable when examining sexual issues, and until that changes, television's portrayal of sex will not undergo a rapid improvement. . . . Adolescents should be encouraged to look critically at the media, and be critical about what they watch."

Sally Steenland, an expert in the media field, concludes that, "Although TV is far from perfect in its treatment of sexuality, it offers more authenticity and equality among the sexes, young and old, than there was decades ago. Alert viewers should catch this progress but will also make their voices heard when lapses occur."

Helen
Lucas
....

GROWING UP GREEK

I was caught in the drama I made of the world in which I lived, the world from which I came, and the world in which I wanted to be.

One of my earliest recollections, when I was about three, is of standing outside our home and wondering what I had done that was so wrong. Why would I go to hell? I wondered if God would take into consideration the fact that I was so little. This sense of having done something wrong—of being wrong—is an impression that has remained with me over the years.

My parents emigrated from a village in Greece, forced by poverty to come to Canada. My two sisters and I grew up in Saskatoon, then a city of 50 000, but our lives revolved around the Greek community of sixty people. Since families from the same village banded together, out of the sixty we were about twenty. Another ten relatives lived in Regina, so these thirty people were the ones that mattered in our lives.

We were raised to respect and slightly fear our elders—fear in the sense that we were taught never give them a reason to talk about us. Of course we were model children—submissive, scholastic, music-lessoned, clean-scrubbed, quiet, with our thick, centre-parted hair in long, lush braids. During national Greek holidays we would don Greek costumes and recite patriotic poetry about a war with the Turks which, of course, we had won.

Everyone was struggling. The effects of the Depression were still around. I wore my cousin Jack's hand-me-downs. I remember wondering what the front slit in the underwear was for. Mother would spend a day washing and drying the clothes. Then she'd spend a day mending. New mending went patiently over previous mending. Yet as little as we had, we'd periodically fill a flour sack with clothing to send to our even poorer relatives in Greece. Supposedly when you are young you are not aware of being poor, but because of our strong ties with impoverished relatives "over there," we were constantly reminded that our roots were poverty.

Letters arrived regularly, addressed in awkward English handwriting, and inside were the onion-thin pages filled with the complicated Greek scribbles only my mother could decipher. Once in a while came the envelope edged in black, preparing us for the news inside. I hated looking at the photographs of everyone grouped around the open coffin of the dead relative. Why did they send such photographs? "So you can see how good he looked when he died," I was told. Black was the colour of death, old women, and priests.

I was caught in the drama I made of the world in which I lived, the world from which I came, and the world in which I wanted to be.

To this day, if you ask me where I come from, I cannot answer precisely. Part of me is from the Canadian prairies where I was born and raised, and part is from Greece, where I have never been. At home I spoke Greek and lived a Greek life. At school I was Canadian but even there the Greek values kept interfering. I could work with my Canadian friends but I could not play with them or behave like them. I kept mostly to myself.

Now I can look back and understand my parents' need to cling to the values of the country they had left behind. Change is frightening and slow. They could not manage to accept, in those early years, even a part of the new without fearing it would be at the expense of what they already believed in.

What was the world I wanted to be in? Next door lived the Evans family. Mrs. Evans was elegant, refined, glamorous, gracious, and soft-spoken. Sunday mornings she put on a riding habit and went off to her horses. She even had a maid. I absolutely worshipped her and wanted to be a lady like her.

But she was English, I was Greek. I came to the conclusion, probably again around three, that anyone not English was second-best. Then and there began my bountiful inferiority complex.

My parents must have felt this too. They came to someone else's country. Did they feel second-best? The message we children got was that we would have a better station in life than they did. Their dream was that we would definitely be first-class citizens. Our entrance to this better world would be through an education. "No one can ever take an education away from you," my father frequently said. It never mattered that we were girls; we were expected to go to university. Marriage would come later. Besides, the education guaranteed a better husband.

After a year of university I ended up in Toronto studying at an art college. It was a natural progression. Being by myself much of the time had given me a chance to develop my imagination. I found enjoyment in making images on paper. This child who felt so insignificant could actually receive attention, even admiration, by bringing a drawing to her teacher.

There were many reasons I became an artist. As a loner I could still work alone; no one else need be involved. I was timid with people. Alone I could do exactly what I wanted with no one to judge me. I was no longer caught between two sets of values; in fact, the conflicts of my youth became subject matter for my studio. The past was working for me. It didn't matter that I had no role models, for this way I had no predetermined boundaries to maintain. Boundaries had been a way of life. I also enjoyed my exclusiveness. I was in unexplored territory; it was exciting, it was freedom.

How has my mother responded? She is pleased and proud of what I do, although she doesn't completely understand it. If I'm a painter, why won't I paint like Leonardo da Vinci? While I was teaching painting it was more comfortable for her to think of me as a teacher. I keep sending home newspaper clippings about me or my work but I don't get the "bravo" I seek. If I were to call and say, "Mother, I'm off to Oslo to accept the Nobel Prize," she'd probably say, "Careful, don't speak to any strangers while you're away."

My values confuse her just as her values once confused me. We will never totally understand each other because we have lived such different lives. That is why the total approval I seek can never come. It could only happen if both of us had similar experiences in related lifestyles. Yet she is unbelievably supportive and whole-heartedly respects my need to paint. More than anyone she has been there to help me with problems that have prevented me from painting.

A friend of mind, on meeting Mother, felt we were not one but two generations apart. That may be so. Yet when I get angry about Greek women kept in black, or the archaic values of the church, or about passivity being death, I remember that my widowed mother wears blue, that she has some of the same lack of tolerance for the church that I have, and that she leads an exceptionally active life.

When I telephone and we talk about something we both understand—a recipe, or how to plant a lily, or whatever—we are again mother and daughter, and there is for a little while no distance between us.

Sangita
Manandhar
. . . .
Student
Essay

That's How It Is: Life For
A Young Asian Girl

*Sometimes I really do feel torn between two countries. I
don't know who I am, a Nepalese girl or an English girl.*

Life for a young Asian girl living in a western country such as England can be
very confusing.

I am a fifteen-year-old Nepalese girl. I have been living in England for the
past twelve years, and I have only returned to Nepal once, and that was
when I was seven years of age. I find that now, as I am growing older and
realizing the differences in the type of life that a Nepalese girl has to lead
compared to a life that an English girl leads, it is hard to decide which life is
more suitable for me.

Asian girls lead a very different life compared to the life western girls lead.
For a start, Asian girls are not allowed to go out, they are not allowed to
smoke, drink or swear, and they are definitely not allowed to go out with
boys. Going out with boys means that they will ruin their chances of getting
a good husband. Husbands are chosen by arrangement. Personally, I find it
really silly, but back in Nepal, even if a girl is just seen talking to a few boys
and being friendly with them, she is considered as something bad and ends
up getting a bad name for herself. Although I have quite strict parents, they
do allow me to go out, though not at night. Sometimes when my friends are
allowed to stay out late at night, I must admit, I envy them a lot. I feel that
because my parents are living in this country and bringing up their children
in it, they must at least make a few adjustments to suit the way of life over
here.

A good education is very important to Asian families, but parents usually
tend to encourage their sons rather than their daughters to work hard at
school (girls are more encouraged to learn how to cook and clean). Because
of this, it is often the girls who study harder and want to go on to higher
education. Most parents do not grant their daughters' wishes, but marry
them off as soon as the suitable match arrives, but I have been lucky in the

fact that my parents have always encouraged me in my studies—though sometimes, just a little too much.

Nepalese girls usually tend to look rather young for their age, but act quite mature, while English girls tend to look much older than their age, but act quite immature.

Back in Nepal, girls of my age are already cooking and cleaning for their family. It is because of this that I usually receive gasps of shock when I tell Nepalese visitors that I cannot cook a meal.

Sometimes I really do want to go back to my own country, as I can learn how to live my life, so I can learn about my own people, our traditions and customs. I want to go back before I, to put it in my parents' words, "ruin myself." Already I find that my thoughts are becoming too westernized.

Another subject which I really feel confused about is equal rights. At school I am taught to believe that women are no less than men and they must have the chance of having equal opportunities; but at home, I am witnessing the fact that women are always being put down. We Nepalese girls are taught to respect the menfolk, because they have the knowledge and capability of doing everything. We are told that women are the weaker sex. Women must always stand by their husbands, whether they are right or wrong. Back in Nepal, the two words "equal opportunities" would not even be heard of, let alone practised!

If I knew more about my own country, maybe I wouldn't feel so confused; but I don't remember a thing. The only Nepalese customs and traditions I know are what my parents have taught me.

I have spent the whole of my life here, more or less, and hardly remember anything of Nepal. It is when my parents try to tie me down with Nepalese customs and traditions that I feel confused. Sometimes I really do feel torn between two countries. I don't know who I am, a Nepalese girl or an English girl. I find that I am leading two separate lives. I am a completely different person at home to the type of person I am at school. At school I feel free and lead the life of an English girl, at home I feel imprisoned with traditions and lead the life of a Nepalese girl. I must admit, I sometimes envy the English girl's way of life. She seems to have so much freedom, and I, none.

I often feel guilty about my own thoughts, and also hate having to lead two different lives. I very much want to act and feel like a Nepalese girl, but how can I when I have no experience? I often ask my parents to send me back to Nepal, but they will not. Instead they are always telling me never to forget who I am and where I came from. How can I when they won't even let me learn?

To tell you the truth, I don't really feel like a Nepalese person at all. I have lived amongst English people for nearly all my life, so is it really my fault if I act and feel like one? I am not saying that I hate being a Nepalese girl, I am just saying that I wish I was allowed a little more freedom and a chance of being independent. How can my parents expect me to be and act like a typical Nepalese girl when I am brought up in a society where the way of life is completely different? Surely our parents cannot expect us to act like pure angels when we are brought up in such a free country as this. Maybe back home we would be angels, because we wouldn't have any chance to be other, but surely not in this country.

So who then is to be blamed? Who is the main cause for the confusion? The parents? Or the children themselves? Should the parents try to understand the western way of life and be lenient in their ways? Or should the children realize that they too have their own culture and try to hold on to it? I only wish I knew.

Ellie
Presner
. . . .

TAKING BACK THE NIGHT:
ONE WOMAN'S EXPERIENCE

The slaughter of 14 women . . . was a catastrophe that brought
women across the country . . . to the stunning realization that
abuse will continue, and escalate, until we all say STOP!

First I buy the candles. They are a bargain at four for a dollar: one for me, one
for my 21-year-old daughter, and one for each of her friends. Tonight I am
going on my very first protest march. It is to be a women-only demonstration against violence towards women, and is called, eloquently, Take Back
the Night.

I am old enough to remember news-casts of fiery anti-war protests, early
Women's Liberation demonstrations, and Ban the Bomb rallies. But I was
never a marcher; merely a spectator. Why? I'm sure I felt as strongly about
those causes as the activists who participated. Perhaps I was too comfortable, too tired, too lazy, in my cozy middle-class nest . . .

Well, that was then. Tonight I will make up for it. I pick up my daughter
and her friends, and we drive to the starting point of the march. We are
several minutes late. As I park the car near St. Denis and Rachel in downtown Montreal, I hear an eerie sound, a tremendous chorus of cheers and
whoops coming from somewhere up the street.

We get out of the car, and the young women with me begin to run towards
the tumult.

"Wait!" I shout. "Wait for me!" Dismayed, I chase after them.

"What's happening?" I ask, gasping, as I struggle to catch up. Ululating
screams swell in the distance, as my daughter tells me: "The march is
starting! Come on!"

Oh.

The noise sounds like war cries. In a way, that is exactly what it is.

Blue and red police car flashers greet us as we round the corner. Then I see
them, a surging mass of women, euphoric, screaming, bearing banners,
candles, noisemakers. We sprint over and slip in among them.

Now it is no longer "us" and "them"; it is only "us." As we walk, the din
takes on a rhythmic shape, a repetitive, forceful chant that propels us
forward:

La rue! (The street!)
La nuit! (The night!)
Les femmes san peur! (Women without fear!)
La rue!
La nuit!
Les femmes sans peur!

Time to light our candles. We borrow a light from the flickering taper of the woman next to us. We smile our thanks; the sharing has begun.

We hold our candles via an ingenious method my daughter somehow knows about. The top third of each candle is pushed up through the bottom of a styrofoam coffee cup. This way, the flame will stand the breeze, and the hot melted wax will fall into the bottom of the cup. Later, other marchers express admiration at our cleverness; a newspaper photographer takes our picture. (It will not run.)

The chanting erupts into cheers. A prancing, pixie-like young woman gaily bangs her pot lid with a stick. This is, I think, ironically appropriate: a pot lid—a kitchen item—as a subversive prop. I glance around me and behold a wild and wonderful scene. I see all sizes, shapes, and ages of females: mothers, daughters, babies in strollers, grandmothers, many with candles, banners, or placards, others clanking cups—and more pot lids.

A new slogan is picked up:

No means no!
Yes means yes!
Wherever we go!
However we dress!

I turn and notice that my daughter and her friends are chanting loudly along with all the others. My vocal cords seem frozen. I look at the spectators on either side of the street, men and women, some gawking, some grinning, a few waving, watching us march. I feel self-conscious. What's wrong with me?

No means no!
Yes means yes!
Wherever we go!
However we dress!
However we dress . . . However we dress . . .

I am walking to the community pool with my best friend. We have on shorts, T-shirts, ankle socks. A man is walking towards us. From a distance, he looks kind of old, like one of my uncles. As he nears us and is about to pass, I see with a start that his pant zipper is undone. He is not wearing underwear. Later, I tell my parents.

They are horrified. They call the police, who say the man is probably long gone by now. I feel confused.

I am nine years old.

A new outpouring of elated whoops and cheers: we reach a point where the street becomes one-way, and the police allow our march to spread across the entire width of brightly lit St. Denis Street. We are powerful! The marchers strike up a vigorous chant:

Women unite!
Take back the night!
Women unite!
Take back the night!

Suddenly, I find my vocal cords unlocked. I chant with the rest; it feels fantastic!

Tonight, we have power. But I remember another night, when I had no power at all.

"Would you like a lift home?" he asks me.

"Oh no," I say, stepping back from his yucky alcoholic breath. I've been babysitting his kids, and just want to go home.

"S'okay," he insists, "Can't have a cute little girl like you walking outside all alone this late, can we?" I say good-night to his wife, and he steers me to the car. I am too shy to stand up to his robust confidence.

We drive towards my house, which is luckily only six blocks away. He chatters loudly, sending clouds of sickly liquor aroma in my direction. Suddenly, his hand is on my knee. My heart stops. Revulsion overtakes me; I squirm my knee away, out of his reach. He gets the message. When I finally reach my front door, breathless with anxiety and nausea, I believe I have narrowly escaped a terrible fate, though I am not sure exactly what that fate would have been. But if I have escaped, why do I still feel so awful?

I am 13.

By now, we have reached a somewhat seedier section of the street. The trendy cafés lining our route have given way to more garish storefronts. Abruptly my eyes are caught by a glittering sign: *Danseuses Nues* (Nude Dancers). Instinctively, I stop and point. I begin to boo, surprising myself by my new initiative. My neighbours have also become aware of the sign and are equally disgusted; they follow my example.

Our booing and pointing are contagious. Some women add hisses and more colourful hand gestures. Male onlookers smirk. The bouncer stands before the offending establishment, defiantly facing us, legs spread, arms crossed, resplendent in his ivory suit, a sultan guarding his harem. Our boos are angry, loud, relentless. Finally, we march on, chanting again:

La rue!
La nuit!
Les femmes sans peur!

La nuit . . . the night . . .

It is dark. I am walking home, shivering, from the bus stop. The streets are empty; my night class ended late. Footsteps echo in the distance behind me. They are not my own. Swiftly I turn around, and I see it is a man. He isn't looking at me—or is he? I speed up my pace, and cross diagonally to the other side of the street. I concentrate: please don't cross the street too. He does. My heart pumps harder; I am walking as fast as I can. But so is he. I reach the corner, my house in view, when I dare to look back. He has disappeared. But my fear has not.

I am 20.

Around me the masses of marchers are cheering; I join in. We are exhilarated, determined. I observe my neighbours. My daughter and her friends hold their candles aloft, vibrant statues of liberty. Off to my far right, a woman walks her bicycle. Riding it would not carry the same beat as marching.

To my left struts a very tall, shaven-headed woman in black leather. She wears one earring. I now notice the stubble on her cheeks. "She" is apparently a "he." This is fine with me: if he shares our terrors of the past, he can share our present joy.

Directly in front of me marches a woman my age, with her sweatered arm looped through that of an older woman. I hear the younger one call her partner *"Maman."*

Maman . . . mother . . . daughter . . .

My daughter tells me something one day about "Frank." He used to be her nursery-school bus driver. "Frank," she says, used to tickle her sometimes. On the bus, after all the others had gone. When this happened, she was four. "Why didn't you tell me then?" I ask. She shrugs.

She is now six.

My reverie is broken by a new, fierce chant. Unprintable words fill the night.

Oh, my. What would my mother say? Such language, and in such a public place. Terrible? No. With all due respect, this is not terrible. Assault and murder, however, are. The slaughter of 14 women on Dec. 6, 1989, was a catastrophe that brought women across the country—including middle-aged women like me who had never marched for anything ever before—to the stunning realization that abuse will continue, and escalate, until we all say STOP!

We have been marching downhill for a while, and the end is in sight. I cannot believe I have marched this distance. I have never been fond of walking before. My throat is sore from shouting.

Our clamour begins to fade as we all congregate at the foot of the hill. Someone I do not recognize speaks French into a microphone. Her words sound fuzzy, and I do not understand. No matter. Our daughters, companions, neighbours, and sisters are here. I know I will do this again someday. The long *nuit* is not yet over.

Bertrand
Russell

WHAT I HAVE LIVED FOR

The whole world of loneliness, poverty, and pain makes a
mockery of what human life should be. I long to alleviate the
evil, but I cannot. . . .

Three passions, simple but overwhelmingly strong, have governed my life: the longing for love, the search for knowledge, and unbearable pity for the suffering of mankind. These passions, like great winds, have blown me hither and thither, on a wayward course, over a deep ocean of anguish, reaching to the very verge of despair.

I have sought love, first, because it brings ecstasy—ecstasy so sweet that I would often have sacrificed all the rest of life for a few hours of this joy. I have sought it, next, because it relieves loneliness—that terrible loneliness in which one shivering consciousness looks over the rim of the world into the cold unfathomable lifeless abyss. I have sought it, finally, because in the union of love I have seen, in a mystic miniature, the prefiguring vision of the heaven that saints and poets have imagined. This is what I sought, and though it might seem too good for human life, this is what—at last—I have found.

With equal passion I have sought knowledge. I have wished to understand the hearts of men. I have wished to know why the stars shine. And I have tried to apprehend the Pythagorean power by which number holds sway above the flux. A little of this, but not much, I have achieved.

Love and knowledge, so far as they were possible, led upward toward the heavens. But always pity brought me back to earth. Echoes of cries of pain reverberate in my heart. Children in famine, victims tortured by oppressors, helpless old people a hated burden to their sons, and the whole world of loneliness, poverty, and pain makes a mockery of what human life should be. I long to alleviate the evil, but I cannot, and I too suffer.

This has been my life. I have found it worth living, and would gladly live it again if the chance were offered me.

Robert Sekuler

·········

FROM QUILL TO COMPUTER

Because it makes it easier both to produce and modify our writing, a word processor may also make it easier to find out what we think.

Every advance in technology manages somehow to transform the creative process. Improved fabrication of steel forms stimulated a new vision of architecture's possibilities. Developments in electronics gave musicians unimagined creative freedom and artistic control. Now, a relatively new technology, word processing, may be transforming the art of writing. It is too early to predict all the ways in which writing will change, but we can get some clues by looking at research in cognitive psychology and by studying the experiences of people who use word processors.

The range of available word processors is large. They vary in size from one small box weighing less than four pounds to a deskload of heavy equipment; their costs are similarly variable—from $1000 up to $20 000. But, basically, they are all the same: electronic devices that allow you to type, store, modify, and print text.

The differences between writing longhand, typing, and word processing are readily apparent even to the most reluctant first-time user of a word processor. Writing with paper and pencil is slow, laborious, and downright painful in time. Composing on a typewriter helps with speed and physical comfort, but correcting a typo, inserting a new sentence, or repositioning a paragraph requires messy erasure, fumbling with correction fluid, or "cutting and pasting"—physically relocating a misplaced paragraph with scissors and tape.

The word processor accomplishes these and several other tasks electronically, and consequently can transform writing in three distinct ways: it can ease the mechanical drudgery of writing; it can enhance our motivation and willingness to spend time writing; and it can produce qualitative changes in the way we go about writing.

Nearly all how-to books on writing stress the importance of revision, typically advising "revise, revise, and then revise some more." Many writers treasure the tools of revision—erasers, scissors, tape, correction fluid, and wastebasket—almost as much as they value the implements of production—

pencils, pens, and typewriters. But, while teaching freshmen composition a few years ago, I rediscovered what teachers of English have long known: most people have a strong aversion to revision. Teachers may deplore this reluctance to revise, but it is easily understood. Ordinarily, revision is both difficult and tedious.

A word processor certainly can make cleaning up typos, misspellings, and punctuation errors easy to do. But good prose, of course, is not just a collection of neatly displayed and properly constructed sentences; to lead the reader from one idea to the next, naturally and without hesitation, the writer must provide appropriate road signs—clear transitions and connections between sentences, paragraphs, and larger sections.

Though these transitions are often as hard to produce as the elements themselves, research has shown that readers (and writers) pay a price when writing does not flow smoothly. Marcel Just and Patricia Carpenter, cognitive psychologists at Carnegie-Mellon University, presented readers with two sentences—either adequately or inadequately linked—as in the following pair.

1. (a) It was dark and stormy the night the millionaire died.   •
   (b) The killer left no clues for the police to trace.
2. (a) It was dark and stormy the night the millionaire was murdered.
   (b) The killer left no clues for the police to trace.

As the participants read, Just and Carpenter tracked their eye movements and found that, on average, readers spent half a second less on the second pair of sentences than on the first pair. Why? In the second pair, the transition is clear: the writer uses the phrase "was murdered" in the first sentence to set the reader up for "the killer" in the second sentence. When transitions are missing, you must stop and mentally create them yourself—a distracting and time-consuming task. If you can imagine reading an entire article with sloppy connections not only between sentences but between paragraphs and collections of paragraphs, you can see why good transitions are so important.

How would a word processor help? As Peter Wason, a psychologist at University College, London, observes, "Writing is difficult for some people because they try to do two incompatible things at the same time: say something and say it in the most acceptable way." In *Writing with a Word Processor* William Zinsser suggests that you forget links and transitions initially. Concentrate instead on "letting your creative motor run the full course at full speed; repairs can always be made later." Following Zinsser's advice, you then mark each place where a transition might be needed (say, with an "XXX"). Later, you can instruct the word processor to locate each "XXX" and display the surrounding text, and then you can develop and insert the needed transitions. Many people, in fact, do the same thing when composing with pen, pencil, or typewriter, but the whole process is less convenient than it is with a word processor and therefore less likely to get done.

Word processors are also helpful because they make it easy to get a clean printed copy of your latest revision. Andrew Fluegelman and Jeremy Hewes, authors of *Writing in the Computer Age*, argue that getting clean copies on demand offers positive psychological benefits. The copy's attractive, professional appearance provides reinforcement: when you have been really struggling with the text, the clean copy holds out a promise of better times ahead. Also, the clean copy makes it easier for you to review the material as any other reader would, without interruptions from complex marginal notes and messy insertions and deletions.

Word processors make an important contribution, improving motivation not only during revision but also during the entire writing process. Once beginners overcome their fear and awe of word processors, they realize that these imposing gadgets can make writing more bearable for several reasons. For one, word processors eliminate one of the more perplexing obstacles for many writers—the blank sheet of paper that seems to stare back reprovingly. Some people claim that a blank word-processor screen actually evokes less terror than does a blank piece of paper. Since few word-processor screens display the equivalent of an entire 8 1/2-by-11 inch page, Fluegelman and Hewes say you can fill a screen faster than you can a sheet of paper, in effect dividing the chore into smaller, more manageable subtasks.

One friend of mine, however, is bothered less by a blank page or screen than by another common problem—writer's block. When he's stuck on one part of an article he must write, he quickly detours to another part that will be easier to complete. Not only does the detour give his writer's block sufficient time to work itself out, but when he's finally got all the parts completed and in place, the word processor can remove all telltale marks of the chaos from which his article emerged. Many people take similar detours when writing longhand or on a typewriter, but both methods tend to promote thinking in one direction—from a document's beginning to a document's end. Inserting material into something you've already written is possible but, again, not convenient.

Though the mechanical and motivational effects of the word processor are powerful in their own right, they may prove minor compared to one potential effect of this new technology: changing the way we think about the writing process itself. To appreciate this fully, we'll have to consider what creative writing is.

Many textbooks and teachers describe creative writing as a series of clearly defined steps. According to this view, you pick a manageable topic, do the required research, compose an outline, flesh out that outline, and, finally, polish what you have written. Though this view encourages the idea that writing can be taught and learned in simple and convenient chunks, many cognitive psychologists—and many successful writers—have a different understanding of the writing process.

The novelist E.M. Forster put it well, asking: "How do I know what I think until I see what I say?" Kurt Vonnegut makes the same point when he observes that when writing, he feels like someone who is "watching a teletype machine in a newspaper office to see what comes out." Fine, for the creative genius, you might say, but what about the average person?

Psychologists Linda Flower and John Hayes of Carnegie-Mellon University asked college students to write essays on women's rights or abortion and, at the same time, to describe aloud what they were doing. Their research suggests that good writers do not do as much detailed mental planning as we might think. In fact, Flower and Hayes found that writers often did not know precisely what they would write until they had written it.

Though these findings are somewhat discomforting, suppose that they are true. What are the implications for writing on a word processor? Because it makes it easier both to produce and to modify our writing, a word processor may also make it easier to find out what we think.

One way to understand this is to consider what Susan Horton, a professor of English at the University of Massachusetts, calls reformulation. In *Thinking Through Writing*, Horn likens revision to tinkering and reserves the term "reformulation" for significant changes in organization, structure, and clarity. Reformulation, then, is a form of creative play, requiring intuition and experimentation. Reviewing the text, you may feel that a change is needed at a particular place without knowing precisely what that change should be.

One way of resolving this dilemma is to ask a series of "what if" questions. This type of question has been popularized by computer programs, such as VisiCalc, used for financial planning. In such programs, the user enters all the relevant data and assumptions—for example, interest rates. You can then ask a "what if" question by telling the computer to recalculate its projections based on some changed assumption: what if interest rates rise, for example.

These programs encourage the same kind of playful, creative experimentation that an experienced word-processor user comes to depend on. You simply examine what you have already written and then try various "what ifs"—"What if I invert this sentence . . . move this paragraph . . . delete this phrase?" and so on. If you've made an improvement, it can be retained; if not, you can try again. By making alternative reorganizations more accessible, a word processor encourages you to experiment where you probably would not bother on a page of typed manuscript.

A word processor can certainly help an individual to write, but often writing involves collaboration with others. Though there haven't been any formal studies, in my experience a word processor can prove equally helpful when collaborating with another author.

When Randy Blake, a colleague at Northwestern, and I collaborated on a textbook, we divided the chapters between us and worked separately to prepare very rough first drafts. When a rough draft was ready, we sat down together at one word processor, using one keyboard but two display screens so that each of us had an unimpeded view of the action. Then we took turns reading aloud, revising and reorganizing the text in tandem. The idea was to encourage joint work before the text had become too polished and therefore resistant to change. Working together in this way, we generated far more "what if" questions than we would have singly. The result is a text that not only reads well (we're told) but appears to be seamless; reviewers say they can't tell who wrote what.

There's little doubt that, when used properly, a word processor can be a valuable tool for writing. But like all stories, this one has another side that should not be ignored. Some writers become so entranced by these devices that the new-found power to revise turns into an obsession. When that happens, the word processor tends to resemble its counterpart in the kitchen—the food processor. Perhaps you know, as I do, cooks who can't resist using their marvellous toy, so that everything they create is sure to be very well sliced, diced, or pureed.

There's a lesson here, not just for cooks and writers, but for all of us. No matter how powerful the technology we may have to help us, we still need good judgment and self-control.

Alan
Stewart
· · · · · · · · ·

Watch Out For The Lure Of Holden

Although he had a certain charm, Holden was clearly a nut.

Holden Caulfield, the hero of J.D. Salinger's *The Catcher in the Rye*, is a sensitive victim of a mendacious and corrupt society. Endearingly vulnerable and neo-picaresque, he typifies adolescent disaffiliation concordant with rebellious refusal of initiation. He is Christ-like, with a quality of self-heedlessness that is nearly saintly, and he turns his naked vision on the world, finding it devoid of peace, charity, and honesty. Withdrawn, yet quixotic, with the fragile innocence of a Huckleberry Finn, ironically but aptly coupled with the gorgeous-yet-damned quality that is almost Gatsby-like, Holden sacrifices his stigmatic blood to indelibly etch . . .

Enough. If you've been halfway awake for any of the 30 years since Holden pouted into print, you can write the rest yourself. Just remember to rely heavily on such terms as alienation, sensitive, and picaresque. You may have had to already, because, after *Of Mice and Men*, *The Catcher in the Rye* is the most frequently taught novel in high schools, and has probably had as many essays written about it as summer vacations. I have never studied it myself, but when I was a teacher I did put it on the reading list once. It went over big with the class, although no one could think of much to say about it or about Holden, and class discussions were little more than group gum-chewing sessions. Occasionally, a student would mutter something like, "Well, Holden is, you know, like, sort of neat."

What can you say about Holden anyway? For one thing, neat is definitely what he is not. In fact, he is a real mess, but a mess in a typically adolescent way, and perhaps this is why adolescents have pounced on him with such collective zest over the years.

However, even as an adolescent myself, I felt nervous reading his snobbish pronouncements. Holden seemed to divide the world into two groups. He was in one group, along with a few other people such as his little sister,

---

NOTE: Also read "When Men Refuse to Grow Up" by Judith Finlayson on page 98.

Phoebe, and Jesus; everyone else was in the other group, the phony vulgarians who sleep with their mouths open and pretend to be scratching their noses when they are actually picking them. I had a feeling that Holden would not include me in his group. I felt Phoebe had it right when she told him, "You don't like anything."

It seemed to me that, although Holden's life was no roaring hell, to use a term in vogue when I read the book, he was ever ready to sit in judgment on the rest of the world, dismissing us in a manner both intolerant and harsh. I felt that I, too, was as sensitive as hell, but I did not keep flunking out of prep school, or run away to New York City to have picaresque adventures, or end up in the bin out West. So, I had to be one of the vulgarians.

Although he had a certain charm, Holden was clearly a nut, or disturbed, as we say nowadays. After all, the action of the book is recollected by him later, and he refers to it as the "madman stuff that happened to me around Christmas." I think this is another clue to his appeal. For some reason, it seems, most of us who plod through life paying our bills, flossing daily, and calling our parents at dutiful intervals, like nothing better than wallowing in accounts of those who are too crazy or too sensitive, or both, to behave similarly.

This lure of the lunatic appears often in fiction, and it is a popular convention to regard the insane as somehow closer to reality than the rest of us. Certainly, Holden is not the only neurotic hero to enjoy the approval of the saner majority. Anyone familiar with mental illness, as either participant or observer, has little sympathy with the presentation of the lunatic as wise seer.

Avoid people who seem to regard the insane as open lines from God. And avoid people who tell you how much they identify with Holden. If you are a woman getting to know a man, and after a good dinner he takes you back to his place for coffee and brandy and gets into that old sensitivity ploy about how much he relates to people like Mother Teresa and Holden Caulfield, get a cab immediately. If you can't get a cab, run, lady.

Lesley
Visser
....
A LOCKER ROOM WITH A VIEW

If society accepts the premise that women in this country can command troops in Saudi Arabia, make policy in Congress, and sit on the Supreme Court, then it's hard to argue about their license to cover sports.

The first time I entered a men's locker room, I was 22—and terrified. My mother, a high-school English teacher, had attended Catholic high school and Catholic college. My father, raised in the Netherlands, had no notion what a sportswriter was. The idea that I would willingly walk into a room full of naked men appalled them beyond belief. In truth, it alarmed me, too. But I knew, as one of the original half-dozen women who first covered sports in this country, that it was a battlefield I'd eventually have to face.

This initiation, however, did not take place in the major leagues. It was 1976, when there were so few women reporters following pro football that locker-room access wasn't even an issue yet. In my main assignment, covering the New England Patriots, after the game I was left to interview players in the parking lot under the rain and snow and sleet—and the icy stares of wives, who wondered what I could possibly be doing hanging around their husband's cars.

But I was also assigned to cover World Team Tennis, and a team called the Boston Lobsters—desperate for coverage and blessed with a progressive owner—didn't care if I went into the locker room after a match. The coach was a crazy Romanian, Ion Tiriac, and he was all for being on the cutting edge. Even so, I remember having a near anxiety attack the first time I had to enter their sacred enclosure. I tried to memorize all the questions I needed to ask, lest I be in the position of glancing around while trying to collect my thoughts. I kept the notebook poised a myopic four inches from my face. And I stared straight into every player's eyes—never below them—with the maniacal intensity of a Charles Manson. Tiriac wasn't the least bit unnerved. He shrugged his shoulders when I came in, put a towel around his waist, and continued to answer questions in six or seven different languages.

The events of the past few months have taught us that not everyone in pro sports shares Tiriac's attitude. Back in September, Lisa Olson, a sportswriter for the *Boston Herald*, was allegedly harassed by members of the New England Patriots in a manner that would be unacceptable in a boardroom, operating room, classroom, or any other place of employment. According to Olson, she was sitting next to one of the players at his locker, conducting an interview, when several naked Patriots approached her, positioning themselves inches from her face and daring her to touch their private parts.

Initially, Olson continued to do her job and tried to handle the paralyzing event through her editor and through the team, but it soon became public knowledge, and she was forced to relive the experience on network television—everything from "Prime Time Live" to "Good Morning America." Because the incident involved two of America's favourite topics, football and sex, controversy soon swept the nation, polarizing people and confusing the issue. When Olson's answering machine filled up with messages every three minutes—often with death threats—she had to get an unlisted number. Finally, she fled to the Caribbean. And even there, she was recognized on the beach.

The commissioner of the National Football League, Paul Tagliabue, appointed a special counsel to investigate the incident; at the same time, Olson quit covering the Patriots and switched to the Boston Celtics. The Patriot players continued to deny their involvement. Days after Olson's travail, there was a second incident: Cincinnati Bengals coach Sam Wyche barred a woman reporter from his locker room, saying, "I'm not doing that to the guys. I'm not doing it to their wives."

Of the hundreds of television and radio shows about the Olson case that I either participated in or listened to, it became clear that most people in America weren't certain just what the issue was. First of all, they weren't aware that being in a locker room is actually only about 10 percent of our job. No matter how many years women have been in the business, no matter how many glorious World Series or dramatic Super Bowls we've covered (the game itself, after all, is the reason we wanted to be sportswriters or sports broadcasters in the first place), everyone's initial question seems to be, "Do you go in the locker room?"

Moreover, the American public had absolutely no concept of what a locker room is like. Well, here's what a locker room *isn't*: It isn't a singles' bar, some sort of Chippendales where 47 men parade around naked, hoping to stir a woman's erotic longing. It's a hot, stuffy chamber, usually in the basement of a stadium, with metal chairs, rolls of tape, and the smell of liniment. It's piles of towels and cans of soda. In the case of baseball, it's often clusters of players standing around a buffet table, eating the insides of sandwiches and throwing the rest away.

The locker room is a kind of fraternity, a comfortable cave where physically gifted men can pad around clothed or unclothed, intimidating each other and the press. In this world, no one thinks it's unusual to see a 30-year-old man play a shaving-cream joke on someone even older than he is.

I remember a basketball-playoff game between the Celtics and the Los Angeles Lakers in the middle of June in the Boston Garden; 25 reporters were pressed against each other in 95-degree heat, trying to get a quote from Lakers forward James Worthy, who was sitting quietly at his locker. Diane K. Shah, then a columnist for the *Los Angeles Herald Examiner*, turned to me, sweat dripping down her face, and said, "We fought for the right to get in here?"

Yes, we did, because the locker room is the place of business after a game. It's where professional athletes and professional reporters review the day's work, where the writers gather anecdotes and capture the emotions of a game. So the real issue in Lisa Olson's case was the violation of her right to be treated with dignity in the workplace.

It wasn't the first time a woman reporter said she had been verbally brutalized in the locker room. Last August, a pitcher for the Detroit Tigers named Jack Morris behaved inexcusably when Jennifer Frey, an intern for the *Detroit Free Press*, approached him for a story. Morris told her that he wouldn't "talk to a woman when I'm naked . . ." And in 1986, outfielder David Kingman of the Oakland Athletics sent a gift-wrapped rat to Susan Fornoff, a highly regarded reporter for the *Sacramento Bee*.

All of us who have lasted more than five years in this business have learned to absorb a certain number of such insults. I think we develop a kind of scar tissue that makes the next humiliation a little easier to take. I got my own lesson in learning to be tough in 1980, while covering the Cotton Bowl, one of the premier events in college football. The University of Houston beat the University of Nebraska on the last play of the game and all of the reporters filed into the locker room to capture the stunning emotional aftermath. Along with 15 or 20 other scribes, all male, I was interviewing the Houston quarterback when suddenly Bill Yeoman, the head coach, screamed out from across the room, "I don't give a damn about the Equal Rights Amendment." With that, he marched me through the room and forced me out the door. Embarrassed and crushed, I kept saying to myself, as all the cameras shifted in my direction, "Oh, please, just don't let me cry on the five o'clock news."

Why do locker-room incidents happen? These players, after all, are professional men who earn more money than half the CEO's in New York, Chicago, or Los Angeles; they have some responsibility for dealing courteously with the ink-stained wretches and microphone-wielding labourers of the world. Besides, any smart athlete knows that women are protected by the 14th amendment of the Constitution and by league policy. In other words, we have a right to do our job.

I have a theory, which I tested on some male friends. I think many men can't believe that for us, being in a locker room is not a sexual experience.

That's because the same might not be true for them. When the Lisa Olson dispute occurred, a number of men said to me, "Hey, I'd like to be in a locker room looking at Chris Evert" (as their eyebrows flew up and down). Boys grow up reading *Playboy*; naked equals sexual is the message they get. Frank Deford, editor-in-chief of the *National*, was honest enough to write that "women don't look when they're in men's locker rooms. No, they glimpse. Men would not look, either, if they were allowed in women's locker rooms. No, our eyes would dwell. That is a major difference." (For the record, all members of the media are allowed into both men's and women's locker rooms at the U.S. Open Tennis Championship in Flushing Meadow, New York, as they are at the women's NCAA basketball championship.)

One of my colleagues at CBS Sports, announcer Tim Ryan, has another hypothesis. He claims that discomfort regarding women in the locker room is more about "ancient cultural hang-ups" than blatant sexuality: "I think most American men are embarrassed about nudity, which has more to do with puritanical attitudes about our bodies than with sexism toward women."

And speaking of puritanism, this does seem to be a time of growing conservatism in this country. An ex-Ku Klux Klan imperial wizard-turned-Republican, David Duke, wins 44 percent of a Senate vote in Louisiana. A court order is needed to exhibit the photographs of Robert Mapplethorpe. And former victims of prejudice may be guilty of prejudice themselves: At least one black player was allegedly involved in the Olson incident, prompting Ira Berkow of the *New York Times* to write, "There was a time when he would not have been allowed into a professional-football locker room. There was a colour barrier in the National Football League until 1946, but it has since been knocked down. And right-minded people cheered."

Not all coaches and players feel that women don't belong. "It doesn't take a very intelligent person to put on a towel or a bathrobe after a game," commented Boomer Esiason, quarterback for the Cincinnati Bengals. "The onus should be on the players to take proper steps to cover themselves. It's my problem, not the reporter's problem." Don Shula, coach of the Miami Dolphins, said of women reporters, "They're professional, they're credentialed, they belong." Perhaps these athletes or coaches have known sisters, wives, or girlfriends who've struggled in the workplace for equal opportunity and equal pay.

There have been suggestions that an alternative to the locker room be arranged: a separate postgame interview area open to all members of the media. The trouble is, past experiments with such "classroom" setups have proven to be sterile affairs that produce canned and boring revelations. The solution could be much simpler: namely, good manners. Says Michele Himmelberg, president of the Association for Women in Sports Media, "For years, women have done their job without incident. Now, all of a sudden, players forgot how to be discreet?"

I've come to wonder, too, why this is an issue only in the world of sports. I've never heard the claim that women who pose nude for art classes represent a threat to decency, or that Calvin Klein or Giorgio Armani leers at runway models as they change their clothes backstage. If society accepts the premise that women in this country can command troops in Saudi Arabia, make policy in Congress, and sit on the Supreme Court, then it's hard to argue about their license to cover sports. In the end, when people ask us, "What's a nice girl like you doing in a locker room?" we'll try to smile and say, "We're working."

RESPONDING TO THE ESSAY

1. In your Response Notebook, react to an essay's style and structure.

Tip • See also "Suggestions for Personal Response" on page 183.

2. Working alone or in small groups, compose questions and activities which cue readers' responses to an essay. Exchange work and complete several suggested activities.

Tip • For ideas, see the conference sheets on pages 185 to 186.

3. Compare two essayists' handling of the same topic, considering which treatment you prefer and the implications for your own essay writing. You and a partner might prepare a tipsheet summarizing your findings.

4. Note characteristics of an essayist's voice you enjoy—stylistic elements which create energy and uniqueness. What might you learn from this writer about projecting your own voice?

Tip • Ask a partner to help determine the characteristics of your voice. Then write a letter to the author about your learning; or express important facets of your writer's voice in a mask.

5. Working independently or with a partner, evaluate an essay using a checklist you've devised or refer to pages 185 to 186. Justify each response with specific textual references.

6. Reflect your understanding of an essay by presenting its ideas or your response to them in another form, for example, a poem, cartoon, skit, role-play, parody, eulogy, collage, script, interview, letter, videotape, radio play, or song.

Tip • See suggestions on pages 189 to 190.

7. With a partner, devise and teach a lesson plan for an essay. Include various approaches to accommodate different learning styles.

Tip • See Resource One on page 178.

8. Research a bibliography for use in the study of a theme or author you enjoy.

9. (Re)read aloud an essay, considering phrasing you enjoy. Compose and tape a sound poem, or create a collage of words and images expressing how you might enliven your diction.

10. Create a poster or three-dimensional object depicting an effective essay's structure and organization through shapes and symbols. Plan an outline for an essay using a similar structure.

11. Compare several thematic treatments; for example, consider an essay, a short story, a film, and a poem about friendship. Express your reactions in an imaginative form.

Tip • ***See the "Guide to Themes" on page 209.***

12. In small groups, prepare an in-role panel discussion in which several essayists discuss their work and offer tips to student writers; or role-play an interview about composing strategies involving several essayists and novelists.

Part Three

RESOURCES

A Potpourri Of Guides And Tips

Like the students who helped prepare this book, you'll probably discover these resources may be used independently, with small peer groups, or under teacher direction. Each resource is a distinct but interrelated package inviting you to explore strategies to strengthen learning or communication. Its purpose is to help you become an independent learner prepared for a lifetime of challenges.

Resource One:
The Autonomous Learner

As a senior student with competing demands for your time and interests, you may ask, "Why does learning matter?" or "How can I use my time economically?" To begin, you might reflect in your Response Notebook about the extent to which your actions demonstrate several of the following traits commonly exhibited by successful learners:

- flexibility
- self-awareness
- responsibility
- decisiveness

- sensitivity
- reflectiveness
- motivation
- curiosity

- persistence
- organization

To acquire or refine such traits, explore strategies from these resources. Discover what works best for you by keeping an open mind, setting reasonable long- and short-term goals, and experimenting with suggestions.

We've discovered no universal recipe for learning. In fact, no two people learn in precisely the same way. For example, you may learn best by *seeing* material, but your friend may need to *hear* it, and your little brother may prefer to *participate*. To explore your learning style and its implications, see "Learning in Style" (page 192).

Regardless of their learning style, however, most people benefit from developing sound work and study skills. You and several peers might begin by composing a tipsheet for building these skills. Then compare it with the following checklist or invite a representative from your school's Student Services or Special Education Department to visit your class.

Work and Study Habits

1. Keep a daily planner.

2. Study in a quiet, well-stocked work area at approximately the same time each day.

3. Once an hour take a brief "stretch" break.

4. Develop reliable study strategies. For example:

   - peruse titles, headings, topic and concluding sentences, and chapter summaries
   - devise queries
   - pinpoint main ideas and supporting evidence
   - write summary notes (or annotate a text you own)

   Student Tip • "Finish reading a piece of work before taking notes; this discourages you from copying word for word." *Alice Ho, Alpha Secondary School, Burnaby, B.C.*

   - review material and relate it to previous learning

5. Allocate plenty of time for exam review.

   Student Tip • "Set goals. If you know what's important for your future, you'll be more likely to control your procrastination." *Ender Cheung, Sir Winston Churchill High School, Calgary, Alberta*

   - post a study schedule
   - ask about question types and weighting
   - annotate your notes
   - summarize information on titled cards
   - doodle visual associations
   - invite a classmate to "test" you
   - devise sample (essay) questions and answers
   - review common instructional verbs

6. During a test or exam, skim the entire paper before beginning. Highlight the marking scheme and key instructional words and divide your time according to the marking scheme.

   - answer in standard formal English
   - proofread your work

Guide to Independent Study

If your course includes a project for independent study, the strategies outlined here may help you get organized. Collaborating with a partner and the teacher enhances your chances of success.

To design a project, brainstorm ideas associated with instructional verbs, then "match" them with items from the product list. Or adapt a project from the generic independent study topics.

Sample Instructional Verbs

assess	design	research	survey
build	enact	review	videotape
create	interview	rewrite	write
debate	justify	sculpt	

Sample Products List

anthology	fable	puppet
article	fairy tale	questionnaire
autobiography	invention	scrapbook
ballad	journal	script
biography	legend	seminar
case study	letter	short story
crossword puzzle	magazine	slides
dial-a-lecture	memoir	speech
documentary	mobile	story-board
editorial	play	storytelling
epilogue	portfolio	transcript
essay	profile	yarn

Generic Independent Study Projects

1. Prepare an exhibit for a booth at your school's Parents' Night. Your project should include visual information about how studying the essay has enhanced your writing potential.

2. In the role of an essayist whose work you've admired, write journal entries which demonstrate your knowledge of the individual's contributions to thought and style. Append a commentary in which you speculate on how the writer's work may help clarify personal goals.

3. Compile a community resource file of volunteers who will share their on-the-job writing experiences with senior students.

4. Compile a resource for future students—perhaps a dictionary of key terms and concepts or a jackdaw or set of flashcards—which reflects your learning about the essay.

5. Plan and implement a Letter to the Editor campaign about an important political or social issue raised by one or more essays.

6. After reading a work of non-fiction prose, design a project with your teacher. For example, write a review or compare the book and film versions of a work such as *Out of Africa*.

7. Create a Hall of Fame for essayists who have made significant contributions to the genre.

8. Develop an on-line set of "We Recommend" mini-reviews of non-fiction prose works.

Your working plan may include the following four stages which you and your teacher may adapt to your needs.

Stage I: Probing
• brainstorm options
• clarify your project's WHAT + HOW + with WHOM and WHEN you'll collaborate
• problem-solve with peers and your teacher

Stage II: Creating
• read, research, and note-take
• record responses
• problem-solve with peers and your teacher

Stage III: Presenting
• prepare and present an imaginative reflection of your learning
• invite and respond to questions

Stage IV: Reflecting
• record reflections on the experience, pondering your strengths and weaknesses and future improvements

RESOURCE TWO:
READING AND WRITING STRATEGIES

An effective reader employs a repertoire of strategies. For example, when reading for pleasure, you may snuggle into bed and listen to your Walkman. But reading for information and ideas requires a critical eye. With essays, especially *argumentation* and *persuasion*, experiment with these guidelines.

The Critical Essay Reader

Warming up: Assemble a pencil, highlighter, and notebook.
• What queries does the title raise?
• What do you know about the author?
• What do you know about this topic?

First reading: Note surprising, interesting, or perplexing aspects.
• Compose a written reaction in your Response Notebook. For assistance, see "Suggestions for Personal Response" on page 183.

Close reading: After completing the following steps, you may wish to extend your initial response entry.
• Paraphrase the thesis or unifying idea.
• Identify the essay's main or skeletal ideas.
• Scrutinize supporting detail or illustration, such as dates, statistics, places, names, allusions, anecdotes, case studies, expert quotations, references to research, publication titles, and so on.

Student Tip • "The principal ideas in essays are seldom extraordinary. It's the author's use of detail, the way he or she has related the idea to your life, that determines its power and profundity." *Alyssa Becker, Sir Winston Churchill High School, Calgary, Alberta*

• Note bias; be alert for undecipherable jargon and illogical or unwarranted comparisons and phrases such as "in my opinion," "everyone knows," and "it's a fact."
• Assess the essay's credibility and overall impact.
• Reflect on the essay's interest and importance for understanding yourself and your world.

You, the Writer

Now, let's move on to writing—a demanding but rewarding activity. As with other aspects of learning, there's no "one right way" to go about strengthening written expression. The remainder of this resource focuses on specific strategies which help you complete writing tasks often required of senior students. It's writing which:

• requires sophisticated thinking
• invites substantiated personal response (that is, you must justify or explain ideas)
• focuses on argumentation.

The following suggestions and checklists may help you accomplish these tasks.

The Writing Variables
- *Purpose*   Why am I writing this piece?
- *Audience*   Who are my anticipated readers?
- *Tone*   What is my attitude towards the subject?
- *Mood*   What (emotional) response do I want to create?
- *Language* What language level and type of diction will create the mood?
- *Voice*   Should I express my writer's voice or aim for a neutral presentation?

Response writing is a first step for developing clear writing which reflects your own voice. Personal responses are neither "right" nor "wrong." Your Response Notebook will likely be evaluated for thoughtfulness, detail, and willingness to experiment with forms and probe ideas. Read, reflect, and write without undue concern for punctuation and grammar.

Suggestions for Personal Response
One of the following sentence lead-ins may help you begin.
- This sentence makes me think about . . .
- I wonder why . . .
- As I read this essay, I felt/thought/imagined . . .
- This anecdote reminds me of the time that I . . .
- I like/dislike the idea that . . .
- The essayist seems to feel/think that . . .
- I am surprised by . . .
- If I were the writer, I would have . . .
- From this author's use of language I learned that . . .
- The structure of this essay shows me how to . . .

Consider experimenting with a variety of forms.

- poems (ballads, limericks, haiku, free verse)
- letters (to the author, an elected representative, the newspaper editor, a television station, a friend)
- interior monologue (the author or a character from an anecdote)
- collages, cartoons, or line drawings
- surveys, questionnaires, or interviews
- diary entries, obituaries, or profiles
- "slice of life" short-stories or skits or vignettes

To practise response writing and reflect on the composing process, you may wish to react to one or more statements and tips.

Famous Quotations for Response
Getting Ideas
• "The best time for planning a book is when you're doing the dishes."
Agatha Christie

Student Tip • "Don't be afraid to use up lots of paper and make a mess when you brainstorm. Some of my best ideas come after four pages of writing about what I *think* my topic is." *Clara Cristofaro, Alpha Secondary School, Burnaby, B.C.*

Audience
• "A writer's problem . . . is always how to write truly and . . . to project it in such a way that it becomes a part of the experience of the . . . [reader]."
Ernest Hemingway

The First Draft
• ". . . bad writing can be revised, [but] white paper can't be helped at all."
Robert Fulford

Student Tip • "After completing the first draft, it's always wise to go back over your work and create options. Experiment with several different opening and closing sentences for each paragraph. Then try combining short sentences, or breaking up long ones." *Julie Anne Abbott, Sir Winston Churchill High School, Calgary, Alberta*

Revising and Editing
• "In composing, as a general rule, run your pen through every other word you have written; you have no idea what vigor it will give your style."
Sydney Smith

Student Tip • "When revising your work, it's vital to eliminate words, phrases, and even paragraphs which do not contribute directly to the thesis or objective." *Tom Borugian, Alpha Secondary School, Burnaby, B.C.*

Peer Conferences
• "No passion in the world is equal to the passion to alter someone else's draft." *H.G. Wells*

Since your attitudes, habits, and emotions influence your writing almost as much as skills and knowledge, it's wise to reflect in your Response Notebook on yourself as a writer. Then you may wish to check your work for perceptions about the following issues.

Your Writer's Mind Map
• childhood writing experiences
• getting started
• peer editors
• collaborative writing

- process of thinking and writing
- topics
- peer conference processes

- strengths and problem areas
- reading habits and preferences
- self-evaluation

Another important strategy for becoming a strong writer is the peer conference. Your teacher may ask the class to brainstorm suggestions for conference etiquette. Your tipsheet might look something like this one.

Conference Tips for Peer Editors

1. Treat your partner's work with respect.

2. Determine who will read the writing aloud.

3. Decide where to place comments, for example, on the draft or a separate conference sheet.

   Tip • Use pencil, not red ink.

4. Ask your partner how he or she *feels* about the piece.

5. Invite your partner to pick the initial focus, for example, clarity of ideas, use of examples, or "show, don't tell" techniques.

6. Offer tactful comments, beginning with the strong points. For example, "I really like . . . " or "I admire. . . ." Then suggest improvements. For example, "How would you feel about resequencing paragraphs three and four? The flow doesn't work for me."

7. Summarize your comments, ending on a positive note.

   Student Tip • " 'This paper is good' may spare a writer's feelings but it doesn't explain *what* is 'good' and what still needs work. If you receive a vague comment, ask your partner questions which will direct her or him towards the answers you need." *Phuong Ngo, Sir Winston Churchill High School, Calgary, Alberta*

If you're asked to develop criteria to guide conferences, the following samples may help you complete this task.

Sample Conference Sheet for Peer Editors (Generic Essay)

1. The Thesis Statement
   - clear and concise
   - significant claim/assertion
   - partner's suggestions

2. The Evidence
   - reputable/reliable sources

- appropriate "show, don't tell" techniques
  - –statistics
  - –quotations
  - –titles (e.g., film and print)
  - –personal opinion
  - –comparison/contrast
  - –figurative language
  - –dates and/or places
  - –dialogue
  - –anecdotes
  - –allusions
  - –definition(s)
  - –rhetorical devices

3. The Structure and Organization
   - introduction
   - body
     - –paragraphs with opening sentence, "meat" or filling, and closing sentence
     - –logical or effective sequencing
     - –transitions
   - conclusion

4. The Expression
   - type and level of language appropriate for
     - –purpose and audience
     - –consistent tone and mood

5. The Overall Impact/Impression
   - interest
   - imagination
   - energy

RESOURCE THREE:
SPEAKING AND LISTENING TECHNIQUES

Why does dynamic speech matter? According to Laura Dariius, president of the Center for Speech Arts in New York City, "sloppy or unsophisticated" speech creates a negative impression about your intelligence, manners, and perhaps even values. Fluent speech may help you win that school election or even impress a member of the opposite sex. In small groups, compose tips to enhance your "speech image," whether you're interviewing for the school paper or a job, or delivering a class presentation. Then compare your list with the tipsheet which follows.

The Dynamic Speaker

1. Adopt an authoritative vocal tone and body posture which says "I'm worth listening to!"

2. Speak in a moderate tone, varying your pace and pitch.

3. Keep your voice level at the end of each sentence; unless you're truly asking a question, don't "rise."

4. Avoid babble by speaking in "thought groups" of about half a dozen words each.

5. Employ crisp, careful diction; don't lose those "ings" or resort to "junk" words such as "um" and "huh."

   Tip • If facilities permit, ask a classmate to videotape a practice session. You'll be able to assess your performance before delivering that important seminar.

The other side of this communication link is, of course, masterful listening. Simultaneously talking on the phone, watching television, and perusing a magazine invite lazy listening habits. Working with a partner, list strategies for listening to class presentations. Then peruse the checklist which follows.

The Active Listener
1. Acknowledge the speaker's message. For example, nod, lean forward, make eye contact.

2. Develop a personal shorthand for note-taking.

3. Organize information under headings and subheadings, highlighting main ideas and distinguishing between fact and opinion.

4. Jot down queries and responses.

5. Keep an open mind.

   Tip • For additional skill-building advice, read the essay "Listen Up! Enhancing Our Listening Skills" on page 202.

   Student Tip • "Look directly at the speaker and concentrate on his or her voice, not the rustling papers and whispering." *Christopher Li, Alpha Secondary School, Burnaby B.C.*

Chances are you'll be assigned a collaborative or individual class presentation. The following hints will get you started. For more detailed information, consult your teacher-librarian.

The Class Presentation
1. Clarify details such as the topic, length, date, and evaluation criteria with your teacher.

2. If you're part of a group, select a responsible leader to organize and coordinate individual tasks and track progress. Exchange phone numbers. Your teacher will likely ask each person to keep his or her own notes.

3. Gather your material. On index cards, note the book's title and publication data. Use one card per topic with the heading clearly printed across the top. Record quotes and the page numbers accurately. Then compile a summary of your points.

4. Prepare an outline for the class. Ask your teacher about photocopying individual copies or showing an overhead transparency.

5. Visualization exercises help you relax.

6. When presenting, *don't read* your work. Follow the tips for effective speaking suggested earlier in this resource.

7. Invite the class's questions and respond succinctly.

Tip • Consult with your teacher to determine the appropriateness of enlivening your presentation with dramatic techniques. See pages 189 to 190 for suggestions.

An effective presentation meets standard criteria. In a practice run, you might invite a classmate to score each of the following areas as *S (strong)*, *A (average)*, or *W (needs work)*. Or you may wish to compose your own checklist.

Evaluating the Oral Presentation
- imaginative handling
- on topic
- general ideas and supporting detail
- brief quotations
- organized
- audio visual resources
- dynamic delivery
- audience participation
- standard, formal English

Student Tip • "I find the most effective way to prepare a seminar is to imagine that I'm having a personal conversation with each student. When presenters sound like the *Brittanica Encyclopedia Power Set* and the *Oxford Dictionary of Science Terms*, they're guaranteed to lose their friends' attention —and bore the teacher, too." *Nicole Ruddy, Alpha Secondary School, Burnaby, B.C.*

The key to effective speaking and active listening is building core skills which help you advance in and beyond school. Oral communication *works for you*—if you help it along!

RESOURCE FOUR: REPRESENTING— DRAMATIC TECHNIQUES AND THE ESSAY

Employing dramatic techniques will enrich your study of the essay. Consult with your teacher to determine which of the following suggestions are appropriate for your course.

Dramatic Strategies

Tip • Enhance your work with appropriate music and lighting.

1. Introduce a group seminar with a brief role-play, tableau, freeze-frame, or mime which dramatizes an essay's thesis.

2. Represent an essay's tone or mood with one of the above techniques. The teacher and your classmates may then interview each participant about his or her role.

3. With a partner, assume the roles of the essayist and an interviewer on a television talk show. Explore relevant issues about thought, style, and structure, or invite several "writers" to compare their work.

4. Divide a narrative essay into sections, each of which represents one anecdote or step in the essay's development. Present the essay through role-play or mime.

5. In small groups, perform pantomimes or tableaux representing words and phrases from one or more essays and invite classmates to "guess the word."

6. Compose a vignette which dramatizes your responses to an argumentative essay. Present it to the class.

   Tip • For "how-to" advice, see Bob Barton's *Tell Me Another: Storytelling and Reading Aloud at Home, at School, and in the Community* (Markham: Pembroke Publishers, 1986).

7. Recreate a narrative essay in a live storytelling session. Perform, don't read.

8. Give a dramatic reading of a speech or persuasive essay.

9. To review for a test, in small groups perform pantomimes depicting an essay's thesis or subject. Invite classmates to identify the source.

10. Use mime, creative movement, and evocative music to "get inside" a writing style.

11. Retell a narrative, enact the conflict of argumentation, or capture the passion of persuasion through tableaux, sock puppets, or pantomime. Accompany the "action" with a live or taped text which captures the essayist's thesis or unifying idea.

12. With a partner, role-play a debate between a controversial essayist and a critical reader or reviewer.

Once you become accustomed to performing for and with your classmates, you'll probably discover additional dramatic techniques to expand your appreciation of essays.

RESOURCE FIVE:
TOWARDS MEDIA LITERACY

Let's face it—most of us watch a great deal of television. We also consume popular culture from mass-market magazines and newspapers, films and rock videos, the radio, and billboards. We can, to some extent, control these forces' impact on our values and lifestyle if we build skills for thoughtful media use. The material in this resource, along with essays about the media in "Perspectives," will help you accomplish this goal.

You might begin by composing a survey about viewing habits for use with peers. Consider the inclusion of issues such as those suggested below.

Thinking about Television Viewing
1. Current weekly viewing time

2. Childhood viewing patterns

3. Types of programs viewed. For example: sitcoms, soaps, action-adventure shows, rock videos, cultural programs, documentaries, news, talk shows, game shows, sports, "yellow journalism"

4. Perceived impact of television on values and lifestyle. For example: heroes, food and beverage preferences, reading habits, clothes, and music

5. Traits of a discriminating viewer. For example: skeptical of claims; distinguishes between fact and opinion and objective and subjective presentation; evidence supports claims; notes appeals to the emotions; searches for hidden biases; seeks "expert's" credentials; notes sex-role stereotyping

Chances are that your language arts program offers opportunities to view and discuss films related to your literary studies. The following information may help you compose a personal response or a formal film review.

Responding to Film

Watch the film closely, perhaps more than once. Then consider:

1. Title and information about the director and other creators

2. Type of film. For example: comedy, western, horror, action-adventure, melodrama

3. Summary statement about the film's effectiveness (your thesis statement)

4. Specific references to strengths and weaknesses of:

- characterization as depicted by cast
- setting and atmosphere
- conflicts and plot
- sequencing and pacing
- unity and cohesiveness (editing)
- sound track
- photography
- themes
- emotional satisfaction
- other work by the director, producer, or cast members

Films for Media Study

Source: *Films and Videos for Language Arts, Grades 7—13*, NFB Resources. For information call:

- Atlantic Canada   1-800-561-7104
- Quebec   1-800-363-0328
- Ontario   1-800-267-7710
- Western and Northern Canada   1-800-661-9867

Video Kits

Media and Society Video Package: A four-hour resource which examines the effects of media on our society. 193C0189 123

Images and Meaning: A nine-part anthology of NFB productions which stimulate discussion and learning about media literacy. C0186 147

ADDITIONAL READING

The essays on pages 192 to 208 may help you build important skills.

Lorene
Hanley
Duquin
·········

LEARNING IN STYLE

My friend Sheila was an ideal student. She always paid attention in class and got good grades in every subject. She took notes and asked questions. She never forgot her homework. She did well on quizzes. Teachers loved her. She could never understand why I was bored a lot, disliked certain teachers, and hated some subjects—like math and science—with a passion. I said school was the problem. She said I was.

Until recently most schools were on her side. High school was basically taught one way, and that's the way students were supposed to learn. But education experts now say that's wrong. The latest research shows that there's more than just one way to learn, and students are definitely *not* the same.

Take Sheila and me. She's logical and fact-oriented—an active learner. She loves doing labs and projects. I'm the exact opposite—the quintessential dreamer. I rely on imagination and intuition, and I drove teachers crazy because I was always talking when I was supposed to be listening.

Our different way of doing things has nothing to do with how intelligent we are, but it has a lot to do with how we responded to school and teachers. Sheila was always considered a good student. Although my grades weren't bad, I was usually considered a troublemaker.

The recent explosion of research on how the brain processes information has done a lot to explain our differences. It has also opened up new ways to make learning easier and more fun. One of the pioneers in the field, Bernice McCarthy, Ph.D., has determined that students actually fall into four different groups: Imaginative Learners, Analytic Learners, Commonsense Learners, and Dynamic Learners. (Gender doesn't play a role—there are an equal number of boys and girls in each group.) These categories aren't rigid —you may feel you have characteristics of more than one type—but they do describe dramatically different ways of learning.

Here's how learning styles work:

Learning Style One: The Imaginative Learner
Jill Sullivan, seventeen, likes to sit and think, but in a subjective way. She gets gut feelings about things and has a vivid imagination. Jill likes to listen to class lectures and to read, "but then I try to figure out how the information fits into my own life," she says, "and why it's important for me to learn it."

Jill also really likes class discussions and brainstorming sessions. She generally bases her opinions on experience—her own and other peoples'. Her favourite courses are public speaking and creative writing.

About 25 percent of high-school students fit into this category.

If Jill had to learn about the Bill of Rights, she would be most enthusiastic about imagining what her life would be like if freedom of speech or freedom of religion were taken away. For a project, she might choose to write a fictional account of a weekend without rights.

Learning Style Two: The Analytic Learner

Lori Bergin, fifteen, likes to sit and think, but unlike Jill, who relates to feelings, people, and experiences, Lori is more logical and relies on facts when she evaluates things. What experts have to say about a subject is important to her. She's impatient with class discussions and isn't interested in the reactions and experiences of other students. "I like to think through an idea by looking at all the information available about it," she says.

Lori's the rational type. She likes doing research, and she feels most comfortable in a traditional classroom—where the teacher does the talking and she takes notes. Her favourite classes are the ones where the information is clear-cut, with right and wrong answers, like math.

About 30 percent of high-school students are in this category (which is pretty low, considering this is the group most schools are designed for).

If Lori were learning about the Bill of Rights, her choice of a project would be a research paper.

Learning Style Three: The Commonsense Learner

Kim Zak, fourteen, is logical and facts are important to her, but she's not content to sit and puzzle things out like Lori is. Kim needs to be doing something more active while she's learning. She likes to test theories and solve problems on her own. She hates being given the answer. She's not happy when she has to listen to someone else talk or watch someone else do a demonstration. She's always the first to volunteer, and she can't understand why some of her friends don't want to participate.

"I like to take something apart and figure it out myself," Kim says. She likes labs, role-playing, and hands-on projects.

About 17 percent of high-school students fall into this category.

Kim would want to test the Bill of Rights to see if it really worked. She'd participate in a demonstration or at least role-play various situations to see for herself how a person's rights are protected.

Learning Style Four: The Dynamic Learner

Christina Nenov, fifteen, learns best when she's active, like Kim, but she doesn't take as standard an approach to learning as Kim does. Ideas and people are more important to Christina than facts and things. She is highly creative and likes to look for new aspects of a subject and raise new possibilities. Then she wants to try those ideas out on other people. "I learn best when I can take a theory or an idea and see what will come of it," she says.

Christina's favourite classes are the ones in which she can move around and talk to people. She's bored when classes are too structured. She likes when classes are broken up into small groups for projects or discussions, and she often volunteers to give the report for her group at the end of the session.

About 28 percent of all high-school students fit into this category.

When studying the Bill of Rights, Christina would want to examine the school rules to see if they violated students' rights, and then set up a committee to write a new school code.

All four learning styles are equally valuable. The bad news, according to Dr. McCarthy, is that many teachers use only one method of teaching, and that method appeals mainly to Analytic Learners. If you find school boring, if you hate certain subjects, if you cram for tests but don't feel you're really learning anything, there's a good chance the problem isn't *what* you're learning but *how* you're learning.

The good news is that when you're able to learn in your own style, you enjoy what you're learning, you feel good about yourself, and you want to learn more. And there *are* things you can do to make school suit *you*. (You may be surprised to find out how many teachers are open to suggestions, too.)

The idea, says Dr. McCarthy, is to always be on the lookout for ways to relate your learning style to every subject. This doesn't mean you try to get out of doing work; it means you think about what would make a subject interesting to you—then see if you can't apply it to the assignment at hand, whether it's reading a chapter in a textbook or doing a special project.

Here are some ideas:

• An Imaginative Learner should always try to relate an impersonal assignment, like graphs in a math class, to something in her own life, like the amount of electricity her family uses. For a French class, she might exchange letters with a pen pal in France. In history she might trace her family tree or interview her oldest relatives.

• An Analytic Learner has the advantage of learning in her own style at school—but that doesn't mean it'll always be easy for her. Some teachers run classes differently, and it's a good idea to work with other people on things she doesn't do as well. Analytic Learners also make good tutors.

• A Commonsense Learner might create a system of flash cards or design a worksheet for studying almost any subject. In math she could try coming up with graphs that make pictures or dot-to-dot drawings. She'd do better making a model of a historic event than writing a report.

• A Dynamic Learner does well organizing field trips or finding and scheduling guest speakers for a class. She would also make a good tutor. In math she might offer to interview people who use math in their jobs and report back to the class. In English she could consider writing and producing a contemporary version of *Romeo and Juliet*.

Now that you know there's a way you learn best and that you can make learning more interesting for yourself, the options are endless. "The big word in all of this is connections," Dr. McCarthy says. "Try to make connections between your own personal style and what you're studying, and you'll make leaps in intelligence."

I often found ways to make the most of being an Imaginative Learner, and I discovered there was room for my ideas in many of my classes. It made school a lot more fun. My friend Sheila? She became a teacher.

**Timothy
Perrin**
· · · · · · · · · ·

Unleashing Your Creativity: Become A Better, More Productive Writer

In the summer of 1985 I was trying to write a profile of Ray Bradbury for *Writer's Digest*. I had made no progress for about a week, so I put the piece aside and worked on other things.

About 11:30 one hot July night, I climbed into the shower to cool off. Suddenly, the lead that had eluded me popped into my head: "Ray Bradbury is a wimp." The first 800 words of the article and the last 100 quickly followed, almost as if someone were dictating to me.

I jumped out of the shower, dried off, ran into my office and turned on the computer. I worked until about 2 that night getting down that beginning and end. Because those parts set the tone of the whole article, it was easy to fill in the middle the next day.

Since then, all that showers have been good for is getting clean—but what happened to me is not unusual. Research into how creative people work shows a common pattern: a) a lot of time collecting material followed by b) a period of apparent inactivity, then c) a sudden burst of "inspiration," and finally d) a period of hard work getting all the new ideas down and organized.

Knowing that, we can learn to make "inspiration" happen, and thereby take better control of the creative process so that we become more productive—and *better*—writers.

Writing calls on two contradictory skills: creativity and critical thinking. Only when we exercise both in balance—and in turn—can we write well. Too much "creativity" and we ignore our readers. Too much critical thinking, especially early in a project, and we might not write anything at all, frozen into inaction by fear of producing something less than perfect.

Researchers like Gordon Rohman at Michigan State University have found that no matter what the genre, successful writers do different things at different times in a writing project, yet virtually all of us use a variation of the same three-stage process: Invention, Drafting, and Revision.

Invention

Invention—sometimes called "prewriting"—is where you figure out just what it is you have to say. It is the most "creative" part of the process, the home of "writer's block," and where most of us get hung up. It is the time for letting our "writer" create and getting our critical "editor" to shut up.

A while back I finished a Drama in Real Life piece for *Reader's Digest* about the rescue of 200 people who had to abandon ship in near hurricane winds and 20-foot seas in the North Pacific. I had a research file more than two inches thick. I interviewed 16 people, plotted two drifting life rafts on nautical charts, and read dozens of newspaper clippings and official reports. I had everything I needed, yet I couldn't get started. Before I could start to write, I had to organize.

Using a computer outline program I was able to weave the 16 stories into one, creating a backbone for my story that allowed me to relax and just tell the tale.

Outlining is just one invention technique. For a large project like my story, it was what I needed to get my mind ready for the actual writing. I've also found outlines useful on technical projects, such as the computer manuals I sometimes do.

Other invention techniques are less structured. Here's one that is perhaps the least structured of them all: Spend just a second thinking about what it is you're writing about. Now start writing *everything* that comes to mind. There's only one rule: You must not stop for ten minutes. You must not pause. You must not correct your spelling or grammar. You must keep going.

If you get off the topic, fine. Follow that train of thought and keep writing. There's no way to do this wrong except to stop.

If you can't think of anything to say, repeat the last word over and over or write, "I can't think of anything to say." It will start again quickly enough.

If you write on a computer, turn off the monitor or cover the screen so you can't see what you have typed and will not be tempted to go back and fix typos.

At the end of ten minutes, stop. Read what you have written, remembering that this isn't meant to be finished copy, not even relevant copy. If a line or idea strikes you, use it as the jumping-off point for another ten minutes of writing. Then another short pause to let things settle down a bit, and another ten minutes of writing.

This process is called "freewriting," and its chief proponent is Peter Elbow, author of *Writing With Power*. Freewriting is an intentionally unstructured activity designed to force you out of your critical mode into your creative mode. In anatomical parlance, it uses your more allegorical "right brain" rather than your more structured "left brain." Occupied with the simple goal of *just writing* without stopping for ten minutes, your conscious mind gets caught up in the immediate task of continuing writing and lets your unconscious mind take care of what you write.

The results of freewriting exercises will often surprise you. Sometimes what you come up with will be trivial; other times you will find insights that startle you.

Freewriting is particularly useful when you're intimidated by the audience you're writing for—some writers are intimidated by their editors. Writing for yourself first, you begin to tap a lode of material you didn't even know was available.

Another inventive technique is called "clustering" and comes from *Writing the Natural Way*, by Gabriele Lusser Rico. At the centre of a sheet of paper, jot the central idea of your article or story. As you think of sub-concepts, note them around the outside of the central circle, and connect them to the centre with a line. As each of those sub-ideas suggest other ideas, cluster them around the parent that spawned them. Soon, you will develop a branching structure. . . .

Like freewriting, clustering is to help you create. Worrying about writing to a certain length can come later.

If you want help in exploring ideas, try *heuristics* (from the Greek word *heuriskein*, "to find out"). Heuristics ask questions that cast a topic in a new light. For them to work, you must spend some time to think about each question, no matter how strange it may seem at first.

Erika Lindemann, in *A Rhetoric for Writing Teachers*, spends more than a dozen pages outlining various heuristics. One of the best sets is derived from the work of Aristotle and focuses around five concepts: Definition, Comparison, Relationship, Testimony, and Circumstance. Each question contains a blank into which you insert the topic you are writing about.

For example, under the general heading of Definition are such questions as "How does the dictionary define _____?" and "What earlier words did _____ come from?" Questions under Comparison ask, "From what is _____ different?" and "_____ is most like what?" Under Relationships, "What causes _____?" and "Why does _____ happen?" Under Testimony, "What have I heard people say about _____?" and "Are there any laws about _____?" Under Circumstance, "Is _____ possible or impossible?" and "If _____ starts, what makes it end?"

Of course, these are just a few of the questions in this one set of Aristotelian heuristics. Other sets of heuristics help you define dramatic motives, identify your audience, analyze a piece of literature, or study a subject from different perspectives. Besides Lindemann's book, another good source of heuristics is Richard Coe's *Form and Substance*.

I used heuristics in doing a piece about hypothermia for *Omni* a few years ago. Hypothermia is the cooling of the body's core. It can kill people in extremely cold weather or cold water. Heuristics asked me the question "What parts can hypothermia be divided into?", which made me think about the stages of hypothermia. Another one, "To what is hypothermia similar?" led me to a whole angle about drug-induced comas that share many symptoms with hypothermia-induced comas.

One other invention technique is the easiest and my favourite: I talk about a project. By explaining what I'm working on, I clarify my thoughts and bring into focus just what it is I have to get across. Also, like many of us, I must fight a tendency to write in loftier (and less understandable) language than I use when speaking. In talking about my story, I usually find simpler, clearer ways of saying what I have to say.

Not all invention techniques work for all people. But every successful writer develops techniques to find out what he or she wants to say. The key is to relax. Don't try to "write." Just let the ideas come with no criticism. . . .

Don't be afraid to spend lots of time on invention. I often spend half of my time on a project in the invention phase.

Drafting

Drafting, on the other hand, is the shortest phase, sometimes taking as little as 10% of my time on a project.

Lewis Carroll had some of the best advice on drafting. In *Alice in Wonderland*, when Alice was trying to tell the Red Queen what has happened but found herself confused, the Queen advised, "Start at the beginning, go through to the end, and then stop."

Change that just a little. Make it: "Start at *A* beginning, go through to *An* end, and then stop."

In other words, don't get hung up on your lead or your conclusion. Start anywhere. Just get down everything you want in your story. Let your momentum carry you. You can reorganize and clean up later. For now, it doesn't have to be perfect, not even close.

Do consider three questions: "What am I trying to accomplish with this writing? To whom am I speaking? Why am I writing this?"

Answering these—purpose, audience, and occasion—will start to bring your work into focus. For instance, knowing that this article is for writers, I am filling it with practical ideas you can use to improve your writing. Had I been writing it for people who *teach* writing, I would have been more theoretical and more concerned with telling how to get the ideas in this article across to students.

Revision

The revision phase puts your internal editor in charge.

The key to making revision work is learning to organize and control it. Do you find yourself correcting grammar, spelling, and punctuation as soon as you start to edit? Don't. Instead, organize your editing into six separate "passes" through the work.

On the first pass, edit for truth and accuracy. Did the governor really say his opponent has a face like a ferrett? Why correct the spelling of *ferret* (only one *t*) if you are going to drop the whole sentence anyway?

On the second, reorganize the building blocks. Did you discuss revision before you discussed drafting? Now is the time to put these sections in their proper places. Again, don't worry about little things. Right now you are moving entire sections, not fiddling with the placement of words.

On the third, carefully examine your paragraph structure. In English, our paragraphs most often move from the general idea to the specific. The most general idea in a paragraph appears in what is called the topic sentence. Each succeeding sentence should relate to that topic sentence in some way or another.

For instance, in the previous paragraph, each sentence is subordinate to and more specific than the sentence just above it. You could chart it like this:

1. On the third, carefully examine your paragraph structure.
2. In English, our paragraphs most often move from the general to the specific.
3. The most general idea in the paragraph appears in what is called the topic sentence.
4. Each succeeding sentence should relate to that topic sentence in some way or another.

Of course, not every paragraph has a purely subordinate structure. Some paragraphs have several sentences at the same level of generality: coordinate structure. Others have both coordinate and subordinate structures. This paragraph is one of the latter.

1. Of course, not every paragraph has a purely subordinate structure.
2. Some paragraphs have several sentences at the same level of generality: coordinate structure.
3. This paragraph is one of the latter.

Notice how the two sentences marked "2" refer directly to the topic sentence. Neither relies on the other for its meaning.

Understanding this principle of increasing specificity helps you understand when a new paragraph should begin. It also helps you keep your facts straight within a paragraph. You'll never have to analyze every paragraph you write, but when you just can't get one to come out right, this analysis will often show you where you have gone wrong and how to fix the problem.

On the fourth pass, ensure that each of your sentences meets three criteria. First, is the central action of the sentence in a verb? Don't say "He made a decision" when you can say "He decided." Second, is your verb in the active voice? The active voice is more vital and easier to understand. Again, "He decided" is better than "A decision was made by him." Third, is the core of the sentence together? Is the subject next to the verb next to the object? Don't say, "The boy, after swinging mightily, hit, with great force, the ball." Just say, "After swinging mightily, the boy hit the ball with great force."

Watch lengths of sentences, as well. Keep them short and to the point. One idea per sentence, no more. It's the easiest way to stay out of trouble.

On the fifth pass, check your diction and usage. Have you used *less* when you really mean *fewer*? Is it the *eldest* or *oldest* sister?

On the sixth, check your spelling and clean up your punctuation.

For those of us with deadlines and word counts remains one last task: paring the piece down to size. For instance, as I draft this piece, I already have more than 3000 words for a 2500-word assignment. Before I finish, I must tighten and select well enough to get this article to something between 2450 and 2550 words. That means another pass (or two) through the piece to throw out everything that isn't essential.

Know When to Quit

Knowing when to quit is as important as knowing where to start. Often we wait too long. Pragmatically, some assignments just don't pay enough to justify spending as much time on them as we do. Also, no piece of writing is ever perfect. No matter how many times you revise, you can still find things to change. When you are done, your editor will find something else to fix.

So, don't be afraid to let it go. As the Red Queen says, "go through to the end and then *stop*."

So I will.

Warren
Shepell
Consultants
••••••••••••

LISTEN UP! ENHANCING OUR LISTENING SKILLS

Have you ever thought about how important listening can be? Just consider that we spend 80 percent of our waking hours communicating and over 45 percent of that time listening to others—spouses, children, friends, co-workers, and acquaintances.

What is listening? Many of us think that listening is what we do while waiting for our turn to talk. Listening is more than being quiet and hearing. Dr. Lyman K. Steil, a well-known authority on the subject of listening, explains that listening involves four stages. First, we hear the message, then, we interpret it, evaluate it, and respond to it.

Studies have shown that most of us understand, evaluate, and retain approximately 50 percent of what is said. And after two days, we remember only half of that. The end result is that we comprehend and retain only 25 percent of what is said.

In the workplace, the cost of poor listening adds up to dollars and cents. It can involve the cost of additional time spent in repeating instructions and having to redo assignments that were carried out incorrectly. Further, some workplace accidents involving physical harm to workers are the result of an individual not listening to directions or warnings prior to acting.

On a personal front, our relationships with people can suffer if we do not listen effectively, or if we do not have people in our lives who will actively listen to us from time to time. We all need someone with whom to share our ideas, thoughts and feelings. If we do not have a listener in our lives, we can begin to feel lonely and isolated.

How would you rate your best friend as a listener? The magic of a warm and sincere friendship is usually one of the rewards of good listening. We are attracted to people who listen. They calm us and support us.

If listening is really this important, then why aren't we better listeners? There's actually a physiological reason for our listening difficulties. Our capacity to listen ranges from 400 to 600 words a minute, while the average speaking rate is about 125 words per minute. This can give us plenty of time to think about other things while a person is talking to us.

A major reason for our poor listening habits may be lack of training. We teach reading, writing, and speaking in our schools. Adults take courses in speed reading, business writing, and public speaking. Yet, despite all of our attempts at improving communications, we often neglect the communication skill which is used the most—listening.

Another reason for poor listening is that we may be too busy to focus exclusively on another individual. Have you ever been too busy to lend a sympathetic ear to a child who has had a tough day at school or to really listen to your mate discuss his or her frustrations?

Sometimes we don't listen to others because we think that they expect us to solve their problems. Yet, few of our friends and relatives really want us to organize their finances, find them new mates, or solve their work frustrations. Oftentimes they are wanting to share their thoughts and feelings with us and want only for us to understand and appreciate what they are going through.

Being able to put ourselves into "someone else's shoes," or someone else's experience, so that we can understand how another may feel, is known as empathic listening. We can let people know that we are listening and do understand them by reflecting back to them how we think they must feel. "You must be so excited" might be communicated to someone who is enthusiastically telling you about a promotion they have just received.

We should be aware that empathic listening is the kind of first aid that many people seek. Leo Buscaglia, a well-known psychologist and author, puts it this way: "When I ask you to listen to me and you start giving advice, you have not done what I asked." Remember, there are times when people want us to listen to them and nothing more.

Before you can become a good listener, you must become a flexible listener. In other words, it's crucial to vary your listening style to suit the speaker, the subject, and the occasion.

Consider your reason for listening. More often than not, your reason for listening will help decide your style of listening. Are you listening for pleasure, to receive ideas and information, to evaluate information, or to show empathy? These are the four basic reasons for listening.

If you listen to a business seminar the same way you listen to a TV comedy, you may not retain much from the seminar. And it stands to reason that the critical listening style that you would use to evaluate information regarding a major purchase you are about to make is not the style you would use when listening to a friend's troubles.

Taking a look at your listening habits is the first step towards becoming a better listener. Most of us have a number of listening faults. So don't be surprised if you identify yourself in more than one of these illustrations.

The biased listener

Usually, the biased listener isn't listening. The biased listener has tuned out and is planning what to say next based on some fixed ideas they have about the subject.

When bias becomes prejudice, we may even tune out a person because of his or her age, accent, or occupation.

Ask yourself: Are my biases a barrier to listening? The road to tuned-in listening begins with a deliberate effort to get rid of preconceived ideas and to give others a fair hearing.

The distracted listener

All of us fit into this category at one time or another. Distracted listeners allow internal or external distractions to prevent them from giving others their undivided attention.

Unfortunately, a lot of distracted listeners don't realize that it's important to get ready to listen. You can't turn yourself into an attentive listener unless you make a deliberate effort to tune out internal distractions and concentrate on what the speaker is saying. If this is not possible, it may be better to set another time to meet with and listen to that person so that he or she can have your undivided attention.

For the most part, external distractions can be eliminated simply by finding a quiet place for your important conversations—one where you'll be free from interruptions.

The impatient listener

The impatient listener is one who interrupts and seldom lets people finish what they have to say. It can be easy to slip into this habit.

If you find it extremely frustrating to listen to people who, perhaps, talk slowly, you are probably an impatient listener. Becoming a patient listener involves making an effort not to interrupt. At first, you'll find it difficult to listen without interrupting. But you'll be pleasantly surprised when the lines of communication open up. Remember, if you have been courteous enough to listen to others, more often than not, they'll listen to you.

The passive listener

The passive listener does not realize that listening is an active process. When we are engaged in conversation with this listener, we are never sure if our message is understood. Why? Simply because we receive little or no feedback. Obviously, this can cause plenty of communication problems.

A telephone conversation with a passive listener is even more difficult than a face-to-face conversation. More often than not, a speaker's words are met with stony silence. That's why people often wonder if their call has been disconnected. If you are having a telephone conversation and have the person on the other end of the line ask "Are you still there?" it may be because you have not been communicating to him or her that you are listening.

If you have a tendency to be a passive listener, try turning yourself into a responsive listener by providing people with more feedback. Just lean slightly forward, establish eye contact, and nod or smile when appropriate. An occasional remark such as "I see," "uh-huh," or "yes" can be used when the conversation is either face-to-face or by telephone.

You may realize that your listening skills need some improvement. Although you're not going to change a lifetime of listening habits overnight, you can, with a little time and effort, learn to become a better listener.

Remember that listening is an important communication skill. It should not be taken for granted. You'll find that your family, business, and social interactions will improve—thanks to better listening!

Stumpie
Stavropoulis
··············
Student
Essay

MACBETH: THE TRAGIC HERO

Sample Literary Essay

Shakespeare's tragic hero has been defined as a principle character who is, in some manner, an individual of exceptional potential. But he possesses a fatal flaw which overcomes his reason and leads to his downfall. Shakespeare's *Macbeth* is just this type of classic tragedy. Its protagonist, Macbeth, is clearly a tragic hero whose exceptional potential is ruined by his obsessive ambition and his failure to act decisively upon his genuine wishes.

Macbeth is exceptional in the complexity of his nature. Consider his physical courage and his inner turmoil, his chameleon being hovering between the forces of good and evil, his darkly fascinating ventures into the realm of the imagination. Each facet of this man's personality clashes with another trait, confusing mind and conscience. For example, Macbeth clearly demonstrates his courage on the battlefield, earning just praise from a peer, the thane of Ross:

Nothing afeard of what thyself didst make
Strange images of death (Act 1, scene iii, ll. 100-101)

Ross betrays his wonderment that someone so accustomed to dealing with death's hand seems so unafraid of death itself.

While physical courage sustains him on the battlefield, it exacts its mental toll. Macbeth's courage is unique in that it forces him to confront his crimes of conscience. Reflect, for example, upon his distress at Banquo's ghost, his frightened and amazed words to Lady Macbeth with whom he is losing his rapport:

. . . you can behold such sights
And keep the natural ruby of your cheeks,
when mine is blanch'd with fear. (Act III, scene iv, ll. 139-141)

Here, Macbeth demonstrates sensitivity when he is forced to face the adverse consequences of his actions. He is both denying and affirming the outcome of his good friend's murder. By trying to accept the consequences of his actions, he shows a certain personal courage.

Similarly, Macbeth's imagination both assists and cripples him. He is capable of prophetic far-sightedness; this power guides his thorny path into the distant future. The wealth of Macbeth's imagination adds depth and dimension of thought. However, his imagination is also his worst enemy, conjuring up tortuous images. Witness, for instance, Macbeth's raging imagination in his dagger soliloquy. He cries out:

> . . . art thou but
> A dagger of the mind, a false creation,
> Proceeding from the heat-oppressed brain? (Act II, scene ii, ll. 44-49)

Macbeth is projecting a dreaded image of future actions which foreshadow his mental anguish following Banquo's murder.

Macbeth's very being is a concoction of confusion and churning emotions which compete to enslave his mind. Foremost is his real essence, that which is good and compassionate. This Macbeth shudders at the thought of killing beloved King Duncan. He tells his soul-mate, Lady Macbeth:

> We'll proceed no further in this business. (Act I, scene vii, ll. 2)

It is this Macbeth who considers the far-reaching consequences of murder and who

> . . . is too full o' the milk of human kindness
> To catch the nearest way (Act I, scene v, ll, 14-15)

That is, he is tortured by the idea of the cold-hearted murder of King Duncan.

But there is another Macbeth, one who is primitive and barbaric, a man who acts upon his instincts for personal survival, not rationality. Upon hearing the witches' second prophecies and their warning to "beware Macduff," Macbeth orders the massacre of Macduff's family and he succumbs to his fatal flaw—ambition—and commits whatever immoral acts advance it.

Ultimately Macbeth's ambitious thoughts and actions lead to his cataclysmic downfall. His passion for the throne blinds him to reality. Almost without self-awareness, his obsessive ambition gradually defiles his mind and soul. He focuses on the tantalizing fruits of his goals; even human sacrifices will not impede his "vaulting ambition."

He realizes the extent of his ambition and is conscious of his need to curb it; yet he dismisses that need, rationalizing that:

> To be thus is nothing
> But to be safely thus: our fears in Banquo
> Stick deep; and in his royalty of nature
> Reign that which would be fear'd: 'tis much he dares . . . (Act III, scene i, ll, 52-55)

Since he has identified Banquo, his former confidant, as an enemy, he must be destroyed.

> It is concluded: Banquo, thy soul'd flight,
> If it find heaven, must find it out tonight.
> (Act 3, scene i, ll, 157-158)

But Macbeth's ambition to retain the throne does not end with Banquo's death. Not long thereafter, Macbeth hires assassins to murder Macduff's wife and children, since Macduff is beyond his reach.

And, indeed, this final heinous act costs Macbeth both his throne and his life. Consumed by rage at the senseless slaughter of his family, Macduff joins Malcolm's military campaign which destroys "black Macbeth's" iron rule. Macbeth's ruthless ambition propels his downfall as the forces of good, represented by Macduff's and Malcolm's rationality and integrity as well as Malcolm's rightful claim to the throne, are victorious. "Natural justice" asserts itself when Malcolm is crowned king of Scotland.

One may question why the witches' prophecies are fulfilled, for if Macbeth lacks the free will to fight the prophecies there is no tragedy. Tragedy, by its very definition, requires the option of choosing between good and evil. But Macbeth lacks the willpower to overcome the witches' prophecies; they tell him what he *wants to hear*. Believing in his destiny, removed from common sense, he *chooses* to believe that the unchangeable actions are unravelling before him. He says:

> Come what may,
> Time and hour runs through the roughest day. (Act I, scene iii, ll, 160)

His vision of the future creates a self-fulfilling prophecy. Furthermore, his complex nature and inner turmoil clearly reduce his will to decide. In one sense, Macbeth has no real choices. His inner turbulence renders him powerless to refute any further wrong-doing. Therefore Macbeth is drawn inexorably into his outcome, by lack of volition, because of his prescience of events and indecision to act.

Clearly, Macbeth is a tragic hero because of his exceptional potential as a soldier, his ambition to be king, and his lack of willpower to overcome his fatal flaws. In Shakespeare's *Macbeth*, the tragic ingredients combine to produce an intricately woven plot revolving around the conflict between good and evil. The "star" character—the tragic hero—is stymied by the conflict among his exceptional personality, his obsessive flaws, and his lack of will.

GUIDE TO THEMES

GUIDE TO PATTERNS

Most Closely Resembles Argumentation

Most Closely Resembles Persuasion

CREDITS

Page 4: "Afternoon of an American Boy" from THE SECOND TREE FROM THE CORNER by E.B. White. Copyright 1947 by E.B. White. Reprinted by permission of HarperCollins Publishers.

Page 9: Copyright © 1991 Erik Savas.

Page 12: The Estate of the late Sonia Brownell Orwell and Martin Secker & Warburg Ltd.

Page 22: Copyright © 1971 by Judy Syfers. "Why I Want a Wife" originally appeared in *Ms. Magazine*, December 1971.

Page 24: Copyright © 1991 Talin Arzumanian.

Page 27: "Why We Crave Horror Stories" by Stephen King. Originally appeared in *Playboy*. Reprinted by permission.